T0178688

Quantitative and Statistical Data in Education

Education Set

coordinated by
Gérard Boudesseul and Angela Barthes

Volume 2

Quantitative and Statistical Data in Education

*From Data Collection
to Data Processing*

Michel Larini
Angela Barthes

WILEY

First published 2018 in Great Britain and the United States by ISTE Ltd and John Wiley & Sons, Inc.

Apart from any fair dealing for the purposes of research or private study, or criticism or review, as permitted under the Copyright, Designs and Patents Act 1988, this publication may only be reproduced, stored or transmitted, in any form or by any means, with the prior permission in writing of the publishers, or in the case of reprographic reproduction in accordance with the terms and licenses issued by the CLA. Enquiries concerning reproduction outside these terms should be sent to the publishers at the undermentioned address:

ISTE Ltd
27-37 St George's Road
London SW19 4EU
UK

www.iste.co.uk

John Wiley & Sons, Inc.
111 River Street
Hoboken, NJ 07030
USA

www.wiley.com

© ISTE Ltd 2018
The rights of Michel Larini and Angela Barthes to be identified as the authors of this work have been asserted by them in accordance with the Copyright, Designs and Patents Act 1988.

Library of Congress Control Number: 2018954296

British Library Cataloguing-in-Publication Data
A CIP record for this book is available from the British Library
ISBN 978-1-78630-228-1

Contents

Introduction

This book outlines the main methods used for a simple analysis, and then a more elaborate one, of quantitative data obtained in a study or a work of research. It is aimed primarily at students, teachers and researchers working in the education sector, but may also be illuminating in the various domains of the human and social sciences.

The book may be viewed as a step-by-step course: it begins with an introduction to the various methods used to gather data and, one step at a time, it touches on the essential aspects of the quantitative analysis techniques used in the field of research in education to extract meaning from the data.

Essentially, the book is designed for readers who are new to these types of methods. Nevertheless, it could also be very useful for doctoral candidates, and even for researchers, who already have experience, if their approach to the data is merely software based, and they wish to gain a better understanding of the fundaments of these methods in order to make better use of them, take their analyses further and avoid certain pitfalls.

Unlike many other books on the subject, which can be rather difficult to read, or which examine one method and one only, we elected to present a range of the most widespread approaches that can be used easily in the area of education. Thus, readers who want a detailed understanding are advised to consult more specialized publications.

This book is not a mathematics book which presents all of the (often complex) theoretical bases of the methods employed. Nor, though, do we wish to limit it to a presentation of the formulae and the procedures for using these methods. At every stage, we have sought to offer a balanced presentation of the method, with the twofold objective of being comprehensible and enabling users to handle the data in full awareness of what they are doing. Thus, when we do go into some degree of mathematical detail, it is not absolutely essential to read these parts (though it may be helpful to some).

In today's world, students and researchers are in the habit of using software packages where all they need to do is input the data and, simply, press a button. This approach carries with it a certain amount of risk, if the people using the software have insufficient prior knowledge of the fundaments of the methods the program employs. Obviously, throughout the presentations herein, we have used software tools, but deliberately chose not to include a discussion about those tools. The ways in which they are used differ from one program to another, and they evolve very quickly over time. It is possible that, by the time you come to read this book, the programs used here will no longer be in circulation or will have evolved, and indubitably, there will be others that have been developed, which perform better and are more user friendly. In any case, before processing any data, readers will need to invest time and effort in learning how to use a software tool properly; that prior investment is absolutely crucial. After all, before you can use a car, you have to learn to drive. However, time and again, we present the calculations manually, because they will help readers to follow the theoretical process, step by step, from raw data to the desired results, and this is a highly enlightening approach.

Without going into detail, we can state that it is indispensable to perform quantitative data analyses when faced with data taken from a large number of individuals (from a few dozen to thousands or more). The researcher or student collects the data they need; those data are entered into a table cross-referencing the individuals sampled with the various parameters (variables) measured: the Individuals/Variables [I/V] table. This is the starting point for the data analysis, because it tends not to be directly interpretable, but we need to extract as much information from it as possible. In order to do so, the researcher takes a series of steps.

The first step is elementary descriptive statistics. It consists of constructing other, more explicit tables, extracted from the [I/V] table, and then generating graphical and cartographic representations of those data. In addition, in the case of numerical variables, it is possible to achieve a more accurate description by introducing mathematical indicators: mean, variance, standard variation for each of the variables, and covariance and correlation coefficient for each pair of variables. After using the tools offered by descriptive statistics, researchers are able to begin to present the data, comment upon them, and compare them to the original working hypotheses.

The second step is confirmatory statistics, also known as statistical inference. At this stage in the process, the researcher is able to present the data in a legible form, and has been able to make observations about the dataset and draw conclusions. However, for obvious practical reasons, these data will have been collected only from a reduced sample, rather than from the entire population, and there is nothing to suggest that were we to look at other samples within the same population, the same conclusions would have been reached. The researcher then needs to consider whether the results obtained on the sample or samples at hand can be generalized to apply to the whole population. This is the question addressed by confirmatory statistics based on fundamental concepts of probability and on the law of coincidence and the law of large numbers. Confirmatory statistics gives us laws that predict the probability of a given event occurring in a population. With that in mind, it is possible to compile probability tables, which can be used as the basis for statistical tests (averages, Student's t-test, χ^2 distribution, ANOVA, correlation test, etc.), which the researcher needs to use to find out whether the results obtained can be generalized to the entire population.

The third step involves multivariate data analysis techniques, which offer overall observation of the links that may exist between more than two variables (3, 4, ..., n). They are being used increasingly frequently. They complement elementary descriptive statistics as they can reveal unexpected connections and, in that sense, they go further in analysis of the data. Principal component analysis (PCA), which applies to numerical variables, is at the root of multivariate methods. Factorial correspondence analysis (FCA) and factorial multiple correspondence analysis (FMCA), for their part, apply to qualitative data, and they are built on the theoretical foundations of PCA.

The fourth step that may be used is statistical modeling. Having demonstrated the existence of links between the different variables, we can attempt to find any mathematical relations that might exist between one of the variables (known as a dependent variable) and one or more other variables (known as explanatory variables). In essence, the aim is to establish a predictive model that can illustrate how the dependent variable will be affected as the explanatory variables evolve; hence, the method is known as statistical modeling. For example, Pascal Bressoux sets out to build a model that determines the opinion that a teacher has of his pupils (the dependent variable) as a function of multiple explanatory variables, such as their academic performances, tardiness to school, their parents' socioprofessional status, etc. Statistical modeling can deal with situations that vary widely with the nature of the explanatory variables and of the dependent variable (normal or logistic regression), depending on whether the explanatory variables act directly or indirectly, or on the effects of context with the existence of various levels of interactions (pupils, class, school, town, etc.).

The book is organized in the same order as the steps that a researcher needs to take when carrying out a study. Hence, it consists of six chapters, each having between two and five sections. Chapter 1 deals with data collection in education. Chapter 2 looks at elementary descriptive statistics. Chapter 3 is given over to confirmatory statistics (statistical inference). Then, in Chapter 4, we examine multivariate approaches, followed by statistical modeling in Chapter 5. Finally, Chapter 6 is devoted to presenting tools commonly used in education (and other disciplines), but are gaining robustness as they become slightly more quantitative than normal, and it is helpful to formally describe this process. The two examples cited here relate to social representations in education and the studies leading from links to knowledge. The basic idea is to show that many methods can be improved, or transformed, to become more quantitative in nature, lending greater reproducibility to the studies.

1

Data Collection in Education

1.1. Use of existing databases in education

A piece of data is an elementary description of a reality. It might be, for instance, an observation or measurement. A data point is not subject to any reasoning, supposition, observation or probability, even though the reason for and method of its collection are non-neutral. Indisputable or undisputed, it serves as the basis for a search, any examination, expressed in terms of a problem. Data analysis is normally the result of prior work on the raw data, imbuing them with meaning in relation to a particular problem, and thereby obtaining information. Data are a set of measurable values or qualitative criteria, taken in relation to a reference standard or to epistemological positions identified in an analysis grid. The reference grid used and the way in which the raw data are processed are explicit or implicit interpretations, which can transform (or skew) the final interpretation. For example, discretizing data (classifying them by establishing boundaries) in a graph enables an analyst to associate a meaning (an interpretation) with those data, and thus create new information in relation to a given problem.

Societies are restructuring to become "knowledge societies" in a context where in the global economy, innovations are based on the storage and exploitation of knowledge (value creation), and on the training and qualifications of actors in knowledge exploitation. Today, our knowledge society is faced with an explosion in the volume of data. The volume of the data created and copied is increasing exponentially, and the actors in civil society and in economics are taking great pains to find solutions allowing them to manage, store and secure those data. The tendency toward the use of *Big Data* to obtain a competitive edge and help organizations to achieve their objectives requires the collection of new types of information (comments posted on websites, pharmaceutical testing data, researchers' results, to cite only a few examples) and examination of the data from every possible angle in order to reach an understanding and find solutions. Education is no exception to this rule, and burgeoning quantities of data are available in this field. Though this is not an exhaustive list, we could point to international databases with which practitioners, students, researchers and businesses can work. Data enables us to act on knowledge, which is a determining factor in the exercise of power. It should also be noted that in today's world, data transmission is subject to rigorous frameworks (for example, issues of data privacy).

Below, we give a few examples of the databases that can be used.

1.1.1. *International databases*

The available international databases are, primarily, those maintained by intergovernmental organizations. For example, the UNESCO Institute for Statistics and the World Bank run a paying service for statistical monitoring in education. They facilitate international comparisons. The main access points are listed in Table 1.1.

UNESCO database: education	http://www.uis.unesco.org/education
World Bank database: education	http://datatopics.worldbank.org/education/
OECD database: education	http://www.oecd.org/education/
United Nations database: for teachers	https://www.gapminder.org/for-teachers/
Eurostat database: education and training for Europe-wide comparisons and longitudinal monitoring	http://ec.europa.eu/eurostat/web/education-and-training/data/database
Eurydice database: institutional information network on educational policy and systems in Europe	http://www.eurydice.org/
Canadian databases on education the world over	https://www.wes.org/ca/wedb/
Database of National Center for Education Statistics	https://en.wikipedia.org/wiki/National_Center_for_Education_Statistics

Table 1.1. *International databases*

Educsol database: education	http://eduscol.education.fr/numerique/dossi er/archives/ressources-en-ligne/bases/bases-donnees
INSEE database: teaching and education by commune	http://www.insee.fr/fr/themes/ theme.asp?theme=7
Databases of the Ministry for National Education and the Ministry for Higher Education and Research	http://www.education.gouv.fr/ bcp/mainFrame.jsp?p=1 https://data.enseignementsup-recherche. gouv.fr/explore/?sort=modified
Statistical data from CAPES (French teacher training qualification) examination	http://www.devenirenseignant.gouv.fr/ cid98479/donnees-statistiques-des-concours-du-capes-de-la-session-2015.html

Table 1.2. *French national databases*

1.1.2. *Compound databases*

The list offered here is by no means exhaustive, and the situation is constantly changing. It shows the main databases compiled by organizations, communes and researchers.

Institutional databases: e.g. that of the Académie d'Aix-Marseille	https://fichetab.ac-aix-marseille.fr/
Emmanuelle database: compiles all editions of textbooks published in France since 1789, for all disciplines and all levels of education	http://www.inrp.fr/emma/web/index.php

Table 1.3. *Compound databases*

Researchers establish numerous databases. A few examples are presented in Table 1.4.

Database of the Center for Study and Research on qualifications	http://mimosa.cereq.fr/reflet/index.php? lien=educ_pres
Databases of rural schools of the Observatory for Education and Territory, longitudinal examination	http://observatoireecoleetterritoire

Table 1.4. *Databases established by researchers*

An analyst working with the data can then construct their own statistical tables and apply their own processes to obtain an answer to a given question.

1.2. Survey questionnaire

In the field of education, it is very common to use questionnaires to gather data regarding educational situations. Think, for example, about the areas of guidance counselling, for school and for work; about the paths taken by the pupils; the social make-up of the community of teachers and parents; knowledge about the establishments; etc.

In all cases, in order to write a useful questionnaire, it is important to know the general rules. Below, we very briefly discuss the general principles, but there are numerous publications in sociology of investigation, which must be consulted to gain a deeper understanding.

1.2.1. *Objective of a questionnaire*

To begin with, it is necessary to very clearly specify the aim of a questionnaire, and to set out the requirements in terms of collecting information. Indeed, questionnaires are always used in response to a desire to measure a situation – in this instance, an educational situation – and their use is part of a study approach which is descriptive or explicative in purpose, and quantitative in nature.

The aim, then, is to describe a population or a target subpopulation in terms of a certain number of criteria: the parents' socioprofessional profile, the pupils' behavior, the intentions of the educational actors, the teachers' opinions, etc. The goal is to estimate an absolute or relative value, and test relations between variables to verify and validate hypotheses.

In any case, the end product is a report, whatever the medium used. The report is made up of a set of information having been collected, analyzed and represented.

As with any production, the conducting of an inquiry must follow a coherent and logical approach to a problem.

1.2.2. *Constitution of the sample*

Very simply, there are two main ways of constructing a sample for an investigation. Either the entire population is questioned – e.g. all the pupils in a school – in which case, the study is said to be exhaustive or else only a portion of the population is questioned – e.g. just a handful of pupils per class – in which case, the study is done by survey.

However, the technique of survey-based investigation necessitates a degree of reflection on the criteria used to select the portion of the population to be surveyed. That portion is called the sample. In order to obtain reliable results, the characteristics of the sample must be the same as those of the entire population. There are two sampling methods. To begin with, there are probabilistic methods, meaning that the survey units are selected at random. These methods respect statistical laws. With simple random surveying, a list of all survey units is drawn up, and a number are selected at random. With systematic sampling, from the list of all survey units, we select one in every n number. With stratified sampling, if the population can be divided into homogeneous groups, samples are randomly selected from within the different groups.

Second, we have non-probabilistic methods. The best-known non-probabilistic method is the quota method, which is briefly described below.

This method involves four steps: studying the characteristics of the base population in relation to certain criteria of representativeness, deducing the respective role of these various criteria in relative value, determining a sampling rate to determine the sample size and applying the relative values obtained to the sample.

The example below illustrates the principle: consider a population of 10,000 residents. The analysis of that population (INSEE) shows that there is 55% of women, 45% of men, 10% aged under 20, 20% aged between 20 and 40, 25% aged between 40 and 60, and 45% over 60.

These percentages are referred to as quotas. If a sampling rate of 1/20 is chosen to begin with, this means that the ratio "sample size/size of population under study" must be 1/20.

The sample size, then, is 10,000/20 = 500 people. The structure of the sample is determined by applying the quotas. There will be 500 × 55% = 275 women, 500 × 45% = 225 men, 500 × 10% = 50 under the age of 20, 500 × 20% = 100 between the ages of 20 and 40, 500 × 25% = 125 people between 40 and 60 years of age, and 500 × 45% = 225 people over 60.

The difficulty lies in setting the sampling rate. An empirical method is to estimate that the sampling rate must be such that the smallest group obtained is at least 30 people. For probabilistic methods, there are formulae in place which relate to statistical functions.

Probabilistic methods allow us to determine the sampling rate as a function of the population size with a sufficiently large confidence interval.

NOTE.– We can also calculate the overall sample size using statistical concepts, which we shall touch upon later on in this book. Therefore, the presentation here is highly simplified.

The sample size that should be chosen depends on the degree of accuracy we want to obtain and the level of risk of error that we are willing to accept.

The accuracy is characterized by the margin of error "e" that is acceptable. In other words, we are satisfied if the value of the sought value A is between A $(1 - e)$ and A $(1 + e)$. Often, e is taken to be equal to 0.05.

The risk of mistake that we are willing to accept is characterized by a term "t", which will be explained in Chapter 3. If we accept conventional 5% risk of error, then t = 1.96.

There are then two approaches to quickly calculate the size of a sample:

– based on a proportion, we can calculate the sample size using the formula:

$$n = \frac{t^2 x p(1-p)}{e^2}$$

where:

– n = expected sample size;

– t = level of confidence deduced from the confidence rate (traditionally 1.96 for a confidence rate of 95%) – a reduced centered normal law;

– p = estimated proportion of the population exhibiting the characteristic that is under study. When that proportion is not known, a preliminary study can be carried out, or else the value is taken to be p = 0.5. This value maximizes the sample size;

– e = margin of error (often set at 0.05).

Thus, if we choose p = 0.5, for example, choosing a confidence level of 95% and a margin of error of 5% (0.05), the sample size must be:

n = $1.96^2 \times 0.5 \times 0.5 / 0.05^2$ = 384.16 individuals

It is then useful to verify whether the number of individuals per quota is sufficient based on a mean. In order to do so, we need an initial estimation of the standard deviation, so we can adjust the sample on the basis of the accuracy of results it obtains and the expected level of analysis:

$$n = \frac{t^2 x \sigma^2}{e^2}$$

where:

– n = expected sample size;

– t = level of confidence deduced from the confidence rate (traditionally 1.96 for a confidence rate of 95%) – a reduced centered normal law;

– σ = estimated standard deviation of the criterion under study. This value will be defined in Chapter 2;

– e = margin of error (often set at 0.05).

1.2.3. *Questions*

1.2.3.1. *Number of questions*

Apart from exceptional cases, if the surveys are being put to people on the street, the questionnaire must be reasonably short: 15-odd questions at most.

If the respondents are filling in a questionnaire in an educational institution or at home, the number of questions may be greater.

1.2.3.2. *Order of the questions*

A questionnaire should be structured by topic, and presented in the form of a progression, leading from the fairly general to the very specific. Personal questions (age, address, class, gender, etc.) must be posed at the end of the questionnaire.

1.2.3.3. *Types of questions*

Remember the different types of questions:

– closed-ended, single response;

– closed-ended and ranged: e.g. enter a value between "1 and n" or between "very poor and very good".

NOTE.– These questions must offer an even number of choices when the goal is to express an opinion; otherwise, there is a danger that the responses will be concentrated around the central option:

– closed-ended, multiple choice: one or more responses out of those offered;

– closed-ended, ordered: the responses are ranked in order of preference;

– open-ended: the respondent has complete freedom to respond in text or numerical form.

It is worth limiting the number of open-ended questions, because they take a long time to unpick with a survey software tool. As far as possible, it is preferable to reduce an open-ended question to a multiple-choice one.

1.2.4. *Structure of a questionnaire*

The questionnaire must contain three parts: the introduction, the body of the questionnaire and the conclusion.

1.2.4.1. *Introduction and conclusion*

The questionnaire needs to be formulated in a way that will draw the respondent in. It generally includes greetings, an introduction to the researcher, the context and the purpose of the study, and an invitation to answer the questions that follow.

EXAMPLE.– (Greeting), my name is Y; I am an intern at company G. I am carrying out a study on customer satisfaction. Your answers will be very helpful to us in improving our service.

The conclusion is dedicated to giving thanks and taking leave. Once written, the questionnaire will be tested in order to reveal any difficulties in understanding the questions or difficulties in the answers.

1.2.4.2. *Body of the questionnaire*

The questions must be organized logically into several distinct parts, from the most general questions to the most specific ones. Generally, information questions or personal identification ones (e.g. age, gender, socioprofessional status, class, etc.) are posed at the end.

1.2.5. *Writing*

1.2.5.1. *General*

The writing of the questionnaire in itself requires great rigor. The vocabulary used must be suited to the people who are being questioned. It is important to use simple words in everyday language and avoid overly technical or abstract words or ambiguous subjects.

The physical presentation must be impeccable and comfortable to read. The questions should be aligned with one another and, likewise, the grids used for the answers. Word-processing tools generally perform very well in this regard.

1.2.5.2. *Pitfalls to be avoided*

The questions posed must invite non-biased responses. Questions that might bring about biased responses are those that involve desires, memory, prestige and the social environment. Generally speaking, the questions should not elicit the response ("Don't you think that...") or contain technical, complicated or ambiguous terms. They must be precise. Indeed, any general question will obtain a general response that, ultimately, gives us very little information.

Below, we present a series of errors that are to be avoided.

The question "Do you play rugby a lot?" is too vague and too general. It could usefully be replaced by "How many times a week do you play rugby?".

"What is your favorite activity?" This question strips the respondent of the freedom not to have a favorite activity. "Do you have a favorite activity?" is better, because it leaves the respondent with the freedom to have one or not.

The question "Do you have daughters, and what age is your youngest?" contains a twofold question. It needs to be broken up into two separate questions.

The question "Don't you agree that adults do not do enough walking?" lacks clarity, because of the double negative and the length of the question. The respondent may not actually have an opinion on the issue, or might respond with a "yes" or "no" carrying little meaning. It would be useful to replace this question with one inviting a scaled response.

"Do you eat vegetables often?" is a bad question, because the word "often" may be interpreted differently by the various people to whom it is put. It is preferable to use a scaled question:

☐ every day   ☐ twice a week   ☐ once a week   ☐ etc.

1.3. Experimental approaches

1.3.1. *Inductive and deductive approaches*

In sections 1.1 and 1.2, we have shown how to obtain data, either by directly consulting the databanks available in the pre-existing literature or by compiling original data based on investigations. In both cases, the researcher acts as an impartial observer, doing nothing more than collecting the data. Theoretically, they should have no direct influence on what they are observing. Once the data have been harvested, the researchers analyze them and attempts, *a posteriori*, to declare results to establish patterns, rules and laws. The approach is inductive. If we observe one variable in particular, and attempt to establish a link with another variable, the link we see is invariably fogged by the presence of parasitic variables.

Experimentation is another way to obtain data. In this case, the approach is deductive, and the researcher is no longer a mere observer. They begin by formulating an initial hypothesis, called the research hypothesis, and implement a procedure and an artificial device to validate or undermine the original hypothesis. They attempt to control the situation in order to see how a variable, known as the dependent variable, responds to the action of one or more other variables, known as independent variables, which the researcher can manipulate, thereby circumventing the problem of parasitic variables, as far as possible. Yet in the human sciences, unlike in the hard sciences, this control is never absolute.

Often, an experiment is cumbersome to put in place and complex to manage; the impact of this is to limit the size of the samples observed. The small size of these samples constantly forces us to wonder: "Had I worked on a different sample, would I still have obtained the same result?" In order to answer this question, we have to use confirmatory statistics (see Chapter 3), the aim of which is to determine whether the results obtained from the sample can be generalized to the whole population.

Below, we present an example drawn from cognitive psychology, which is a pioneering discipline in the field and frequently uses the experimental approach, before going on to talk about the form that the experimental approach might take for research in education.

1.3.2. *Experimentation by psychologists*

Psychologists are adept with the experimental approach – particularly in cognitive psychology. They place the individuals in their sample in situations that favor the observation of a link between a dependent variable and an independent one. To illustrate this approach, below, we present an example drawn from Abdi [ABD 87].

The study relates to the effect of the use of mental imagery for memorization. The question posed is: do subjects have better retention of information memorized with the help of images than information memorized without images? To answer this question, an experiment is set up. Subjects are asked to learn pairs of words, such as "bicycle-carrot" or "fish-chair". They then need to give the associated second word – for instance, if the tester says "carrot", they should answer "bicycle", and so on.

Two groups of 15 subjects are set up: the experimental group (EG) and the control group (CG). Each of the groups is shown the pairs of words on a screen, represented by an image for the EG and the written words for the CG. Afterwards, they are questioned about what they have memorized.

The dependent variable is the "number of word pairs memorized", and the independent variable is the "learning method", with two facets: "with images" and "without images".

In this study, the experiment demonstrated that memorization was far greater in the EG than in the CG. Thus, it appears that the more visual method aids memorization.

1.3.3. *Experimentation in education*

As we shall show later on, research in education can take multiple and diverse paths, but all sharing a common goal: to collect data in order to draw conclusions about certain phenomena pertaining to the human sciences in general, and education in particular. One of these avenues is experimentation, and the aim is to construct theoretical models that can help understand, and even predict, different aspects of education, and particularly to improve educational practices. Measurement of the "effectiveness of teaching" is one of the fundaments of such work.

Below, to demonstrate the form an experiment may take, we present two situations in the field of research in education.

1.3.3.1. *A simple example: fictional, but realistic*

We wish to test the effectiveness of a new method for teaching reading, and to find out whether it is more effective than the method conventionally used.

We construct an experiment

Consider two primary school classes with 26 and 23 pupils, respectively. The first, the CG, will learn with the conventional method, while the second, the EG, learns with the new method.

After 2 months of teaching, an identical test is put to both classes. An assessment grid is used to precisely grade each pupil, and that grade serves as a performance indicator. We may decide that the performance indicator for each of the two classes is the mean obtained by the pupils. In this case, the dependent variable is the "mean grade obtained" and the independent variable is the "group", which has two facets: CG and EG.

By comparing the two means, we can tell which of the two groups has performed better. However, is it the learning method which has made the difference, or other, parasitic variables?

Before drawing a radical conclusion, there are a number of factors that need to be taken into account such as the initial "level" of the two classes, the teacher's influence (teacher effect), the sample size and, indubitably, other parasitic variables as well. Although we cannot absolutely avoid parasitic effects, it is wise to identify them and minimize their effects as far as possible. For example, to ensure that the two classes are of the same level to begin with, we could choose them in the wake of preliminary testing before the start of the experiment. For the teacher effect, while it is not always possible, the ideal is that the same teacher should dispense the education to both classes.

1.3.3.2. *A real-world example in the context of an experiment at university*

The real-world example on which we wish to focus relates to a third-year undergraduate course in engineering sciences, in the sector of mechanical engineering. It compares the effectiveness of conventional teaching techniques (classes and supervised work) with the same education, on the same content, but using problem-based learning (PBL). In PBL, students work in small groups. They are given a problem to solve and must pull together the information necessary to solve it, and even independently acquire the essential new concepts, whereas in conventional education, new knowledge is imparted in class and through guided work.

The questions which are posed are as follows:

– is the acquisition of fundamental academic knowledge as effective, in PBL, as it is in conventional education?

– is the memorization of knowledge as significant, in PBL, as in conventional education?

In other words, we want to know whether it is more effective to obtain fundamental academic knowledge independently (through PBL) or by structured teaching (classes and guided work), and also find which of the two approaches best aids memorization.

We construct an experiment

We have two groups: the EG (54 students), working by PBL; and the CG (46 students), following the usual path of classes and directed work. To answer the first question, a longitudinal measure is put in place, running from the start of March to the end of May. It mainly comprises a general level test before the course starts (pretest) and a test after the course (posttest) relating to the discipline-specific academic content retained from the course.

In the pretest, the two groups obtain an equivalent average score, and the posttest shows that after the course, the two groups are still equivalent, on average. However, a more detailed analysis of the results clearly shows that the best students in the EG have made more progress than the best students in the CG, and conversely, that the weakest in the EG have less success than the weakest in the CG. This experiment shows that when it comes to fundamental academic teaching, problem-based learning is more effective for the stronger students, but risks leaving the weaker ones behind.

To answer the second question, a memorization test is organized for when the students return in September. The results demonstrate that, overall, the EG was better able to memorize the knowledge than the CG.

In all cases, data are recorded about the individuals, and to begin with, those data are entered into a binary table (Individual/Variable). The same is true for all data collection methods.

This table is not legible. Hence, the rest of this book examines the various approaches that can be used to extract information from it, formulate hypotheses and even draw conclusions.

Elementary Descriptive Statistics and Data Representation

2.1. Tables and graphic representations

The goal of descriptive statistics is to make the dual-input individual/variable [I/V] table legible, directly generated from the data readings. It uses different approaches (specific tables, graphs, curves, mathematical indicators). Beyond simple presentation of the results, it must enable the users to comment on those results, formulate hypotheses and even draw conclusions in relation to the sample or samples studied. This part is known as elementary descriptive statistics, as opposed to multivariate analyses, presented in Chapter 4, which are based on more complex processing, but which can also be considered descriptive statistics.

Before going onto the presentation, it is worth clarifying a few concepts relating to the objects of research and the concept of a variable.

2.1.1. *Population, sample and individuals*

Researchers are interested in individuals (subject, object, etc.) belonging to a population. The term "individual" must be understood, here, in the sense of a statistical unit. The population is a set, comprising a large number of individuals, considered to form a whole. That whole may be different in nature depending on the problem at hand – for example "Europeans", "French people", "Marseille residents", "Swiss students" and so forth. Most of the time, researchers cannot possibly have access to the whole of the population, so must be content with working on a sample, of a reasonable size, made up of individuals selected from within the population. The selection of individuals for a sample is crucially important, because this choice may influence the nature of the results; this is a topic which was discussed in the first chapter, and an issue which shall be illustrated throughout this book.

We often have to compare samples to one another, and two situations may arise. The first is to compare samples composed of different individuals at the same time; in this case, we say that we are dealing with independent samples. The second occurs when the samples are made up of the same individuals to whom the questions have been put, before and after one or more actions; in this case, we wish to measure the effect of the action, and say that we have two matched samples. We then speak of longitudinal analysis.

2.1.2. *Variables*

A researcher takes information from each individual in the sample in order to provide elements of responses to the research questions they are examining. Each of those pieces of data is referred to as a variable. Naturally and practically, the data collected are presented in a table which cross-references the individuals with the different variables; this is the first step in descriptive statistics. This table is known as the individual/variable table, represented as [I/V].

Table 2.1 is an example, where we have collected information (variables) about the n pupils (individuals) in a class.

Pupils	Gender	Age	Grade in math	Grade repetition	Parents' SPC	....
1	F	12	10	No	Farmer	
2	M	14	13	Yes	Sr. exec.	
...	...	...	...	...	...	
I	M	12	16	No	Mid. exec.	
...	...	...	...	...	...	
n-1	F	14	18	Yes	Employee	
N	F	13	8	No	Laborer	

Table 2.1. *Example of an individuals/variables [I/V] data table*

The variables (gender, age, grade in math, grade repetition, socioprofessional category of the parents [SPC], etc.) are highly disparate in nature and are worth looking at in greater detail, as this plays an essential role in how the data can be processed.

2.1.2.1. *Quantitative variables (age, grade in math)*

A quantitative variable (also known as a numerical variable) is a variable that expresses a measurement; it is expressed in the form of an integer or a real number. In Table 2.1, this is the case with the variables "age" and "grade in math". It would have also been the case with "weight", "height", "income" or "number of children" recorded for the various individuals. As we shall see later on, the numerical nature of these variables means they can be subjected to a wealth of mathematical treatments, which cannot be applied to other types of variables.

2.1.2.2. *Qualitative variables (gender, grade repetition, socioprofessional categories)*

A qualitative variable is one that expresses a "state", as is the case with the variables "gender", "grade repetition" and "parents' SPC". They are expressed by means of modalities. The variable "gender" has two modalities [F, M]; the variable "grade repetition" has two modalities [yes, no] and the variable "parents' SPC" has five modalities [farmer, sr. exec, mid. exec, laborer, employee]. When a qualitative variable has two modalities, it is said to be dichotomic; if it has more than two, it is said to be polytomic.

It is common practice to distinguish nominal qualitative variables and ordinal qualitative variables. The former merely reflect a state, as is the case with the qualitative variables in the table; the latter express a state in which it is possible to define an order, a hierarchy and, therefore, a ranking. It would also be the case with a variable such as "level of education reached" with the six modalities [level I, level II, level III, level IV, level V, level VI].

2.1.2.3. *Quantitative variables expressed in modalities*

Quantitative variables can be represented in the [I/V] table as qualitative variables. In order to do this, we need to define modalities. For example, the quantitative variable "age" in the first table, if we accept that its values may range between 12 and 17, can be transformed into age groups or classes: class 1 [12–13 years], class 2 [14–15 years], class 3 [16–17 years]. In that case, the variable "age" would have three modalities. In the table, for each individual, there would be, for example, "yes" in the corresponding box and "no" in the others, or simply an X in the corresponding box.

2.1.2.4. *Random variables*

Here, we touch on a crucially important point. When we sample a variable with an individual, taken at random, it is impossible to know the result we will obtain in advance, but most of the time, we know the probability that the variable will take such and such a value (or such and such a modality). We then say that the variable is a random variable; it is on this concept that all statistics is based, being an important part of analyses of quantitative data.

Being able to say that we know the probability of obtaining this or that value recorded for an individual taken at random is based on the combination of the laws of chance and of large numbers. There are numerous probability laws, linked to the phenomena studied and the populations concerned. The simplest is the law of equiprobability; the best known and the most commonly encountered is the normal law (the bell curve). This part, which is fundamental for statistics, will be discussed in detail in section 3.1.

2.1.2.5. Dependent/independent variables

Often, studying a phenomenon involves showing the link which may exist between two or more variables observed on a sample – for example, the link between individuals' ages and short-term memory, or simply between the height and weight of the individuals in a sample.

We say that we have two independent variables if, when one of them changes, it has no effect on the other. That is what would occur, certainly, if we were to study the individuals' height in conjunction with their short-term memory. We say that we are dealing with two dependent variables in the opposite case.

2.1.3. Tables

In this section, we discuss the first step in descriptive statistics. It involves presenting multiple types of tables constructed on the basis of the [I/V] table and giving the graphical representation of those tables. To illustrate the idea, we imagine a fictitious study to characterize an average enterprise comprising 32 people working in new technologies.

2.1.3.1. [I/V] table

In the present case, the [I/V] table contains a number of variables taken for each individual in the company: "gender", "salary", "level edu.", "age", "category" (hierarchical rank), etc. We can also detect "absences", and even include subjective data such as a "level of esteem".

We shall focus on the three variables "gender", "salary" and "level edu.". "Salary" is a quantitative variable, while the other two, "gender" and "level edu.", are qualitative variables with, respectively, two modalities [M, F] and four modalities [A, B, C, D]. Those modalities are defined by A (low. bac), B (bac to bac + 2),

C (bac + 2 to bac + 4) and D (masters, engineering degree, etc.). The individuals are numbered 1–32.

It is highly advisable to copy Table 2.2 with an Excel spreadsheet and to process the data offered, step by step.

Individuals	Gender	Salary	Level edu.	......	......	....
1	M	1,550	A	....	....	....
2	F	1,250	A			
3	F	2,200	C			
4	M	1,250	A			
5	M	1,550	A			
6	M	2,500	B	....	....	....
7	F	1,480	A			
8	F	2,100	C			
9	M	1,900	B			
10	F	2,990	C			
11	M	2,850	D			
12	F	1,420	A	....	....	....
13	F	2,250	C			
14	M	3,200	D			
15	M	2,900	D			
16	F	1,300	A			
17	F	1,600	B	....	....	....
18	F	2,550	C			
19	M	1,230	A			
20	M	3,800	D			
21	M	2,600	C			
22	F	1,700	B			
23	M	2,000	B	....	....	....
24	F	2,600	C			
25	F	1,350	B			
26	M	1,400	B			
27	M	2,100	B			
28	M	2,300	B			
29	F	1,260	A	....	....	....
30	M	2,450	C			
31	M	2,400	C			
32	M	2,800	D			

Table 2.2. *[I/V] table of the data from the enterprise*

The [I/V] table is illegible. As it stands, it is not possible to draw lessons from it. Hence, in order to make progress, from the [I/V] table, we shall extract specific tables which are easier to read: population tables and contingency tables.

2.1.3.2. *Population tables*

Population tables tally the number of individuals in each of the modalities, making it easier to interpret the qualitative or quantitative variables expressed in modalities.

2.1.3.2.1. Population tables for qualitative variables

The variable "gender" is a qualitative variable with two modalities [M, F]. It is also interesting to express the populations in percentages.

Gender	M	F	Total
Population	18	14	32
%	56.25	43.75	100

Table 2.3. *Population table: gender*

The variable "level of education" is a qualitative variable with four modalities (A, B, C and D).

Level edu.	A	B	C	D	Total
Population	9	9	9	5	32
%	28.125	28.125	28.125	15.625	100

Table 2.4. *Population table: level of education*

2.1.3.2.2. Population tables for the quantitative variable

The variable "salary" is a quantitative variable that cannot be used directly to generate a population table. For that, we start by defining classes of salaries (modalities). For example, we might define six classes (or modalities).

I: 1,200–1,500 (salaries between 1,200 and 1,500); II: 1,500–1,800; II: 1,800–2,100; IV: 2,100–2,400; V: 2,400–2,700; VI: >2,700 (salary over 2,700).

In these conditions, we can establish the population table that counts the number of individuals per modality defined:

Salary	I	II	III	IV	V	VI	Total
Population	9	4	4	4	5	6	32
%	28.125	12.5	12.5	12.5	15.625	18.75	100

Table 2.5. *Population table: salary*

2.1.3.3. Contingency tables cross-referencing two variables

Contingency tables are dual-input tables that cross-reference the populations of two variables. In each cell, at the junction of two modalities of these variables is the population of individuals who simultaneously belong to both modalities of each of those variables. Below, we show the contingency tables for the three variables, compared two by two.

2.1.3 3.1. Gender and salary

In each of the cells, we find the number of individuals (M or F) whose salary falls within each of the categories (I, II, III, IV, V, VI). The table also shows the total for each of the rows and columns.

We see that there are three men who have a category-III salary and that, in total, there are four people with a category-III salary.

	I	II	III	IV	V	VI	Total
M	3	2	3	2	3	5	18
F	6	2	1	2	2	1	14
Total	9	4	4	4	5	6	32

Table 2.6. *Contingency table: gender/salary*

2.1.3.3.2. Gender and level of education

For example, we can see from the table that three women have a level of education B (bac to bac + 2).

	A	B	C	D	Total
M	4	6	3	5	18
F	5	3	6	0	14

Table 2.7. *Contingency table: gender/level of education*

2.1.3.3.3. Salary and level of education

We see that of the six highest paid employees, five of them have a level of education D and one has C.

	I	II	III	IV	V	VI	Total
A	7	2	0	0	0	0	9
B	2	2	3	1	1	0	9
C	0	0	1	3	4	1	9
D	0	0	0	0	0	5	5
Total	9	4	4	4	5	6	32

Table 2.8. *Contingency table: salary/level of education*

To make it easier to write the contingency tables, we have only shown the cross-referenced populations, expressed in %. By way of example, see Table 2.9, which cross-references gender with salary, including the %: we can see, for instance, that six women have a salary in modality I – that is, between 1,200 and 1,500 euros – which represents 42.9% of the women.

	I	II	III	IV	V	VI	Total
M	3	2	3	2	3	5	18
M %	16.7	11.1	16.7	11.1	16.7	27.8	100
F	6	2	1	2	2	1	14
F %	42.9	14.3	7.1	14.3	14.3	7.1	100
Total	9	4	4	4	5	6	32

Table 2.9. *Contingency table: gender/salary with %*

2.1.3.4. Analysis and conclusions

Population tables and contingency tables reveal information that is not visible in the [I/V] table. What is this new information?

2.1.3.4.1. Population tables

There is no significant imbalance between men and women, though there are more men (18, which is 56.25%) than women (14, which is 43.75%).

The level of training of personnel is of high quality: 23 have postsecondary qualifications, which is 72%. Of those, 14 (44%) have an undergraduate degree or greater. This level of qualification is not surprising for a company working in the area of new technologies.

With regard to salaries, we see that there are nine employees with a low salary, probably representing low-qualified staff having maintenance or subordinate logistics jobs. At the other end of the scale, we have six highly paid staff who are, undoubtedly, the highest qualified and the executives in the company. The salaries appear to correspond to the level of qualification of the staff.

2.1.3.4.2. Contingency tables

Women's salaries are lower than those of men; 42.8% of the women have a salary under 1,500 euros, as opposed to only 16.7% of the men, and only 7.1% of the women have a salary higher than 3,000 euros, as opposed to 27.8% of the men. For lower incomes, this trend, although it is less marked, is confirmed.

The pay scale is strongly linked to level of education. We can clearly see that the salaries are an increasing function of the level of education.

The women have a good level of education, but none of them is within the ranks of the highest qualified people.

The analysis could continue by taking account of other variables in order to further improve knowledge of the company. In terms of what is of interest to us here, this example must be considered only as a "toy" example – a pretext to present tools that can be used for an initial analysis of the raw data given in the [I/V] table.

2.1.4. *Graphic representations*

2.1.4.1. *Introduction*

It is often helpful, and sometimes absolutely essential, to present the data contained in the different tables in graph form. In any case, we must take account of how easy the representation is to read, as well as the esthetic aspect of the documents, not to mention the fact that graphic representations can reveal information, which has been previously hidden.

In turn, we shall touch on the graphic representations of the population tables and then contingency tables, and we shall finish with the use of point clouds, which only exist for quantitative variables, and show any link that may exist between quantitative variables.

The results presented below were computed using an Excel spreadsheet, in which it is enough to copy the data table in question and use the set of graphic possibilities available in the "Insert" menu, followed by the "Charts" menu.

The examples processed below are merely a small sample of the possibilities afforded by Excel, for both the type of graph and the style and colors of presentation. It is highly advisable to take a look at Excel to discover all the possibilities offered, which are easy, user-friendly and quick to master.

2.1.4.2. *Graphic representations of a population table*

The illustrations correspond to the above survey regarding the organization of the fictional enterprise. Each figure is a representation of the population tables presented above.

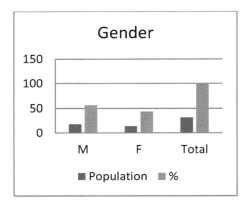

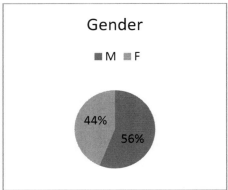

Figure 2.1. *Graphic representations, histogram and pie chart, of the population table with gender. For a color version of this figure, see www.iste.co.uk/larini/education.zip*

There are many different ways in which to represent a population table. The most widespread but also the most explicit are the histogram (also known as a distribution) and the famous pie chart (or sector graph). Figures 2.1–2.3 show the graphic representations corresponding to the population tables presented above.

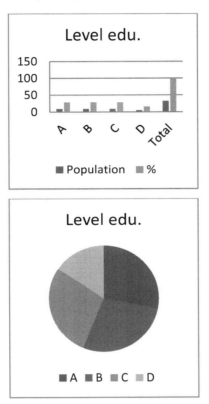

Figure 2.2. *Graphic representations, histogram and pie chart, for the population table with level of education. For a color version of this figure, see www.iste.co.uk/larini/education.zip*

2.1.4.3. *Graphic representations of a contingency table*

To graphically represent a contingency table that cross-references two variables, it is possible to use a histogram. To illustrate the point, let us take another look at one of the contingency tables above, cross-referencing the modalities [M, F] of the variable "gender" with the modalities [I, II, III, IV, V, VI] of the variable "salary".

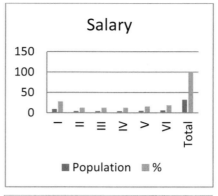

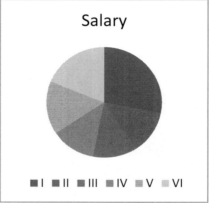

Figure 2.3. *Graphic representations, histogram and pie chart, from the population table with the salary. For a color version of this figure, see www.iste.co.uk/larini/education.zip*

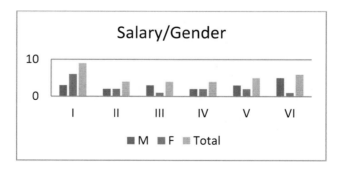

Figure 2.4. *Graphic representation of the gender/salary contingency table. For a color version of this figure, see www.iste.co.uk/larini/education.zip*

We can see that many women have a low salary (I) and very few have a high salary (V and VI).

2.1.4.4. *Point clouds for two quantitative variables*

We shall now take a look at a different type of graphic representation, which will frequently be used in the rest of this book: point clouds. Point clouds can be used when we are dealing with two numerical quantitative variables extracted from an [I/V] table.

The graphical representation is based on the fact that if we are operating in a planar space with two dimensions (X , Y), we can represent each individual, on that plane, as a point, where X and Y are two variables characterizing the individuals.

It is also advisable that readers themselves generate point clouds, based on the table below, using an Excel spreadsheet.

Consider the grades obtained in math, physics and history/geography by 12 pupils in the same class.

Pupils	Math	Physics	HG
1	10	10	8
2	15	14	4
3	8	8	4
4	9	9	12
5	19	18	13
6	2	3	15
7	14	14	14
8	5	6	6
9	4	5	7
10	8	8	3
11	2	3	2
12	1	4	4

Table 2.10. *Record of grades for math, physics and history/geography (HG)*

We first construct the point cloud to represent the physics grades (Y) as a function of the math grades (X) (Figure 2.5), and then the physics grades (Y) as a function of the history/geography grades (X) (Figure 2.6).

For example, pupil 5 has the coordinates $X = 19$ and $Y = 18$ in the plane representing physics grades as a function of the math grades. The same pupil has the coordinates $X = 18$ and $Y = 13$ in the plane representing the history/geography grades as a function of the physics grades.

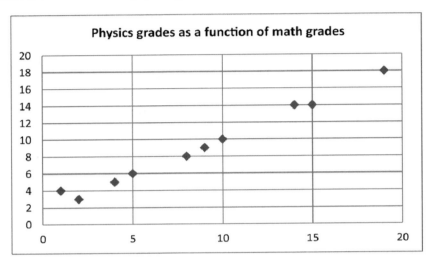

Figure 2.5. *Math/physics point cloud*

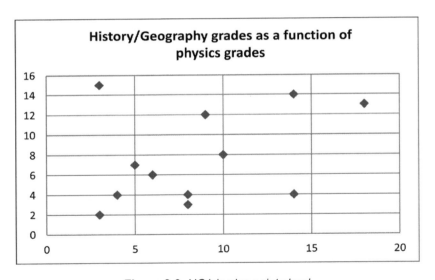

Figure 2.6. *HG/physics point cloud*

This simple illustration shows what we can learn from point clouds. In our case, here, we see that there is a strong linear link between physics grades and math grades. This link suggests that the better a student understands math, the better they perform in physics. On the other hand, there is no demonstrable link between the grades obtained in history/geography and the grades obtained in physics.

2.2. Mathematical indicators

2.2.1. *General points*

Mathematical indicators apply only to quantitative variables. A significant portion of the statistical approaches studied in the rest of this book is based on such indicators.

We define a number of properties (values) that give us a precise mathematical description of the data found in a sample. In turn, we shall look at values characterizing a single variable (monovariate mathematical indicators: mean, variance, standard deviation, etc.) and then values characterizing the interaction between two variables (bivariate mathematical indicators: covariance and correlation coefficient).

It may be that this section will pose a few problems for readers with a purely "literary" background, because it uses mathematical language with which they are unfamiliar. For those who fall into this category, note that not a great deal of effort is required to fill that gap. Simply reading over section 2.2.2 and getting to know the Excel spreadsheet to perform the calculations will allow users to understand well and be able to apply these concepts. Readers already familiar with mathematical language may skip section 2.2.2.

2.2.2. *Some fundamentals of mathematical language*

2.2.2.1. *Index variables*

We record data from six individuals. The result is shown in Table 2.11, where, for each individual, we can see the value of the variable X.

Individuals	I_1	I_2	I_3	I_4	I_5	I_6
X	$x_1 = 6$	$x_2 = 9$	$x_3 = 12$	$x_4 = 7$	$x_5 = 9$	$x_6 = 11$

Table 2.11. *Monovariate index [I/V] table*

Often, for brevity of formulation, we introduce an index (for example, i). We say that the value of the variable X associated with individual I_i can be written as x_i, where, in this case, i can assume the values [1, 2, 3, 4, 5, 6]. For example, for individual I_4, the value of X is $x_4 = 7$. This formulation is used for general definitions and in calculations where it is not possible to explicitly state all the terms contained in the table during an operation.

2.2.2.2. Summation of indices

Staying with the above example, we might, for instance, want to find the sum of the values of the variable X for each individual – i.e. perform the following operation: $6 + 9 + 12 + 7 + 9 + 11 = 54$.

We can also briefly write that $\sum_{i=1}^{i=6} x_i = 54$, which is read as: "The sum of the x_i values where i ranges from 1 to 6 is equal to 54".

We might also, for example, wish to express the sum of the squares of the values taken by the variable X: $\sum_{i=1}^{i=6} x_i^2$, read as: "The sum of the squares of x_i for i ranging between 1 and 6", and this operation would give us a value of 512.

2.2.2.3. Generic tables with one index

Here, the term *generic* means that something is supposed to represent all situations.

Consider a situation comparable to the one we looked at above (Table 2.12), but now with an undefined number (n) of individuals, instead of six. We can write a generic table – i.e. one capable of representing all situations of the same type.

It is read as follows: the value of x for the individual I_1 is x_1, the value of x for the "general" individual I_i is x_i and for the last individual I_n, the value is x_n.

Individuals	I_1	......	I_i	......	I_n
Variable X	x_1	......	x_i	......	x_n

Table 2.12. *Generic [I/V] table with one index*

We can find the sum S of the n terms in the table by: $S = \sum_{i=1}^{i=n} x_i$. If we know each of the x_i values, then we can calculate S. The indexed representation and the operations of summation are perfectly suited to the calculation procedures offered by an Excel spreadsheet.

2.2.2.4. *Generic tables with two indices*

We can also use tables with two indices to represent contingency tables. In Table 2.13, we have a table that cross-references voter intentions in five cities across France for three candidates (A1, A2, A3).

The population in each of the cells is of the form n_i^j. The subscript represents the candidates (rows) and the superscript represents the cities (columns).

Candidate/cities	Marseille	Lyon	Bordeaux	Lille	Toulouse	Total
A1	n_1^1	n_1^2	n_1^3	n_1^4	n_1^5	N_1
A2	n_2^1	n_2^2	n_2^3	n_2^5	n_2^5	N_2
A3	n_3^1	n_3^2	n_3^3	n_3^4	n_3^5	N_3
Total	N^1	N^2	N^3	N^4	N^5	N

Table 2.13. *Contingency table with two indices: candidate/cities*

It can be read as follows: "In the city of Bordeaux (column 3), there are n_2^3 electors who declare that they intend to vote for candidate A_2 (row 2)".

We often need to know the sums of the populations for the rows and those of the columns. We speak of knowing the *margins*. In the total cells for the rows, we see terms of the type N_2, expressing the sum of the populations of row 2 – that is $\sum_{j=1}^{5} n_2^j = N_2$. Similarly, in the total cells for the columns, we see N^4, for example, which expresses the sum of the populations for column 4.

In the more general case where we have n individuals, from whom we record p variables, we would have the following generic [I/V] table. It can be read as follows: the value of the variable V^j recorded for individual i is x_i^j.

	V^1	V^2	......	V^j	......	V^p
I_1	x_1^1	x_1^2		x_1^j		x_1^p
I_2	x_2^1	x_2^2		x_2^j		x_2^p
......						
I_i	x_i^1	x_i^2		x_i^j		x_i^p
......						
I_n	x_n^1	x_n^2		x_n^j		x_n^p

Table 2.14. *Generic table with two indices*

Another operation with which it is important to be familiar (it will be discussed later on in the book) is double summation. It consists of adding together all the values of the p variables for the n individuals. It is represented thus, mathematically:

$$S = \sum_{j=1}^{p} \sum_{i=1}^{n} x_i^j = \sum_{i=1}^{n} \sum_{j=1}^{p} x_i^j$$

Equality means that we can start by adding up each of the columns, and then add together the results obtained for each column, or we can begin by adding up each of the rows and then add together the results obtained for each row.

2.2.3. *Monovariate mathematical indicators*

2.2.3.1. *Definitions*

Consider the generic [I/V] table resulting from the collection of data from n individuals, pertaining to the variable X.

Individuals	I_1	....	I_i	....	I_n
Variable **X**	x_1	....	x_i	....	x_n

Table 2.15. *Generic monovariate table for individuals/variables*

We now define values that can be used to characterize the sample defined in the generic monovariate table.

Mean of the variable X:

$$\overline{X} = \frac{1}{n} \sum_{i=1}^{n} x_i$$

By definition, it is the sum of the x_i for all the individuals, all divided by n (the number of individuals). Conventionally, it is written with a bar above the variable.

Going back to Table 2.11:

$$\overline{X} = \frac{6 + 9 + 12 + 7 + 9 + 11}{6} = 9$$

Variance of the variable X: The variance measures the dispersion of the values around the mean value. It is defined as follows:

$$\text{Var}(X) = \frac{1}{n} \sum_{i=1}^{n} (x_i - \overline{X})^2$$

It is the sum of the squares of the differences $x_i - \overline{X}$ calculated for each individual, all divided by n, the number of individuals. We choose the sum of the squares because otherwise, the positive and negative values would cancel one another out and, for instance, in the event of a symmetrical distribution, we would obtain a variance of zero.

Still looking at Table 2.11, we find:

$$Var(X) = \frac{1}{6}\{(6-9)^2 + (9-9)^2 + (12-9)^2 + (7-9)^2 + (9-9)^2 + (11-9)^2\} = 4.3$$

We also define a variance known as the unbiased variance:

$$Var(X) = \frac{1}{n-1}\Sigma_{i=1}^{n}(x_i - \overline{X})^2$$

Unbiased variance will be used in the second half of this course, when we discuss mean tests.

Standard deviation of the variable X:

$$S(X) = \sqrt{Var(X)}$$

The standard variation of variable X is the square root of its variance. Depending on whether we use variance or unbiased variance, we will be dealing with the standard deviation or the unbiased standard deviation.

2.2.3.2. Meaning and properties of the variance and standard variation

We have defined the variance and standard deviation; now, we shall gain an understanding of their meaning and, thereby, how it is useful to know them in order to give a description of the data collected.

Imagine a class of 12 pupils who have undergone three written math tests. The mean of the grades obtained is the same for all three tasks (i.e. 10/20). However, the nature of the tests is such that test Math1 is not discriminating (all pupils obtained the same score of 10/20); yet the grades obtained in Math2 range from 6/20 to 14/20 and for Math3, the grades range between 2/20 and 18/20. Hence, it seems that Math2 allows us to tell the students apart, and Math3 even more so. The grades obtained are represented in Table 2.16.

Pupils	Math1	Math2	Math3
1	10	6	2
2	10	10	15
3	10	7	3
4	10	11	13
5	10	8	5
6	10	13	14
7	10	13	18
8	10	12	17
9	10	7	4
10	10	10	6
11	10	14	16
12	10	9	7

Table 2.16. *The three series of math grades in the imaginary tests*

The calculations of the means, variances and standard deviations give:

$\overline{Math1} = 14$ Var (Math1) = 0   S (Math1) = 0

$\overline{Math2} = 14$ Var (Math2) = 0, 67   S (Math2) = 0, 82

$\overline{Math3} = 14$ Var (Math3) = 2, 66   S (Math3) = 1, 63

We can see that the variance of a variable is linked to its dispersion around its mean value. The more tightly the values are grouped around the mean, the lower the variance. In the extreme case (Math1) where all the values are equal, it has a value of 0. On the other hand, the more widely the values are dispersed around the mean, the higher the variance – this is what we observe for Math2 and Math3.

The standard deviation, which is the square root of the variance, qualitatively behaves in the same way as the variance. These are values that we shall use time and again throughout this book.

2.2.3.3. *Application exercises: calculations with Excel*

In the previous section, we saw how to calculate means, variances and standard deviations *manually*. This exercise is helpful for readers to familiarize themselves with these values, but in practice, the calculations are performed with more elaborate tools. In the present case, we suggest practicing with the spreadsheet software Excel.

Consider the math, physics and history/geography grades recorded for 12 pupils (Table 2.17).

Pupils	Math	Physics	HG
1	10	10	8
2	15	14	4
3	8	8	4
4	9	9	12
5	19	18	13
6	2	3	15
7	14	14	14
8	5	6	6
9	4	5	7
10	8	8	3
11	2	3	2
12	1	4	4

Table 2.17. *[I/V] table showing data for math, physics and HG*

Try and answer the following two questions:

1) find, in turn, the means, variances and standard deviations of the variables "math", "physics" and "HG", using only the basic calculation functions in Excel;

2) perform the same calculation using the macros in Excel.

To answer the first question, we must do the same as we do for the *manual* calculation, but the detail of the calculations is handled automatically by the spreadsheet. The calculation is presented in the form of a table. The operations are performed on the cells in the first row (after typing "=") and the calculation is performed automatically on the other rows when we move the cursor. The calculation of the variance of the grade in math is represented in Table 2.18.

The calculation is performed in accordance with the definition:

$$\text{Var (Math)} = \frac{1}{12}\sum_{i=1}^{12}\left(\text{Math}_i - \overline{\text{Math}}\right)^2$$

The first two columns in Table 2.17 represent the pupils and their grades in math. We begin by calculating the mean grade for the variable "math" ($\overline{Math}$). In the third column, we calculate D = (Math $-\overline{Math}$) and in the fourth, we square D. Then we simply need to find the sum of all the D^2 values and divide that sum by 12.

Pupils	Math	D	D^2
1	10	1.91667	3.67362389
2	15	6.91667	47.8403239
3	8	−0.08333	0.00694389
4	9	0.91667	0.84028389
5	19	10.91667	119.173684
6	2	−6.08333	37.0069039
7	14	5.91667	35.0069839
8	5	−3.08333	9.50692389
9	4	−4.08333	16.6735839
10	8	−0.08333	0.00694389
11	2	−6.08333	37.0069039
12	1	−7.08333	50.1735639
Mean	8.08333333		
Sum			356.916667
Variance	29.7430556		

Table 2.18. *Excel calculation table for the variable "math"*

Standard deviation: 5.45371942.

The above calculation is instructive, because it is based on the mathematical formulation of the definition of the variance, but it is possible to perform it much more easily by using macros in Excel. That is the subject of the second question.

The path is as follows: go to *Formulas*, then *More functions*, then *Statistical*. From the dropdown menu, find VAR.P, which gives the variance. VAR returns the unbiased variance.

For physics and history/geography, we obtain the following results:

Var (Physics) = 21.08333   Standard deviation (Physics) = 4.5916591

Var (HG) = 19.88888   Standard deviation (HG) = 4.4596905

Obviously, in practice, when the indicators are assimilated, we use macros, which produce a result almost instantaneously.

2.2.4. *Bivariate mathematical indicators*

We shall now define bivariate indicators, then examine their properties, and finally present a few examples of calculations.

2.2.4.1. *Definitions*

With a bivariate approach, we have n individuals I_i (i = 1,..., n) and two quantitative variables X and Y recorded for each individual. The generic data are represented in Table 2.19.

Variable/individuals	I_1	.....	I_i	.....	I_n
X	x_1	.....	x_i	.....	x_n
Y	y_1	.....	y_i	.....	y_n

Table 2.19. *Generic bivariate table*

2.2.4.1.1. Covariance of two variables X and Y

By definition, the covariance of the two variables X and Y is:

$$Cov(X, Y) = \frac{1}{n}\sum_{i=1}^{n} (x_i - \overline{X})(y_i - \overline{Y})$$

For example, if we consider Table 2.20, which gives the values obtained when two variables are measured for 10 individuals, we can calculate the covariance of the two variables "manually".

X	1	8	1	18	14	20	8	40	21	14
Y	6	13	9	5	17	20	14	2	17	2

Table 2.20. *Bivariate table: calculation of covariance*

$\overline{X} = 14.5$ $\overline{Y} = 10.5$

$$Cov(X, Y) = \frac{1}{10}[(1 - 14.5)(6 - 10.5) + \cdots . +(14 - 14.5)(2 - 10.5)] = -9.85$$

2.2.4.1.2. Correlation coefficient for two variables X and Y

The correlation coefficient is deduced directly from the covariance and the standard deviations of X and Y, by dividing the covariance by the product of the two standard deviations:

$$Cor(X, Y) = \frac{1}{n}\sum_{i=1}^{n}(x_i - \overline{X})(y_i - \overline{Y})/s(X)s(Y)$$

Thus, in the case of Table 2.17, having calculated the standard deviations:

$S(X) = 10.8834$ and $S(Y) = 6.2489$

We find:

$$Cor(X, Y) = -\frac{9.85}{10.8834*6.2489} = -0.1448$$

2.2.4.2. *Properties of covariance and correlation coefficient*

To demonstrate the properties of covariance and the correlation coefficient, we have "fabricated" five series of pairs (A, B, C, D, E) of variables X and Y. In each of the series, we impose a link of varying degrees of strength between the two variables. For each of them, let us now examine the impact this link has on the covariance and on the correlation.

Series A: we impose Y = X

X	1	2	3	4	5	6	7	8	9	10
Y	1	2	3	4	5	6	7	8	9	10

Series B: we impose Y = −2X + 1

X	1	2	3	4	5	6	7	8	9	10
Y	−1	−3	−5	−7	−9	−11	−13	−15	−17	−19

Series C: we impose Y = (X, X + 1, X − 1)

X	1	2	3	4	5	6	7	8	9	10
Y	1	3	2	4	6	5	7	9	8	10

Series D: we impose Y = (X, X + 2, X − 2)

X	1	2	3	4	5	6	7	8	9	10
Y	1	4	1	4	7	4	7	10	7	10

Series E: chance (random draw)

X	1	8	1	18	14	20	8	40	21	14
Y	6	13	9	5	17	20	14	2	17	2

Table 2.21. *Series A, B, C, D, E: covariance and correlation*

For series A and B, there is an absolute link between variables X and Y. For series C and D, there is a link, but it is somewhat "deconstructed". For series E, the variables result from a construction at random.

For each of the series, Table 2.22 indicates the standard deviations of X and of Y, the variance of the couple (X, Y) and the correlation coefficient.

	S (**X**)	S (**Y**)	Cov. (**X, Y**)	Cor. (**X, Y**)
Series A	3.03	3.03	+9.18	+1.00
Series B	3.03	6.06	−18.36	−1.00
Series C	3.03	3.03	+8.81	+0.96
Series D	3.03	3.24	+9.82	+0.87
Series E	3.03	10.50	−9.85	−0.14

Table 2.22. *Calculation results for series A, B, C, D, E*

By looking at the table, we can see just what is expressed by the correlation coefficient. However, it is more difficult to interpret the values of the covariance.

Analysis of series A and B shows that when the variables are linked by a strict linear relation, the correlation coefficient has a value of 1 with a "plus" sign if the two variables share the same direction of variation, and a "minus" sign if they change in the opposite direction.

Series C is constructed on the basis of series A, but slightly "bucking" the linear law by adjusting the variable Y. We can see that in this case, the correlation coefficient stays close to 1, but decreases slightly (0.96). This means that X and Y are no longer linked by a "perfect" linear relation, but the link is strong and the linearity is also good.

Series D is also constructed on the basis of series A, but the initial linear law is "broken" more significantly than for series C. We can see that the correlation coefficient falls to 0.87. The linearity is degraded but still remains significant.

Series E is constructed at random. The correlation coefficient (−0.14) is very low. It expressed the fact that the linear link between X and Y is non-existent.

Generally speaking, we can hold up the following properties:

– cor $(X, Y) = +1$ when a variable is a strict increasing linear function of the other;

– cor $(X, Y) = -1$ when a variable is a strict decreasing linear function of the other;

– the closer the correlation coefficient is to the extreme values -1 and $+1$, the stronger the link between the variables;

– cor $(X, Y) = 0$ means that the variables are linearly independent;

– the closer the correlation coefficient is to 0, the less of a link there is between the variables.

NOTE.– The two variables X and Y may be linked by a nonlinear relation, such as $Y = X^2$ or $Y = \frac{1}{X}$. In this case, although there is a strong link between the two variables, the correlation coefficient may be low, because, as must be remembered, the correlation coefficient only measures the linear relation linking the two variables. Also, although it is generally referred to as the "correlation coefficient", its true name is the "linear correlation coefficient".

2.2.4.3. *Application exercises: calculations of covariance and standard deviation with Excel*

Look again at the values in Table 2.17, and answer the following questions:

1) calculate the covariances and the correlation coefficients of the variables "math", "physics" and "HG", taken pairwise, using only the basic calculation functions in Excel;

2) perform the same calculation using the macros in Excel.

For the first question, the calculation is performed directly using the equations of definition:

$$Cov(X, Y) = \frac{1}{n} \sum_{i=1}^{n} (x_i - \overline{X})(y_i - \overline{Y})$$

$$Cor(X, Y) = \frac{1}{n} \sum_{i=1}^{n} (x_i - \overline{X})(y_i - \overline{Y})/S(X)S(Y)$$

Table 2.23 illustrates the approach to calculate the covariance and the correlation coefficient of the two variables "physics" and "HG". Having calculated the respective mean values, $\overline{Physics}$ and $\overline{HG}$, followed by the standard deviations,

S(Physics) and S(HG), we define $A = (\text{Physics}_i - \overline{\text{Physics}})$ and $B = (HG_i - \overline{HG})$. Then, using the same approach as for monovariate indicators, we construct Table 2.23.

Pupils	Physics	HG	A	B	A × B
1	10	8	1.5	0.33333	0.499995
2	14	4	5.5	−3.66667	−20.166685
3	8	4	−0.5	−3.66667	1.833335
4	9	12	0.5	4.33333	2.166665
5	18	13	9.5	5.33333	50.666635
6	3	15	−5.5	7.33333	−40.333315
7	14	14	5.5	6.33333	34.833315
8	6	6	−2.5	−1.66667	4.166675
9	5	7	−3.5	−0.66667	2.333345
10	8	3	−0.5	−4.66667	2.333335
11	3	2	−5.5	−5.66667	31.166685
12	4	4	−4.5	−3.66667	16.500015
Means	8.5	7.6666666			
Standard deviation	4.591659	4.4596960			
Cov. (physics, HG)					7.1666667
Cor. (physics, HG)					0.3499792

Table 2.23. *Excel spreadsheet to calculate cov. (physics, HG) and cor. (physics, HG)*

For the second question, we need to find the covariance and then the correlation coefficient in the "Statistical" dropdown menu.

Responses:

Cov (Math, Physics) = 24.875   Cor (Math, Physics) = 0.9933

Cov (Math, HG) = 8.27777   Cor (Math, HG) = 0.34034

2.3. Spatial data representation methods

2.3.1. *Maps to understand the geography of educational phenomena*

Cartography is a graphic representation of the world that enables the reader to identify and understand, among other things, the logic of the locations of things or processes studied. A map is a spatial representation of statistical data. It adds knowledge to the territorial dynamics of educational processes. A map can help to inform and illuminate choices and aid decision making.

There are many different types of maps. Maps based on population data or statistics, which are the best known, are so-called "topical" maps; they describe a specific topic – e.g. the percentage of potential school dropouts per establishment. One of the aims of these topical maps is to graphically represent simple or complex phenomena combining multiple statistical indicators. At the same time, a map can prove to be a source of information to pinpoint localized data, a tool to reveal underlying structures and, finally, a communication channel aimed at "showing". A map is a mediation of statistical data onto the geographic plane.

Reading a map as a whole helps to understand the overall structure of the spatialized information and extract explanations with regard to the general processes. Sparse data or details may emerge when we look again in greater depth. By reading the map, we are able to formulate hypotheses about the geography of an educational situation.

2.3.2. *Statistical data represented on a map*

Cartography is used in addition to representations of data in the form of tables or graphs when the data can be localized (the data are then associated with places or addresses). The individual, in the statistical sense of the term, may be associated with a spatial unit (or geographic unit – e.g. a commune, a school, an establishment). Indeed, cartography is the main mode of representation of the spatial distribution of numerical values calculated or observed, per unit.

Statistical tables or graphs offer a general overview of the tables, but are not sufficient to spatially represent the information. Hence, a map is a complementary means of representation when data tables have spatial units (e.g. communes) and variables (e.g. the number of pupils per commune). The individual, in the statistical sense, represents a spatial unit without taking account of its location. The form of the spatial unit is represented either by a surfacic, linear or punctual vectorial form (e.g. a commune, a neighborhood, a plot of land, a road, a school), or by pixels in a raster format. The individual has a specific nature to which we attribute variables (quantitative or qualitative) in the form of numeric or textual data.

Cartography consists of making a series of maps, *a priori* and therefore hypothetical, demonstrating the explicative information and constituting an element of a solution to the problem at hand. Having collected a data set, it is necessary to identify those that are most pertinent for the analysis. The definition of the topic and of the space being studied is based on proposed hypotheses and a definition of a central and secondary issue. Who are these pupils? Why do they have different school careers? How many are there? Where do they go? etc.

The intellectual construct that is cartography has a graphic language of its own, made up of signs and precise rules [BÉG 10]. Graphic semiology is that indispensable knowledge in cartography about the rules of that graphic language. The map requires learning and knowledge to distinguish the forms of spatial distribution and to understand it. The division of a series of relative quantities into slices or classes is known as discretization. In general, a series is discretized into three, four or five categories, depending on the desired degree of fineness. Thus, we find a representation of the effective numbers of responses for each of the questions. The legend, a scale and an orientation aid in the reading of the map.

2.3.3. *Range-based and point-based maps*

The cartographic representation that uses graphic semiology requires choosing forms of visual variables as a function of the types of data being charted. Communal data whose values are the results of ratios/residents per km², number of pupils dropping out of school per commune, etc., are represented by maps known as range maps. Between these relative data, there is a relation of order. The value (or lightness) being the visual variable that is best suited to represent the order, a series of relative data is represented by a range of values (from dark to light). When the series contains negative values, opposing colors are used (cold colors for negative values and warm colors for positives).

This kind of map was used in a vast statistical study aimed at elucidating the relationship between the territorial context and the results achieved by schools. Here, the study marked the position of the schools surveyed and characterized the demographic dynamism of its location in order to draw the connection between it and the cultural customs of the families.

Absolute quantitative data, which are values of populations, quantities found by a measurement, are charted in point implantations in the form of proportional circles. These maps are known as point-based maps. Between the absolute values, there is a relation of proportionality and a relation of order. Consequently, the relation of proportionality is unique. As the size is the only visual variation that can give an account of the relations of proportionality, the absolute quantities are represented by points whose sizes are proportional to the quantities.

In the same study, the goal was to identify the primary and secondary schools and colleges surveyed.

Evolution of the population from 1999 to 2009

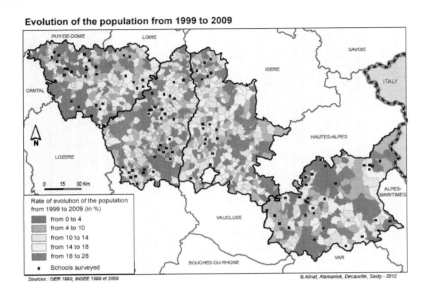

Figure 2.7. *Example of a range-based map. For a color version of this figure,*
see www.iste.co.uk/larini/education.zip

Pupils surveyed in CM2, 5th, 3rd and final year

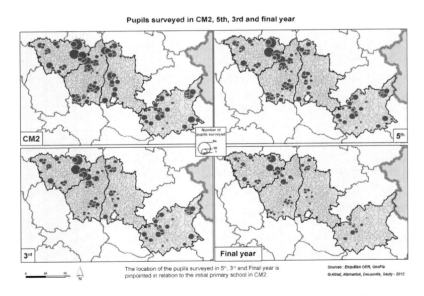

Figure 2.8. *Example of a point-based map. For a color version*
of this figure, see www.iste.co.uk/larini/education.zip

2.3.4. *Other maps*

Without going into detail, there are other types of maps, of which we show a number of examples here.

The maps measure distances to accessibility of the schools in a mountainous region, prior to another study on the impact of transport on school attendance.

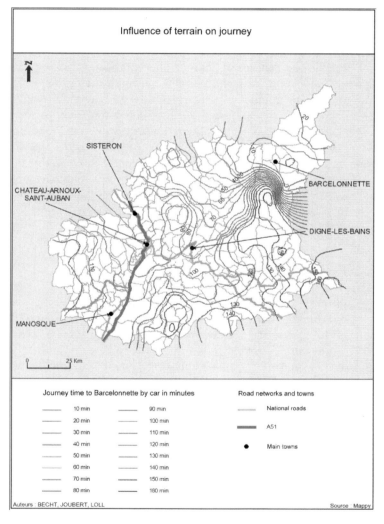

Figure 2.9. *Example of an isohypse map. For a color version of this figure, see www.iste.co.uk/larini/education.zip*

2.3.5. *Geographic information systems*

We shall not go into detail about the construction of a geographic information system (GIS), but simply note that such systems do exist for people who want to investigate in greater depth. The use of a GIS requires a certain amount of learning, but that learning is not particularly complicated. There are simple, free software tools that can be downloaded from the Internet – for example, QGIS. GISs can be defined as a means of managing geographic databases in the form of spreadsheets, integrated into a data system so that the relations between them can be drawn. Cartographic representation is solely the result of superpositions, cross-referencing, spatial relating of various types of geographic features (surface features, linear features or points). The concept of a geographic information system, born of the union between computing, mathematics and geography, aims to use the mass calculation capacity of computers to harvest, store, organize, manage, process, multiply, analyze, represent and disseminate spatial information, of all different types. In geography, GISs have the ability to simultaneously examine several aspects of the same space, to articulate the relations between them, and the spatial organization existing between the geographic features. Spatial analysis of spatial data using statistical or mathematical methods underlies GIS tools. Geographic data, once they are interpreted, become information, which contributes to the building of knowledge. By building a GIS based on educational topics, we are able to garner dynamic and real-time information about educational processes.

2.3.6. *Specific map-analysis methods*

Analysis of maps, and therefore of geographic data, can be done in a number of different ways. A simple description of the distribution of the data, and of the spatial organization of the educational processes which they underpin, is a good first step.

Beyond this, a comparative examination of the charted data is of interest, notably in the event of maps with opposite modalities [ALI 13]. Preponderance refers to a choice of rate of meaningful responses regarding the opposing modalities to define a relevant indicator for a given school. These maps show only the schools which conform to a single selection criterion (that is one modality), which is stated in the title of the map. Maps showing a very small number of schools provide us with only a limited amount of information, but are still of interest, because they identify schools with very specific characteristics – e.g. schools where the pupils and their families go to the theater. Thus, it is possible to find relations between the socioeconomic data for the surrounding areas and those of the families whose children attend the schools.

CM2: over half of pupils have gone to the theater with their families

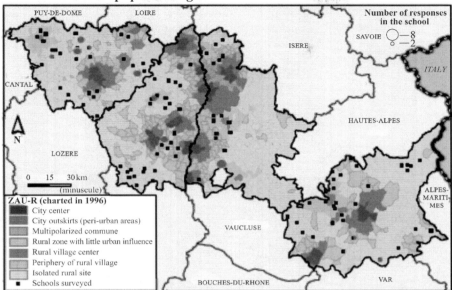

CM2: over half of pupils have gone to the theater on a school trip

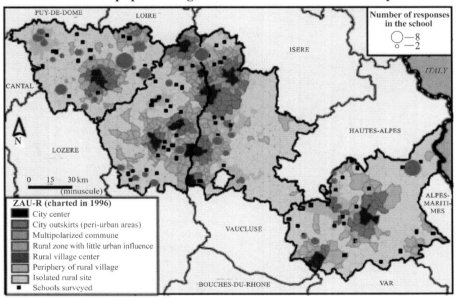

Figure 2.10. *Map of preponderant modalities. For a color version of this figure, see www.iste.co.uk/larini/education.zip*

Furthermore, a chronological analysis of certain maps is helpful when the results of the surveys vary over time. Pupils' responses to identical questions evolve depending on their age. For instance, it is possible to draw the connection between the career paths the pupils wish to follow, the socioeconomic circumstances of the geographic surroundings and the reality of the career paths taken.

Schools of CM pupils (1999), where at least half of the pupils intend to pursue long-term education later on

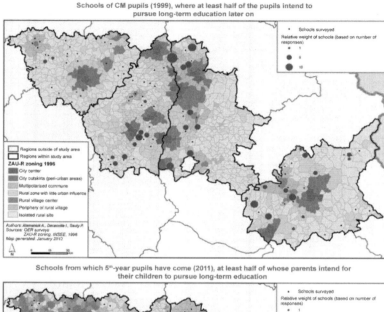

Schools from which 5ᵗʰ-year pupils have come (2011), at least half of whose parents intend for their children to pursue long-term education

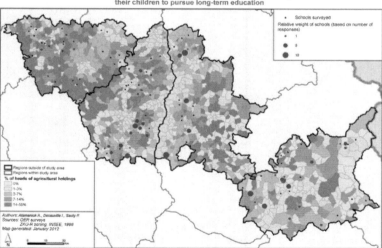

Figure 2.11. *Chronological map. For a color version of this figure, see www.iste.co.uk/larini/education.zip*

3

Confirmatory Statistics

Confirmatory statistics comes into play after the collection of data (Chapter 1) and the shaping and representation of those data as tables, graphs and mathematical indicators (Chapter 2). Researchers can then analyze their results and draw some initial conclusions. These conclusions cannot be disputed, as they are limited to the samples actually observed. However, usually, a study is conducted to produce conclusions that can be generalized to apply to the whole of a population. By way of example, let us examine which types of situations might arise.

Let us begin by coming back to the fictitious study cited in the previous chapters, where the aim is to compare the effectiveness of two reading methods (A and B). In the experiment, method A is used in one class and method B in another class. To prevent the influence of the *teacher effect*, the same teacher will lead both classes. After 3 months of work, a series of identical tests is carried out with the two classes, and it is found that class A has achieved better results than class B. However, as things stand, we cannot conclude that method A is more effective than method B, because there exists the possibility that the choice of samples has influenced the results greatly; had different sample classes been chosen, the result might have been quite the opposite. If we want to show that the result obtained holds true generally (we also say, in this case, that it is proven), we need to use a statistical test that allows us to move from the restricted conclusion, *the results obtained in class A are better than those obtained in class B*, to the more general one, *method A is more effective than method B*.

Along the same lines, we might wonder whether girls perform better in mathematics than boys. To determine this, we need to choose a sample of girls and a sample of boys, and after evaluation, notice, for example, that the group of girls performs better. However, in order to be able to generalize that result and conclude that *girls perform better than boys*, again, we need to conduct a statistical test. We could, for instance, envisage an infinite set of examples, where a study must end with a statistical test showing that the results obtained on a sample are generalizable to the whole of the population.

Statistical tests are based on the fact that there are principles that can be used to predict the probability of an event occurring. These principles are based on two laws: the law of random chance and the law of large numbers.

In the coming discussion, in section 3.1, we shall base our thinking on the laws of random chance and of large numbers to uncover the origin of the main statistical laws, and see how they can be used to construct tables to implement "tests" in confirmatory statistics. In addition, the approach is based on tests using a methodology, which will be presented at the end of that section.

In subsequent sections, we present confirmatory tests. The presentation is by no means exhaustive, but we do discuss those tests that are most commonly used in human and social sciences, and more specifically, in research in the field of education. Readers will require a good knowledge of the mathematical indicators presented in the section on elementary descriptive statistics.

In sections 3.2–3.4, we present the main tests pertaining to quantitative variables: mean, Student's T test, analysis of variance (ANOVA) and Bravais–Pearson for inter-actions between two variables. In section 3.5, we present the tests relating to qualitative variables – mainly χ^2 tests.

In writing this chapter, we have drawn inspiration from numerous specialized publications in the field of confirmatory statistics, especially *Statistique théorique et appliquée* (Theoretical and Applied Statistics), volumes 1 and 2 [DAG 07, DAG 11] and *Manuel statistique pour psychologues* (Psychologists' Guide to Statistics) [GUE 97]. Many of the examples presented herein are taken from these books; others have been harvested from unidentified online resources.

3.1. Law of random chance and law of large numbers: hypothesis tests

3.1.1. *General points*

Events occurring in nature are such that, because of random chance, combined with the law of large numbers, numerous variables characterizing a population are distributed in accordance with probability laws. The existence of the probability laws is attributable to numerous forces influencing the events and individuals in the population. This set of actions determines the values taken by the variables, and distributes them across each individual in a way which is not individually predictable, but is perfectly codified for the population considered as a whole. This is crucially important and touches on the concept of scientific determinism. This complex problem, even today, is at the heart of scientific debate: determinism, the concept of entropy, chaos, etc. It creates a bridge between all the sciences, and as part of this debate, we can point to the existing body of literature:

"If we take a deterministic view of the sciences, any and all phenomena necessarily have a cause. Hence, the term "random" can only be applied to dynamic systems as level of complexity is such that the human mind cannot determine their outcome (e.g. the movement, or the output of balls from a lottery machine). We can say that random chance applies to systems which obey chaos theory".

"A random variable is a function defined on the set of eventualities (possible results) of a random experiment (that is, based on random chance). It is impossible, in advance, to predict which eventuality will apply to a given action or individual, but if we conduct a large number of experiments, we can define probability that a given result will be obtained".

Confirmatory statistics, which is the subject of this chapter, is based on the fact that, using probability laws, it is possible to establish theoretical statistical tables whose values can be compared to experimental observations made on samples. This comparison, based on tests, enables researchers to confirm or invalidate hypotheses formulated using a methodology, which will be presented later.

3.1.2. Probability laws

This section, the contents of which are largely based on the reference [DAG 07], sets out to demonstrate the foundations of the statistical laws. The presentation below is occasionally complex from a mathematical point of view for non-experts. For these readers, it is not absolutely crucial that they understand everything, but we do recommend that they read the section, even if only superficially, as it explains the logic and the rigor upon which the statistical laws are based.

3.1.2.1. *A little history*

Historically, probability laws have often been studied for the purposes of games of chance (card games, drawing of balls, etc.). This has been a subject of interest for centuries, but the first known works on the subject data from the 18th and 19th Centuries. Nicolas Bernoulli's thesis, in 1711, contained the first mention of the concept of a uniform distribution. Then, among others, came the binomial distribution and even the normal distribution (bell curve). However, the largely experimental methods were not always very rigorous. It was in the 18th Century that the great figures of science, such as d'Alembert and Lagrange, made major contributions to the construction of this new science. However, rigorous use of the probability laws largely developed around the 19th Century, in particular, through the work of Karl Pearson and Ludwig Boltzmann. In the early 20th Century, the mathematicians Borel and Lebesgue, in particular, established the idea of measuring probability, and in 1933, Kolmogorov formulated the probability axioms. It was from that point on that the foundations of statistics can be considered to have been in place.

We might legitimately ask ourselves how the normal distribution and other statistical laws were obtained. First, they were obtained experimentally, by repeating extremely numerous simple experiments, such as the drawing of black and white balls, heads or tails with a coin, throwing of dice, observations in nature, distribution of height, weight, milk production of a very large number of individuals, etc. In parallel, though, mathematicians basing their arguments on fundamental theorems were able to recreate these "natural" laws and use the formulas to deduce others, relating to parameters constructed using primary random variables (Student's T values, the χ^2 parameter, Fisher's coefficient, Pearson correlation coefficient, etc.).

Below, we present a number of probability laws. Some of them will be used specifically in the context of this book, but all played a part in establishing the ideas and concepts of what we call the "law of random chance" and the "law of large numbers". We begin by presenting discontinuous, or "discrete", probability laws, and then we demonstrate how to transition from the logic of discrete laws to continuous probability laws. Finally, we shall give a detailed presentation of the crucially important continuous laws: the normal distribution and then the truncated centered normal distribution (TCND), both of which we refer to often.

3.1.2.2. *A number of discrete probability laws*

Below, we present a number of the best known discrete probability laws. They are discrete in the sense that they express the probability that a particular event will occur: heads or tails, rolling a 6 (or throwing heads a second time) with a die, obtaining four of a kind in poker, obtaining a 6 three times after throwing the die five times.

In turn, we shall look at the equiprobability law, the binomial distribution, the polynomial law and Poisson's law, which may be considered an extreme case of the binomial distribution, and which, ultimately, takes the form of a continuous law. The sole purpose of presenting these laws is to give the reader a gradual understanding of how the statistical laws emerged and the fundaments of them.

3.1.2.2.1. Equiprobability law or uniform distribution

The equiprobability law was derived from experimental observations, through the game of heads or tails, or dice games; undoubtedly, this is the easiest to understand of all the statistical laws. It expresses the fact that each event (or modality of the variable) has an equal chance of occurring as any other. This can be seen in the game of heads or tails (two modalities), with a one-in-two chance of obtaining a particular result, or the game of dice (six modalities), where each result has a one-in-six chance of occurring. That is, of course, if the coin or die used is not loaded. The problem of the loaded die will be presented in full later on in this section.

More generally if, for a given phenomenon, we look at a variable with n modalities and that variable obeys a uniform distribution, this means that each modality has a $1/n$ chance of occurring in a draw, throw or sample.

We can look at the case of the distribution of men (M) and women (W) in the population. When a person is selected at random, we have a one-in-two chance of obtaining a woman.

Let us now come back to the example of the die. Consider the variable X, which has six modalities $X = [1, 2, 3, 4, 5, 6]$, with an equal probability $p = 1/6$. We can construct the following table:

x	P(x)	F(x)
1	1/6	1/6
2	1/6	2/6
3	1/6	3/6
4	1/6	4/6
5	1/6	5/6
6	1/6	6/6

Table 3.1. *Table of probabilities and partition function of the uniform distribution for a six-faced die*

We can see from the table that the probability P(x) of obtaining a given value x of the variable X is equal to 1/6 no matter what that value is. We can also see, for example, that the cumulative probability F(3) of obtaining 1, 2 or 3 is 3/6. Similarly, the cumulative probability F(6) of obtaining 1, 2, 3, 4, 5 or 6 is 6/6. The function F(x), which expresses the cumulative probability up to a value of x inclusive, is called the theoretical distribution function.

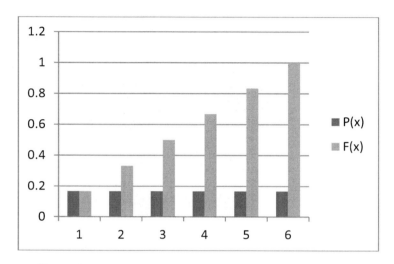

Figure 3.1. *Histograms representing the probability and the partition function of the uniform distribution for a six-faced die*

If we represent the table in graph form, we can see the difference between the probability P and the cumulative probability F.

Law of large numbers

Now imagine that we throw a die N number of times, where N is a very large number. The law of large numbers tells us that we should, for each modality, see a tendency toward a score of N/6. Suppose we actually carry out the experiment. The scores obtained for each of the modalities will certainly be different from N/6 – all the more so if N is not sufficiently large. The question that then arises is whether the differences observed are "normal", implying that had N been sufficiently large, everything would have fallen into place as expected, or whether the difference observed is abnormal. In the latter case, this would mean that either the die is loaded or the thrower is experienced and has some sort of technique, which allows him to cheat. Confirmatory statistics enables us to distinguish between the two situations:

the deviations observed are due to random chance, or the deviations observed are demonstrable, and are due to a real cause.

3.1.2.2.2. The binomial distribution

The binomial distribution is a discrete law that applies to actions taking place in accordance with a diagram known as the "Bernoulli graph", from the name of the 18th-Century scientific great, responsible for numerous advances in multiple fields – mechanics in particular.

Consider an experiment repeated n times (readings taken for n individuals or n throws), for which the variable measured can only have one of two values: A or B. If the probability of obtaining A is $P(A) = p$ and the probability of obtaining B is $P(B) = q$, then we have $p + q = 1$.

Figure 3.2. *Bernoulli plot*

For example, if we look again at one of the previous examples, if the variable is "gender", the two modalities are $A = M$ and $B = W$. Thus, we have $P(M) = 0.5$ and $P(W) = 0.5$. Yet if we consider the problem of the die once more, the two modalities are $A =$ "obtaining a 3" and $B =$ "not obtaining a 3". We have $P(A) = 1/6$ and $P(B) = 5/6$. In both cases, the sum of the two probabilities is indeed equal to 1.

Mathematical expression of the binomial distribution

In a Bernoulli plot, if we conduct n measurements or throws, mathematicians have shown that the probability that the variable X (number of occurrences of event A after the n measurements or throws) will take the value x is (for informational purposes):

$$P(X = x) = C_n^x p^x q^{n-x}$$

This expression is known as the binomial distribution; we then say that the variable X obeys a binomial distribution.

C_n^x represents the number of ways of obtaining event A over the course of n random experiments. A relation, which is taught in secondary schools in combinatorial analysis, can be used to calculate that value.

EXAMPLE.– Only for those who are interested in little mathematical calculations, but it is not overly complicated.

Consider a "balanced" coin. We can define the two eventualities as A "Heads" and B "Tails".

The variable X: "number of times that the event A occurs if I toss the coin three times".

We then wonder: "If we toss the coin three times, what is the probability of obtaining heads three times – i.e. X = 3?"

In the above relation, we have p = 1/2; q = 1/2. We can easily verify that $C_3^3 = 1$. Indeed, there is only one way in which we can obtain "heads" three times after three throws. The calculation then shows us that:

$$P(X=3) = C_3^3 \left(\frac{1}{2}\right)^3 \left(\frac{1}{2}\right)^{3-3} = 0.125$$

which represents a 12.5% chance.

Similarly, we might have asked: "what is the probability of obtaining 'heads' two times (X = 2) after three throws?"

In this case, $C_3^2 = 3$, and the calculation shows us that:

$$P(X=2) = C_3^2 \left(\frac{1}{2}\right)^2 \left(\frac{1}{2}\right)^{3-2} = 0.375$$

which is a 37.4% chance.

EXAMPLE.– Using a simple Excel spreadsheet.

Though it is not absolutely crucial, readers are welcome to continue to practice.

Consider a die with six faces [1,…, 6]. We throw it four times (n = 4). We shall look at the binomial variable X: "number of '1's observed after four throws" and x the number of occurrences of X. Thus, X can take one of five values [0, 1, 2, 3, 4].

The probability P of obtaining a 1 on every throw is 1/6. The variable X is a binomial variable with the parameter p = 1/6 (q = 5/6) and n = 4.

We want to know the values of $P(X = x)$ for $x = [0, 1, 2, 3, 4]$ – that is the probability of obtaining the value '1' zero times, or one time, …, or four times, after four throws.

To answer the question, we can directly use the "formula", as shown in the previous example, but this time, without going into details, the calculations are performed by the Excel spreadsheet using the "binomial distribution" function, with the path:

Formulas → More functions → Statistical → BINOM.DIST
(from the dropdown menu)

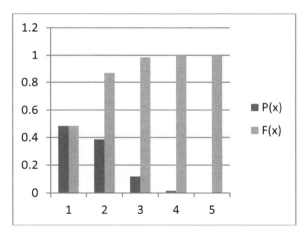

Figure 3.3. *Histograms – probability and partition function: number of "1"s observed after four throws*

x	P(x)	F(x)
0	0.4823	0.4823
1	0.3858	0.8681
2	0.1157	0.9838
3	0.0154	0.9992
4	0.0008	1
Total	1.0000	

Table 3.2. *Probability and partition function: number of "1"s observed after four throws*

For example, we can read: the theoretical probability of obtaining a 1 twice after four throws is 0.1157, and the cumulative probability F(2) is 0.9838, which means there is a 98.38% chance of obtaining a 1 zero, one or two times after four throws.

Dealing with large numbers: Imagine that we actually conduct the experiment. We repeat the series of four throws N times. For each of them, the variable X may take one of the five values x= [0, 1, 2, 3, 4].

The experimental results would certainly be different from the theoretical results obtained from the table, i.e.,

"Total number of times that 1 is thrown" [0 times] = N × 0.4823, [1 time] = N × 0.3858, [2 times] = N × 0.1157, [3 times] = N × 0.0154 and [4 times] = N × 0.0008.

The question that arises is whether the difference observed are normal, which implies that had N been sufficiently large, the order would ultimately have been respected, or whether the difference observed is abnormal, meaning that it does not conform to the binomial probability law, which it ought to obey. In the latter case, it would mean that the die is loaded, or the experienced thrower has a technique that allows him to cheat. In that case, of course, the binomial distribution no longer applies.

3.1.2.2.3. Generalized binomial or polynomial law

Later on, more complex systems were developed. Here, we present the polynomial law that applies to Bernoulli plots that could be described as generalized, with n possible modalities Ai whose respective probabilities are P(Ai) = pi:

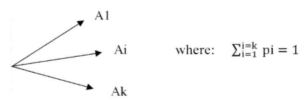

$$A1$$
$$Ai \qquad \text{where:} \quad \sum_{i=1}^{i=k} pi = 1$$
$$Ak$$

Figure 3.4. *Diagram illustrating the polynomial law*

For inexpert readers, the polynomial law is more difficult to understand, but we are quite deliberately discussing it here, because it illustrates the historical journey of researchers developing probability laws to reflect ever more complex situations.

In accordance with the generalized Bernoulli plot with k modalities, we take n independent readings or draws, and define the variable Xi, with the number of occurrences of the event Ai after the n samples or draws, so there are k variables Xi with i ranging from 1 to k. We use the notation x_i to denote the numerical value taken by each Xi. Here again, for the little historical exploration, a combinatorial analysis calculation gives us:

$$P(X_1 = x_1 \text{ and } X_2 = x_2 \text{ and } ... \text{ and } X_k = x_k) = \left[\frac{n!}{x_1! ... x_k!}\right] p_1^{x_1} ... p_k^{x_k}$$

This relation must be read as: "The probability that, after n throws, the number of occurrences of modality 1 will be x_1, and the number of occurrences of modality 2 will be x_2, and the number of occurrences of modality k will be x_k, is equal to the right-hand side of the relation". In the relation, $n! = 1 \times 2 \times 3 ... x(n-1)xn$ is the factorial of n. For the $x_i!$ (factorial x_i), it is the same definition. Each term of the type $p_i^{x_i}$ represents the probability that modality i will occur, and it is raised to the power of x1, which is the number of times the modality needs to occur... This is by no means simple, but let us move on to the next step.

EXAMPLE.– Still using our six-sided die, we conduct a generalized Bernoulli experiment with three modalities: A1: "We obtain face 1"; A2: "We obtain face 2"; Aa; "We obtain another face". We throw the die n = 4 times... and define the three variables X1, X2 and Xa that, respectively, represent the number of times that modalities A1, A2 and Aa are obtained after the four throws.

For instance, let us calculate the probability of obtaining after four throws $x_1 = 0$, $x_2 = 2$ and thus $x_a = 2$. Indeed, because $x_1 = 0$ and $x_2 = 2$, the value of x_a is imposed, because $x_1 + x_2 + x_a = 4$.

If we take account of the fact that the singular term $0! = 1$ and a high number raised to the power of zero is also equal to 1, we obtain:

$$P(X_1 = 0 \text{ and } X_2 = 2 \text{ and } X_a = 2) = \frac{4.3.2.1}{1.2.2}\left(\frac{1}{6}\right)^0 . \left(\frac{1}{6}\right)^2 . \left(\frac{4}{6}\right)^2 = 0.0741$$

This is read as the probability, after four throws, of obtaining 1 zero times, 2 twice and thus the other faces twice as well is 0.0741 or 7.41%.

We can now perform an identical calculation for the set of combinations x_1, x_2, each imposing a value of x_a, and obtain tables and graphs, as we did for the quiprobability law or simple binomial distribution. We could also make the transition to large numbers, meaning performing the n = 4 throws N times, and we would observe the same results as for the previous laws. Hence, we shall leave it there.

3.1.2.2.4. Poisson's law

Poisson's law is obtained as an extreme case of the binomial distribution, and it has the peculiarity of presenting in a form identical to the continuous statistical laws. It is a simple example of the link that may exist between the various laws in extreme but commonplace situations.

To view Poisson's law in relation to the binomial distribution, let us look again at the example of the die thrown n = 4 times, and where we are looking at the probability of a given face coming up 0, 1, 2, 3 or 4 times. This time, though, the experiment is such that:

– n → ∞; we throw the die, or a large number of dice, a large number of times;

– p → 0; for that, the die would need to have a very large number of facets, so that the probability of one of them coming up is very low indeed.

Materially speaking, this experiment is not very realistic, but it helps to understand the context of Poisson's law. We can rigorously demonstrate that in these conditions, i.e.,

$$n \to \infty$$

p → 0 and also n×p → m = const. > 0.

The relation for the binomial distribution:

$$P(X = x) = P(x) = C_n^x p^x q^{n-x}$$

finally becomes:

$$P(X = x) = P(x) = e^{-m} m^x / x!$$

This last equation is Poisson's law, where e = 2.718, the exponential constant, and m is a parameter that can be shown to be the mean value of the distribution of the variable X. Thus, if the above conditions are met, the discrete binomial distribution becomes a continuous law. Indeed, x is no longer just an integer; it can take any integer value or a value of 0.

3.1.2.2.5. Other discrete probability laws

The laws we have looked at here are the best known, but there are many others, each corresponding to different types of events: the Pascal or Fisher distributions, geometric series, etc.

For further information on this subject, readers could consult [DAG 07].

3.1.2.2.6. Section overviews: what we have learned

We have presented probability laws, which manifested themselves naturally, often linked to games of chance, and relating to discrete variables – i.e. variables that can only assume discrete values (heads or tails, one of the six faces of the die, etc.). We have seen that in each of these cases, combinatorial analysis can be used to rigorously establish the theoretical probability that an event will occur. The results can easily be represented in the form of histograms, which show the probability or cumulative probability of obtaining the modalities of the variable in random draws or samples.

In addition, Poisson's law is an example that shows that discrete laws can, in certain cases, for a large number of draws and low probabilities for each modality, appear like continuous laws – that is to say, definite, regardless of the rational value of the variable.

If we conduct the experiment, when the number N of samples or draws is very large, the number of times the event takes place is similar to what is predicted by the theoretical probability law. Should this not be the case, it would mean that the events do not obey the theoretical law; such is the case, for example, with a loaded die.

3.1.2.3. *Introduction to continuous probability laws*

Imagine a continuous quantitative variable, such as the height of the individuals in a population, expressed in centimeters. This variable is continuous, because it can take any of the possible values along the spectrum of real numbers. However, to begin with, we can try a discrete approach that allows us to present the results in line with the presentations we saw above. Thus, we define a number of height ranges or classes. Figure 3.5 illustrates the results, with seven modalities and a step of DX = 10 cm [I = 140–150; II = 150–160; III = 160–170; IV = 170–180; V = 180–190; VI = 190–200; VII = 200–210].

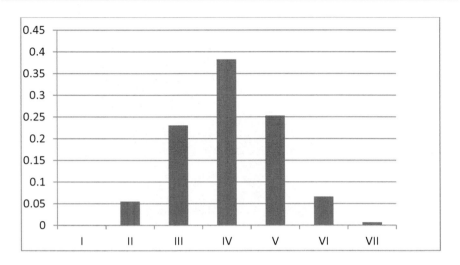

Figure 3.5. *Histogram of height distribution with seven modalities:*
I–II–III–IV–V–VI–VII

We are free to choose the number of modalities and therefore the incremental step DX between one modality and the next. If, for the sake of greater accuracy, we increase the number of modalities (we decrease DX by a certain amount), then the probability of belonging to each modality decreases. We might even go so far as to imagine a scenario where the number of modalities tends toward infinity. In this case, DX → 0 and the probabilities of belonging to any particular one of the modalities tend toward 0. Evidently, this kind of representation is not suitable for the situation, and therefore cannot be implemented in practice.

To avoid this obstacle, instead of representing the probability Pi of belonging to a modality i, it is helpful to define the probability density fi = Pi/DX, which is, in a manner of speaking, the probability of belonging to the modality i "per unit of the variable X". Thus, fi.DX is the probability, in a sample, of finding a value X of the variable within the interval DX; we also speak of the probability of obtaining the value X to within DX.

Now, let us increase the number of modalities; for instance, say we increase the number of modalities from seven to 70, and DX is reduced from 10 to 1 cm; the probability density fi = Pi/DX takes the form shown in Figure 3.6.

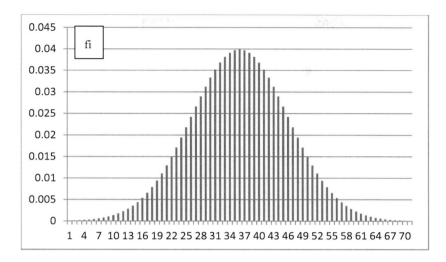

Figure 3.6. *Probability density of height distribution for 70 modalities*

We can see that the graphic representation has an outline, which is almost a continuous outline. If we continue to increase the number of modalities as DX→ 0, the curve representing the probability density then rigorously tends toward the continuous curve shown in Figure 3.7.

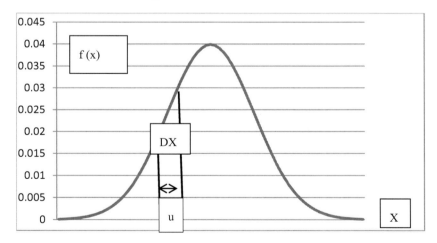

Figure 3.7. *Continuous probability density for size distribution*

MATHEMATICAL POINT.– (Crucially important for the coming discussion). In light of the definition of the probability density, based on the relation fi = Pi/DX, we can see that from the probability density, we can work back to the idea of probability.

The quantity P(u) = f(u) DX, which is the probability that the variable X will assume the value u, within DX (u ± DX/2), can be approximated by the area beneath the curve between the two vertical lines spaced a distance DX apart.

For example, if X is still the height found for the individuals in our sample, the probability of randomly encountering an individual of height u within the range DX is equal to the area underneath the curve between the two vertical lines spaced DX apart.

3.1.2.3.1. Section overview: what we have learned

For continuous random variables, it is not possible, as it is with discrete variables, to directly express the probability of obtaining a given value of the variable.

Therefore, we define the probability density fi(x) = Pi/DX, which, in a way, is the probability of obtaining the value x of the variable in the interval DX of that variable. We also speak of the probability of obtaining the value X to within DX.

The probability of obtaining a given value u of the random variable is equal to the surface beneath the curve between the two vertical lines, spaced a distance DX apart around the value.

This result is at the root of the mathematical calculation by which we can establish statistical tables.

3.1.2.4. *The normal distribution*

The continuous statistical law that is most commonly encountered in the real world is the "normal distribution", which is the well-known bell curve. It was predicted, and even used to produce representations, in the early 18th Century by Bernoulli. It is a continuous law whose definitive mathematical form was discovered through the work of Laplace (1809) and Gauss (1812). Yet the best, most easily comprehensible definition of the normal distribution was given by Émile Borel in the 1920s, in the following terms: "we speak of a normal distribution when we are dealing with a continuous random variable depending on a large number of independent causes whose effects are cumulative and none of which is discernibly dominant over the others".

It happens that numerous "natural" phenomena obey this definition, and thus can be said to obey a normal distribution. This special and central role played by the normal distribution is conclusively and rigorously demonstrated by the central limit theorem, a simplified statement of which is given in the following:

"Consider X1, X2, ..., Xi,..., Xn – a series of n independent random variables, whose mean is $\overline{X1}, \overline{X2},$ ...$\overline{Xn}$, whose variance is Var(X1), Var(X2), ..., Var(Xn), and which obey any sort of probability law. Their sum obeys a law which, as n increases, tends toward a normal distribution with the mean $\overline{X} = \sum_{i=1}^{n} Xi$ and variance $Var(X) = \sum_{i=1}^{n} Var(Xi)$. There is only one restrictive condition: the variances must be finite, and no one of them must be dominant over the others".

To illustrate the practical consequences of this theorem, let us look at the example of the operation of a precision lathe. The settings of the lathe are designed to obtain parts with a very precisely defined shape, but we know that there are numerous causes of perturbation that come into play during the machining process: vibration, wear and tear, fluctuation in the electrical supply, temperature, etc. If the causes of disturbance are numerous, if their effects act additively, and if the disturbances caused by each of them are of the same order of magnitude, then the central limit theorem states that we should observe a "total" disturbance obeying a normal distribution. In addition, as this mechanism of action of causes of disturbance is very widespread in nature, the normal distribution has a favored position.

To take another example: an animal's body size depends on numerous "perturbing" factors in its environment (food, climate, predation, etc.) and a host of genetic factors. Since those determining factors are extremely numerous, independent and no one of them is dominant over the others, we can assume that animal body size obeys a normal distribution.

Mathematically speaking, when a random variable X obeys the normal distribution, this means that the probability density Y of the variable X is written as:

$$Y = f(x) = \frac{1}{S(X)\sqrt{2\pi}} e^{-1/2(\frac{x-\overline{X}}{S(X)})^2}$$

It is read as the probability density that the variable X will take the value x is equal to the expression on the right of the above relation.

The graphic representation is a "bell curve", as shown in Figures 3.8 and 3.9. It depends on the two parameters: S(X) (standard deviation of the variable X) and $\overline{X}$ (mean of the variable X). The first determines the flatness of the curve and the second the position of the axis of symmetry. Hence, while the formulation of the function and the general shape remain the same, there is a different corresponding curve for each pair of these parameters. For this reason, it is common to express a normal distribution in the summary form N($\overline{X}$, S).

Figure 3.8 shows the influence of the mean $\overline{X}$ on the shape of the distribution for a value of the standard deviation S(X) = 1.

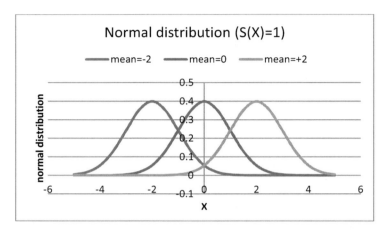

Figure 3.8. *Normal distribution for three values of the mean with a standard deviation equal to 1. For a color version of this figure, see www.iste.co.uk/larini/education.zip*

Figure 3.9 demonstrates the influence of the standard deviation S(X) on the shape of the distribution for a value of the mean $\overline{X}$ = 0.

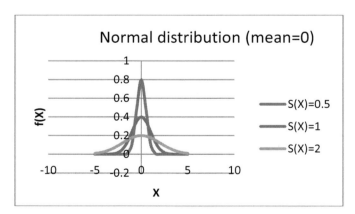

Figure 3.9. *Normal distribution for three values of the standard deviation and a mean of zero. For a color version of this figure, see www.iste.co.uk/larini/education.zip*

Often, nature gets things right. In the discussion below, we shall see that it is possible to obtain a single representation of the normal distribution for all pairs $(\overline{X}, S(X))$: TCND.

3.1.2.5. *The truncated centered normal distribution*

To introduce the truncated centred normal distribution (TCND), we need to change the variable with which we are working. Let X be the initial variable; we begin by defining the centered variable:

$$x_c = x - \overline{X},$$

where $\overline{X}$ is the mean of the variable X.

Now, we can define the truncated centered variable (TCV):

$$X_{tc} = \frac{x_c}{S(X)} = \frac{x - \overline{X}}{S(X)}$$

where $S(X)$ is the standard deviation of the variable X.

TCVs have 2 + 1 remarkable properties. Their means are always equal to 0, their variances are always equal to 1 and because the standard deviation is equal to the square root of the variance, their standard deviations are always equal to 1.

For readers who like mathematical demonstrations:

– the mean $\overline{X_{tc}}$ is always equal to 0 irrespective of the variable X. Proof:

$$\overline{X_{tc}} = \frac{1}{n}\sum_{i=1}^{n} x_{tc_i} = \frac{1}{n}\sum_{i=1}^{n} \frac{x_i - \overline{X}}{S(X)} = \frac{1}{S(X)}(\overline{X} - \overline{X}) = 0 \text{ QED}$$

– the variance $Var(X_{tc})$ is always equal to 1 irrespective of the variable X. Proof:

$$Var(X_{tc}) = \frac{1}{n}\sum_{i=1}^{n}(x_{tc_i} - \overline{X_{tc}})^2$$

However, because $\overline{X_{tc}} = 0$, we obtain:

$$Var(X_{tc}) = \frac{1}{n}\sum_{i=1}^{n} x_{tc_i}^2 = \frac{1}{n}\sum_{i=1}^{n}\left(\frac{x_i - \overline{X}}{S(X)}\right)^2 = \frac{Var(X)}{Var(X)} = 1 \text{ QED}$$

This also means that:

$$S(X_{tc}) = \sqrt{Var(X_{tc})} = 1$$

For all readers: whatever the variable X, which obeys a normal distribution N $(\overline{X}, S(X))$, we have just shown that its truncated centered form X_{tc} has a mean of zero, $\overline{X_{tc}} = 0$, and a standard deviation equal to 1, $S(X_{tc}) = 1$. Thus, the TCV, X_{tc}, obeys a specific kind of normal distribution $N(0,1)$, which is the TCND, and which is the same no matter what the variable X. This property is crucially important, because it means that we can use a single law, the TCND ($N(0,1)$), to study the behavior of all variables that obey a normal distribution N $(\overline{X}, S(X))$.

The TCND is therefore written as:

$$X_{tc} \rightarrow f(X_{tc}) = N(0,1) = \frac{1}{\sqrt{2\pi}} e^{-\frac{1}{2}X_{tc}^2}$$

The TCND curve is shown in Figure 3.10. It represents the probability density of the centered truncated variable X_{tc}. $f(X_{tc})$.

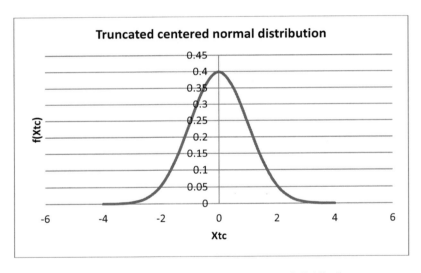

Figure 3.10. *The truncated centered normal distribution*

3.1.2.5.1. Section overview: what we have learned

There is a remarkable probability density law that plays a very important role in nature: the normal distribution, which is none other than the well-known bell curve. This law, for a given variable, depends on two parameters: the mean value of the variable and its standard deviation.

One remarkable property is that it is possible, by switching a variable, to reduce all the normal distributions to just one: the TCND N(0,1).

Based on the TCND, we can establish a table showing the theoretical probability valid for all random variables obeying a normal distribution when we transform them into TCVs, and it is always possible to do so.

3.1.2.6. From the TCND to the statistical table of the TCND

In this section, we show how to establish the statistical table for the TCND on the basis of its probability density N(0,1). The approach presented here is a general one: it applies to all probability density laws. Knowing the principle behind the construction of the statistical tables, although it is not absolutely crucial for a user, it helps in understanding exactly what the statistical tests are.

Statistical tables for the different laws are used throughout this book, and in particular, in the context of confirmatory statistics, i.e. statistical tests (mean, Student's T test, ANOVA, χ^2, etc.).

3.1.2.6.1. Calculation bases: area beneath the curve

In the interests of conciseness in the formulae used, where no danger of confusion exists, we shall refer to X instead of Xtc, and write f(X) for the probability density law N(0,1).

Consider the probability density f(X) of the TCND for the normed centered random variable X. Let a and b represent two arbitrary values of the variable X.

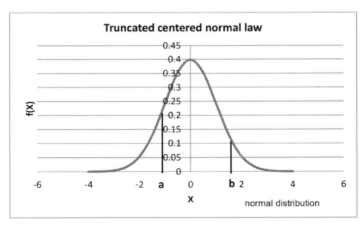

Figure 3.11. *Truncated centered normal distribution: area beneath the curve between X = a and X = b*

Mathematically, this property can also be formulated in mathematical language:

$$P(a < X < b) = [\text{area beneath the curve}]_a^b = \int_a^b f(x)dx$$

The term on the right is the integral of the probability density between the two bounds a and b.

If f(X) is the probability density that represents the height distribution of the individuals in a population, $P(a < X < b)$ indicates the probability of an individual having a "truncated centered height" between a and b.

Consequence 1: Normalization of f(X).

The function f(X) is constructed in such a way that:

$$P(-\infty < X < +\infty) = 1 = [\text{area beneath the curve}]_{-\infty}^{+\infty} = \int_{-\infty}^{+\infty} f(x)dx = 1$$

This means that, in a random draw, the probability that the value of X will be between $-\infty$ and $+\infty$ is equal to 1. We say that the probability density is normalized at 1.

Thus, the probability that an individual's truncated centered height will be between $-\infty$ and $+\infty$ is equal to 1.

Consequence 2: Unilateral probability.

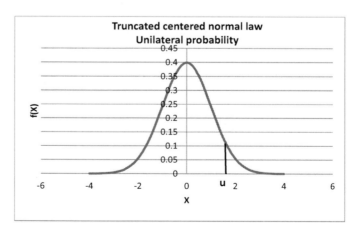

Figure 3.12. *Truncated centered normal distribution: unilateral probability*

Consider an arbitrary value u of the random variable X. In light of the above, we can write:

$$P(X < u) = [\text{area beneath the curve}]_{-\infty}^{u} = \int_{-\infty}^{u} f(x)dx = F(u)$$

The area F(u) beneath the curve from $-\infty$ to u (integral of $-\infty$ at u) represents the probability that, in a random draw, X will be less than u. Mathematicians refer to F(u) as the "partition function", which is the equivalent of the cumulative probability found with the discrete probability laws. F(u) is called the unilateral probability.

For example, if we look again at the previous example, $P(X < u) = F(u)$ represents the probability that an individual will have a truncated centered height less than u.

Consequence 3: Bilateral probability.

Consider an arbitrary value u of the random variable X. In light of the above, we can write:

$$P(-u < X < +u) = [\text{area beneath the curve}]_{-u}^{+u} = \int_{-u}^{+u} f(x)dx = G(u)$$

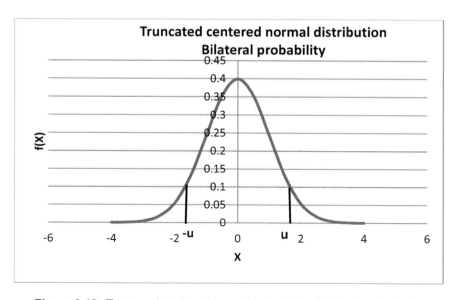

Figure 3.13. *Truncated centered normal distribution: bilateral probability*

The area G(u) beneath the curve between –u and +u (integral of –u to +u) represents the probability that, in a random draw, the variable X will have a value between –u and +u. The property G(u) is called the bilateral probability.

Still looking at the case of the height distribution of the individuals, $P(-u < X < u) = G(u)$ represents the probability that an individual will have a "truncated centered height" between –u and +u.

3.1.2.6.2. Establishing the TCND tables

In the case of the TCND, it is possible to establish two statistical tables: the unilateral table and the bilateral table.

When we know the F(u) = [area beneath the curve]$_{-\infty}^{u}$ for all values of u, we can write the unilateral table for the TCND. F(u) is always between 0 and 1.

Similarly, by knowing G(u) = [area beneath the curve]$_{-u}^{+u}$ for all values of u, we can write the bilateral table for the TCND. G(u) is always between 0 and 1.

If you trust mathematicians, they will provide you with these values by calculating the integral of f(X) for x between $-\infty$ and u or between –u and +u. If not, you merely need to measure the surfaces beneath the curve between $-\infty$ and $+u$ or between –u and +u.

There are many different presentations of these tables. Some give the internal probability, i.e. the probability of obtaining a value between $-\infty$ and $+u$ for the unilateral tables or between –u and +u for the bilateral tables. Others give the external probability, i.e. the probability of obtaining a value outside these different ranges. This variety, for non-experts, can lead to confusion, so we shall limit ourselves to presenting and using the external bilateral table.

3.1.2.6.3. Presentation of the external bilateral table for the TCND

Table 3.3 gives the probability of obtaining, in a random draw, a value of the TCV outside of the area [–u, +u] beneath the curve.

u	0.00	0.01	0.02	0.03	0.04	0.05	0.06	0.07	0.08	0.09
0.0	1.00000	0.99202	0.98404	0.97607	0.96809	0.96012	0.95216	0.94419	0.93624	0.92829
0.1	0.92034	0.91241	0.90448	0.89657	0.88866	0.88076	0.87288	0.86501	0.85715	0.84931
0.2	0.84148	0.83367	0.82587	0.81809	0.81033	0.80259	0.79486	0.78716	0.77948	0.77182
0.3	0.76418	0.75656	0.74897	0.74140	0.73386	0.72634	0.71885	0.71138	0.70395	0.69654
0.4	0.68916	0.68181	0.67449	0.66720	0.65994	0.65271	0.64552	0.63836	0.63123	0.62413
0.5	0.61708	0.61005	0.60306	0.59611	0.58920	0.58232	0.57548	0.56868	0.56191	0.55519
0.6	0.54851	0.54186	0.53526	0.52869	0.52217	0.51569	0.50925	0.50286	0.49650	0.49019
0.7	0.48393	0.47770	0.47152	0.46539	0.45930	0.45325	0.44725	0.44130	0.43539	0.42953
0.8	0.42371	0.41794	0.41222	0.40654	0.40091	0.39532	0.38979	0.38430	0.37886	0.37347
0.9	0.36812	0.36282	0.35757	0.35237	0.34722	0.34211	0.33706	0.33205	0.32709	0.32217
1.0	0.31731	0.31250	0.30773	0.30301	0.29834	0.29372	0.28914	0.28462	0.28014	0.27571
1.1	0.27133	0.26700	0.26271	0.25848	0.25429	0.25014	0.24605	0.24200	0.23800	0.23405
1.2	0.23014	0.22628	0.22247	0.21870	0.21498	0.21130	0.20767	0.20408	0.20055	0.19705
1.3	0.19360	0.19020	0.18684	0.18352	0.18025	0.17702	0.17383	0.17069	0.16759	0.16453
1.4	0.16151	0.15854	0.15561	0.15272	0.14987	0.14706	0.14429	0.14156	0.13887	0.13622
1.5	0.13361	0.13104	0.12851	0.12602	0.12356	0.12114	0.11876	0.11642	0.11411	0.11183
1.6	0.10960	0.10740	0.10523	0.10310	0.10101	0.09894	0.09691	0.09492	0.09296	0.09103
1.7	0.08913	0.08727	0.08543	0.08363	0.08186	0.08012	0.07841	0.07673	0.07508	0.07345
1.8	0.07186	0.07030	0.06876	0.06725	0.06577	0.06431	0.06289	0.06148	0.06011	0.05876
1.9	0.05743	0.05613	0.05486	0.05361	0.05238	0.05118	0.05000	0.04884	0.04770	0.04659
2.0	0.04550	0.04443	0.04338	0.04236	0.04135	0.04036	0.03940	0.03845	0.03753	0.03662
2.1	0.03573	0.03486	0.03401	0.03317	0.03235	0.03156	0.03077	0.03001	0.02926	0.02852
2.2	0.02781	0.02711	0.02642	0.02575	0.02509	0.02445	0.02382	0.02321	0.02261	0.02202

2.3	0.02145	0.02089	0.02034	0.01981	0.01928	0.01877	0.01827	0.01779	0.01731	0.01685
2.4	0.01640	0.01595	0.01552	0.01510	0.01469	0.01429	0.01389	0.01351	0.01314	0.01277
2.5	0.01242	0.01207	0.01174	0.01141	0.01109	0.01077	0.01047	0.01017	0.00988	0.00960
2.6	0.00932	0.00905	0.00879	0.00854	0.00829	0.00805	0.00781	0.00759	0.00736	0.00715
2.7	0.00693	0.00673	0.00653	0.00633	0.00614	0.00596	0.00578	0.00561	0.00544	0.00527
2.8	0.00511	0.00495	0.00480	0.00465	0.00451	0.00437	0.00424	0.00410	0.00398	0.00385
2.9	0.00373	0.00361	0.00350	0.00339	0.00328	0.00318	0.00308	0.00298	0.00288	0.00279
3.0	0.00270	0.00261	0.00253	0.00245	0.00237	0.00229	0.00221	0.00214	0.00207	0.00200
3.1	0.00194	0.00187	0.00181	0.00175	0.00169	0.00163	0.00158	0.00152	0.00147	0.00142
3.2	0.00137	0.00133	0.00128	0.00124	0.00120	0.00115	0.00111	0.00108	0.00104	0.00100
3.3	0.00097	0.00093	0.00090	0.00087	0.00084	0.00081	0.00078	0.00075	0.00072	0.00070
3.4	0.00067	0.00065	0.00063	0.00060	0.00058	0.00056	0.00054	0.00052	0.00050	0.00048
3.5	0.00047	0.00045	0.00043	0.00042	0.00040	0.00039	0.00037	0.00036	0.00034	0.00033
3.6	0.00032	0.00031	0.00029	0.00028	0.00027	0.00026	0.00025	0.00024	0.00023	0.00022
3.7	0.00022	0.00021	0.00020	0.00019	0.00018	0.00018	0.00017	0.00016	0.00016	0.00015
3.8	0.00014	0.00014	0.00013	0.00013	0.00012	0.00012	0.00011	0.00011	0.00010	0.00010
3.9	0.00010	0.00009	0.00009	0.00008	0.00008	0.00008	0.00007	0.00007	0.00007	0.00007
4.0	0.0000	0.0000	0.0000	0.0000	0.0000	0.0000	0.0000	0.0000	0.0000	0.0000

Table 3.3. *External bilateral statistical table for the truncated centered normal distribution*

3.1.2.6.4. Reading the external bilateral table for the TCND

The value of u can be read from the first column for the first two significant digits (example: 1.4) and the first row for the third significant digit (example: 1.47).

The probability of obtaining, in a random draw, a value of the TCV outside of the interval −1.47 and +1.47 is given at the intersection of the rows and columns in question. We read the value 0.1415. This means we have a probability of 14.15% (0.1415 × 100) of obtaining a value outside of the range [−1.47, +1.47], that is falling in one of the two areas outside of that range.

Extreme example

The table tells us that the probability of obtaining a value outside of the range $[0^-, 0^+]$ is equal to 1. This result is to be expected, because the two verticals are exactly the same, and the surface area in question is the total surface, whose area is equal to 1 by definition (normalization of the probability density).

If u increases

The external surface area decreases, and thus the probability of obtaining it, in a random draw, decreases with u. When u becomes very high (4, for example), the external area becomes so small that the probability of the result falling in that range domain is zero, to four decimal places.

An important special case

Probability of obtaining a value outside of the domain [−1.96; +1.96]. From the table, we read 0.05, which is 5%. This value plays an important role because, as we shall see later on, it often serves as a reference value for the acceptable risk level, in statistical tests.

3.1.2.7. *There are other continuous statistical laws*

Although the normal distribution and, consequently, the TCND offer one way of describing the statistical behavior of a very large number of variables in nature, there are other continuous distributions which can be used. However, while the laws (discrete and continuous) that we have encountered up to now focus on directly observable variables, in games or in nature, other laws describe the statistical behavior of "parameters", constructed artificially from the variables at play in a particular problem.

For instance, we could cite Student's statistical law, which describes the behavior of Student's T parameter; the χ^2 statistical law developed by Pearson, describing the statistical behavior of the χ^2 parameter; the Fisher–Snedecor statistical law, which characterizes the statistical behavior of Fisher's famous F parameter; and so on.

Each of these laws, using the same method as that employed for the TCND, enable us to establish probability tables which, as we shall see later on, are used in the context of confirmatory statistics.

Here, we shall not detail all the developments and mathematical properties of these laws; they will be briefly introduced when the time comes to use them. There are relations that exist between all of these statistical laws, which have been the subject of numerous specialized publications, which it is simply not possible to discuss in detail here. We recommend that readers interested in the topic consult *Statistique théorique et appliquée*, volume 1 [DAG 07].

3.1.3. *Hypothesis tests*

3.1.3.1. *Introduction*

In a study, a researcher looking at a population, including one or more samples, collects data relating to one or more variables. As previously mentioned, the data are compiled into an [I/V] table, and are made easier to interpret by a range of specific tables (population tables, contingency tables, etc.) and graphs but also, where necessary, mathematical indicators. The analysis then leads the research to formulate hypotheses, and even put forward conclusions on the basis of the findings. The results obtained are absolutely valid on the specific samples that have been observed, but as those samples were taken as a subset of a larger population, in order to extend the conclusions to the whole of the population, we need to ensure that, had we based the study on different samples, the conclusions would have been the same.

Thus, we need to answer the question: "Are the results and the conclusions reached actually down to the simple random chance of the sample selection?"

In other words, the method must allow us to decide between two statements, which may be formulated in different ways depending on the problem at hand:

– the values observed on this sample do not appear (or do appear) to fit with the accepted values for the population;

– the results that we observe do not appear (or do appear) to correspond to a standard (a theoretical law, a value accepted after numerous experiments, etc.);

– the values observed on two (or n) samples show (or do not show) that the samples are identical, i.e. that they belong to the same population;

– the variables observed are independent (or dependent);

– the link observed between the two variables examined on a sample is not due to the random chance of sample selection.

To make the decision, we can employ statistical tests that are based on tables, such as the TCND table. In any case, if we can show that the results are not attributable to random chance in sample selection, we say that the results are proven, or that they are significant. In this case, the conclusions drawn for the sample or samples can be generalized to the whole population.

3.1.3.2. *The null hypothesis and the alternative hypothesis*

Hypothesis tests are related to the idea that science can only prove that a hypothesis is wrong, but can never prove that it is correct. Science can only state that, in view of the known aspects and in a given context, a theory, an idea, a formula may be taken as an authoritative reference until such time as proof is offered in refutation of it. An excellent example is Newton's law(s), which stood as the very foundation of science until Einstein introduced his theory of relativity, which tore down all previous ideas, relegating Newtonian ideas to a mere approximation in a specific case delimited by human perception. Since then, however, researchers have spent a great deal of time wondering whether relativity is, itself, an approximation of a more general law.

To confirm or invalidate hypotheses, in statistics, we have numerous tests at our disposal, all of which are tailored to the nature of the variables at hand and the situations being analyzed. They are based on probability laws, and for each of the probability laws there is one or more corresponding statistical tables that tell us the probability, in a random draw, of obtaining a particular value of the parameter. In all cases, we must formulate two contradictory hypotheses, H_0 and H_1. The first is called the null hypothesis, and the second the alternative hypothesis.

3.1.3.2.1. Null hypothesis H_0

The null hypothesis holds that the random chance of the sample selection, by itself, accounts for the differences observed between the values obtained on the sample and those expected for the whole population. In other words, this means that, despite the differences, what is observed on the sample is identical to what would be observed on the whole population. In this case, the differences observed are merely fluctuations corresponding to an effect of sampling – a random "background noise", which is added to the signal – rather than to systematic factors.

3.1.3.2.2. Alternative hypothesis H_1

The alternative hypothesis is opposite to the null hypothesis. It expresses the fact that the random chance involved in sampling cannot, in itself, alone account for the differences observed between the sample and the population. In this case, the sample does not behave like the rest of the population. This suggests that there are systematic factors that are responsible for that difference. If H_1 is adopted, we say that the differences observed are proven or significant.

3.1.3.3. *Example of a choice between H_0 and H_1*

Before presenting the main statistical tests, we shall look at an example to see, without going into detail, how to decide between H_0 and H_1, and what the consequences of that choice are.

The CEO of a toy factory wants to know whether children are more attracted to a soft toy in the form of a rabbit, a tortoise or an elephant. To find out, he conducts a study in which a sample of 54 2-year-old children is observed. The results obtained are compared to a theoretical law that postulates that, over the whole population, on average, children do not have any particular preference. Thus, the random sample of 54 children is compared to an imaginary population in which children have no preference between the three figures.

The null hypothesis H_0 is the differences observed between the sample and the fictitious population are attributable to the randomness of the sampling.

The alternative hypothesis H_1 is the differences observed between the choice made in the sample and the theoretical law cannot be entirely attributed to the randomness of the sampling.

In order to decide between the two hypotheses, we must determine what level of risk of error is acceptable if we reject H_0, often equal to 5%. Statistical tables tell us the level of risk we are running, and depending on the acceptable level of risk, we can choose between H_0 and H_1.

	Rabbit	Tortoise	Elephant
Choice of children in sample	10	23	21
Theoretical law for population	18	18	18

Table 3.4. *Data table: choice of soft toys*

The second row of the table tells us the choice made by the sample of 54 children. The third row expresses what would be the theoretical choice of the children in the population if there were no preference at work. Looking at the table, we seem to see that there is an influence that should lead the manufacturer to produce fewer rabbit toys and a little more tortoises and elephants.

In order to decide between H_0 and H_1, we perform a χ^2 test (which we shall study later on, pertaining to populations) and paradoxically, the result of the test, after consulting the statistical table for χ^2, shows that rejecting H_0 carries with it a risk of over 5%. Thus, it is the null hypothesis H_0 which must be adopted, although it seems paradoxical. In this case, the results obtained do not indicate that the production chain needs to be altered, because the risk of error is too great. Now, it is up to the CEO to decide whether the 5% risk is suitable for the situation.

3.1.3.4. *Parametric and non-parametric tests*

The various tests used depend on the type of variable and on the type of measurement scale used. With this in mind, we can distinguish between two categories of statistical tests: parametric tests and non-parametric tests.

3.1.3.4.1. Parametric tests

Parametric tests pertain to quantitative, that is numerical, variables, which express a measurement scale (height, weight, salary, etc.).

Parametric tests are based on probability laws that hold that the variables at play obey a normal distribution across the population. Therefore, we need to check whether the data distribution curve has a shape close to that of the normal distribution. Otherwise, the test becomes significantly less powerful.

To compare two means, the variances must be homogeneous – the dispersions must not be overly different.

If these three conditions are satisfied (which needs to be the case before we make any use of the distribution), then there is a whole range of very powerful tests available. If one, and *a fortiori*, all three are not satisfied, then we run the risk of inappropriately rejecting, or failing to reject, the null hypothesis H_0.

To test the normality of a distribution, there are numerous methods, and the majority of statistics software packages are capable of performing that test. The easiest software to use for the purpose is certainly XLSTAT, which is integrated into the Excel spreadsheet program, and at time of writing, offers the Shapiro–Wilk, Anderson–Darling, Lilliefors and Jarque–Bera tests.

To test the "uniformity" of the variances, XLSTAT is capable of Fisher's F test, Bartlett's test and Levene's test.

3.1.3.4.2. Non-parametric tests

Only non-parametric tests can be used to work with qualitative data expressed in rank order (ordinal scale) or nominal data. Such tests are based on their own forms of statistics, but there is no constraint as to the form of the distribution of the observed variables. However, certain application conditions must be satisfied. The samples in question must be random (i.e. all the individuals have the same probability of belonging to the sample) and simple (i.e. all the individuals who are to make up the sample are selected independently of one another). Non-parametric tests exhibit numerous advantages, but they are less powerful than parametric tests.

The use of non-parametric tests is justified when the application conditions of other methods are not satisfied, even after transformations of variables and, in particular, in cases where the sample is very small.

3.1.3.5. Choice of a test

The appropriate tests are chosen on the basis of the type of measurement, the form of the frequency distribution and the number of samples available. The diagram below illustrates the path leading to the choice of an appropriate test to use for a given situation. It is harvested from [RAM 96].

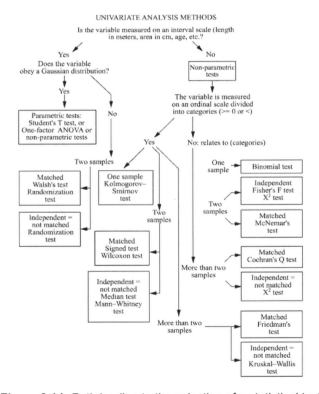

Figure 3.14. Path leading to the selection of a statistical test

3.2. Tests on means: Student's tests

3.2.1. *General*

In this section, we shall begin by presenting mean tests, in the true sense, followed by Student's famous T test derived from these methods. The latter can deal with instances of samples from small populations (n < 30). Both compare a mean value obtained on a sample against a standard, or compare the means obtained for two samples.

Mean tests apply to quantitative variables for which we can define, *a minima*, the mean and the variance. They are parametric tests that look at whether the variables studied obey a normal distribution "closely enough", and have "equivalent variances". If the conditions are respected, these tests can be a very powerful tool.

The below presentation of mean tests and Student's T test is highly detailed, because they must serve as a model to understand the logic and the theoretical bases governing all confirmatory tests. For the continuation, in sections 3.3 and 3.4, dedicated to ANOVA and to the Bravais–Pearson test, the presentation will be less detailed, because we make the assumption that readers are already familiar with the logic of a confirmatory test.

The presentation takes account of the broad range of situations which might arise:

– one or two samples in question;

– the size of the sample(s) n > 30 or n < 30;

– the nature of the samples (independent or matched).

3.2.2. *Comparison of a mean and a norm*

In this case, only a single sample is at issue: the goal is to compare the mean of a variable taken from a sample to that of the whole population, which is described as the norm. The conclusion will be either that the sample is identical to the population (H_0) or that the sample is different from the population (H_1).

Consider a sample k; we are interested in a variable X measured in that sample. The mean value of the variable, observed on the sample k, is written as $\overline{X_k}$. The population has a corresponding "norm" that is the mean, either known or supposed to be known, of the variable X over the whole population, written as $\overline{X}$.

A classic example of a problem which might arise is finding whether a group of pupils belonging to one or more classes is "identical" to the school's population (or the national population) in relation to attainment in math, for example. For this purpose, an indicator (achievement in a series of recognized relevant tests) is determined at school level (or national level). Thus, we know the mean grade $\overline{X}$ obtained in the whole population. The question is whether the mean $\overline{X}_k$ obtained by the sample, extracted from the population, actually reflects the overall context, with some allowance for the influence of sampling (H_0), or whether that mean cannot be explained by the sampling effect (H_1). In the latter case, the difference is said to be "significant"; it is due to external factors, which it would likely be helpful to identify.

To answer this question, we must begin by defining the *gap*, the *distance* between the sample k and the population. As we are working on the basis of mean values, the natural first thought is to find the value of $(\overline{X}_k - \overline{X})$: the mean observed on the sample less the mean of the population (norm). This distance would be zero in the event of a perfect fit between the population and the sample, but this is never the case in practice.

However, to assess the distance, we do not directly use $(\overline{X}_k - \overline{X})$, but instead a parameter Z_k, the truncated distance, based on the very same difference, and whose mathematical properties can be used to implement a simple, powerful tool.

In the coming discussion, we shall, in turn, look at various situations that are subject to slightly different approaches:

– the variance (standard deviation) of the population is or is not known;

– the sample has a large population ($n > 30$) or a small population ($n < 30$).

3.2.2.1. *The variance of the population is known*

In this section, for the sake of clarity, we only present the case of a single sample, with a population of $n > 30$, which is described as a large population. The case of small populations (Student's T) is dealt with below only in the event that the variance of the population is unknown, but adapting to the current case poses no problems.

The population is known, as are its mean and variance. As stated previously, a simple way of expressing the "distance" between the population and the sample observed k would be to look directly are the value $(\overline{X}_k - \overline{X})$, but in practice, we use the truncated distance Z_k that, when the population is perfectly known, is defined as follows:

$$Z_k = \frac{(\text{mean of sample k}) - (\text{mean of population})}{\frac{(\text{standard deviation of population})}{\sqrt{(\text{population of sample})}}}$$

Recap of some mathematical definitions: the population is made up of N individuals, and the sample k of n individuals. If the variable observed is X, we use the notation X_i to speak of the value taken by the variable for individual i; thus, we obtain:

– (population mean): $\overline{X} = \frac{1}{N}\sum_{i=1}^{N} X_i$ (supposed to be known);

– (sample mean): $\overline{X_k} = \frac{1}{n}\sum_{i=1}^{n} X_i$ (calculated from the data);

– (standard deviation of the population): $s(x) = \sqrt{\frac{1}{N}\sum_{i=1}^{N}(X_i-\overline{X})^2}$ (supposed to be known).

We can therefore calculate the truncated deviation of the sample k:

$$Z_k = \frac{(\overline{X_k} - \overline{X})}{\frac{S(X)}{\sqrt{n}}}$$

3.2.2.1.1. Role and properties of the truncated deviation Z_k

Choosing the truncated deviation Z_k instead of $(\overline{X_k} - \overline{X})$ comes at a price; indeed, it has a remarkable mathematical property upon which the method is founded: *if the variable X obeys a normal distribution, then Z_k obeys the TCND.* For the mathematically minded, we can easily verify that, in particular, $\overline{Z_k} = 0$ and $Var(Z_k) = 1$.

The truncated deviation Z_k is a parameter that characterizes the sample k; its value is a measurement of the distance between the sample and the norm. To find out whether that distance is small (H_0) or not (H_1), we need to determine a critical distance beyond which H_0 is rejected.

The critical value Z_T is obtained directly from the TCND table for the value of the risk of error that is deemed acceptable. Though it is not compulsory, this acceptable risk is often taken to be equal to 5% (a 5% chance of being wrong is acceptable). If the experimental distance $Z_k > Z_T$, then we reject H_0 and adopt H_1; otherwise, we stick with H_0.

3.2.2.1.2. Problem-solving with the TCND table

As we saw in the previous section, there are multiple kinds of statistical tables relating to the TCND (unilateral/bilateral; internal/external probability). In the coming discussion, as previously stated, we shall work with the external bilateral probability table, which gives the probability that a centered normed random variable will have a value greater than a given value.

We have made the choice to base this presentation on an example drawn from research done in cognitive psychology:

"Individuals are presented with a series of words. The study involves evaluating their short-term memory capacity. To do so, we count the number of words recalled after a well-known experimental protocol where the individuals tested are presented with 16 common words.

Many earlier studies have shown that with this experimental protocol, immediate memorization capacity obeys a normal distribution with a mean value of 7 and a standard deviation of 2: N(7,2). These values shall be taken to be the norm, as they are "recognized" by the scientific community. The variable (the number of words memorized) thus obeys a normal distribution whose mean is 7 and whose standard deviation is 2: N(7,2).

A researcher wants to know whether these values also apply to schoolchildren. He extracts a sample of 210 pupils in their third-to-last penultimate and final years of school, and puts them through this classic experiment. The mean of the scores obtained by the sample is 6.91".

SOLUTION.– We can calculate the truncated distance observed on this sample:

$$Z_{schoolchildren} = \frac{6.91 - 7.00}{\frac{2}{\sqrt{210}}} = -0.65$$

We want to know whether the sample of schoolchildren (in light of the criterion under study) behaves like the rest of the population (H_0) or whether, on the other hand, it must be considered that this sample of schoolchildren does not belong to the population (H_1).

Looking at the TCND table, we see that for a risk level of 5%, $Z_{T5\%} = 1.96$. The observed value of $Z_{schoolchild} = -0.65$, but as the law is symmetrical, which is important in a bilateral test, it is the absolute value.

The value 0.65 is "within" the interval −1.96, +1.96 (Figure 3.15). We can also say that the distance between the norm and the sample of schoolchildren is less than the critical distance of 1.96; in this case, at a 5% risk of error, we adopt the hypothesis H_0: *the difference observed between the norm and the sample is attributable to the fluctuations in sampling, and thus nothing statistically separates this sample of schoolchildren from the whole population.* The situation is illustrated in Figure 3.15.

Now imagine that the sample of schoolchildren had obtained a mean of 7.33 instead of 6.91. What conclusion would we have drawn?

In this case:

$$z_{schoolchildren} = \frac{7.33 - 7.00}{\frac{2}{\sqrt{210}}} = 2.39$$

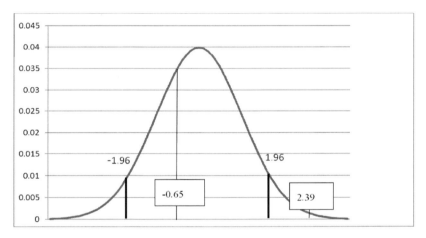

Figure 3.15. *Short-term memory capacity of schoolchildren: score = 6.91 and score = 7.33*

If we look to the bilateral TCND table, we can see that this value is outside of (above) the acceptability range of H_0 at the accepted risk of 5% (−1.96, +1.96). Hence, we are led to reject H_0 and preserve H_1. In this case, the difference observed cannot be explained by the effect of sampling. We say that the difference is proven, so we need to look for the causes of that difference. The situation is illustrated in Figure 3.15.

3.2.2.2. *The variance of the population is unknown*

The mean of the population (norm) is still known, but the variance is unknown. In this case, the above relation that defined the truncated deviation must be slightly modified, in the denominator, replacing the standard deviation of the population, which was supposed to be known, with the standard deviation calculated on the sample. Yet close attention must be paid to the following caveat.

NOTE.– In this case, the standard deviation of the sample is the "unbiased" standard deviation presented above with the mathematical indicators. Remember that if n is the population of the sample, the unbiased standard deviation is defined by the following relation.

Unbiased standard deviation of the sample:

$$S(X) = \sqrt{\frac{1}{n-1} \Sigma_{i=1}^{n}(X_i - \bar{X})^2}$$

If n is large, the difference between the standard deviation and the unbiased standard deviation is slight; on the other hand, where n is small, it may play a not-insignificant role.

Below, we examine two situations: first n > 30 and then n < 30.

3.2.2.2.1. Case of large samples n > 30

The situation is the same as for the previous section, except the fact that we calculate the truncated deviation using the unbiased standard deviation of the sample, and, as before, we refer to the TCND table.

$$Z_k = \frac{(\text{mean of sample})k - (\text{mean of population})}{\frac{(\text{standard deviation of sample})}{\sqrt{(\text{population of sample})}}}$$

EXAMPLE.– "School psychologists in a region where there is a high pass rate for the baccalauréat hypothesize that the differences observed are also to be found earlier on in the students' schooling. With this in mind, they administer a general knowledge test to 104 CE2 children. The national mean on this test is 316.28, but the variance is not known".

The results obtained on the sample are:

– mean: 334.21;

– standard deviation: 112.37.

At first glance, the results in the sample appear to be better than the national mean. Can we, though, state that "the differences observed in the baccalauréat results are also observable earlier in the students' academic career"? Is it not the case that the result can be explained solely by the effect of sampling (background noise)?

Thus, they decide to carry out a mean test to compare the sample to the national population. They begin by calculating the truncated deviation:

$$Z_{observed} = \frac{334.21 - 316.28}{\dfrac{112.37}{\sqrt{104}}} = 1.627$$

Within the 5% error margin, the truncated deviation, as in the previous case, is $Z_T = 1.96$. The value of the truncated deviation observed is less than the threshold value at the 5% risk, so we must adopt the null hypothesis H_0 (the differences observed may be due to a sampling effect). In other words, the distance between the sample and the population is not sufficient to state that the population and the sample are different.

3.2.2.2.2. Small samples n < 30: Student's T law

In the case of small samples, when we wish to compare the mean obtained by a variable on a sample with the same mean obtained on the whole population, we begin by defining a new parameter: Student's T.

$$t = \frac{(\text{mean of sample})k - (\text{mean of population})}{\dfrac{(\text{standard deviation of sample})}{\sqrt{(\text{population of sample})}}}$$

As is evident here, the definition of Student's T is identical to that of the mean deviation. Why, then, should we bring Student's T into play? The reason is simple: the parameter Z_k defined for large samples (n > 30) obeys the TCND, but if the population is small (n < 30), it no longer applies.

Student's T obeys a different statistical law – Student's law – which is presented below. It is a continuous statistical probability law, as is the TCND, but it depends on the sample size. As with the TCND, we can calculate a Student's statistical table. We can show that if n > 30, then Student's law is identical to the TCND.

Thus, in this case, we calculate Student's T, in the same way as for the mean deviation of the sample, as in the previous example, but in order to analyze the result, we must refer to the table for Student's probability law, especially designed for small samples. First, though, here are a few explanations regarding Student's statistical law.

3.2.2.2.3. Student's statistical law

If the number of individuals is low (< 30), the truncated deviation no longer obeys the TCND, even if the variable in question obeys a normal distribution. It obeys a different probability law: Student's law. This is a continuous law whose probability density, for the random variable u, is written as:

$$f(u) = c\left(1 + \frac{u^2}{k}\right)^{-\frac{(k+1)}{2}}$$

The constant c is calculated in such a way that the probability of u falling within the interval $[-\infty, +\infty]$ is equal to 1; it is the distribution normalization coefficient.

The constant "k" is the number of *degrees of freedom,* $k = dof = n - 1$, where n is the number of individuals in the sample.

The graphic representation of Student's law (Figure 3.16) is made up of different curves for each of the values of dof $= n - 1$; they resemble a slightly deformed TCND. It is more heavily deformed when the number of dof is small. Beyond dof $= 30$, the curves are identical to the TCND.

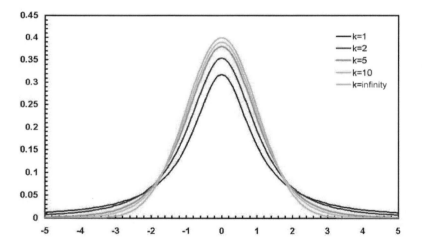

Figure 3.16. *Student's statistical law. For a color version of this figure, see www.iste.co.uk/larini/education.zip*

3.2.2.2.4. Table of Student's statistical law

For each of the values of dof, we can, using the same approach as for the TCND, obtain a table of the same type as those for the TCND. In reality, it is common to bring together all the results for dof $= 1,...,30$ in a single two-way entry table (dof/external probability).

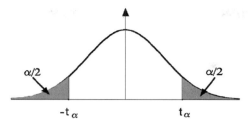

Figure 3.17. *Exclusion zones of H0
for Student's T external bilateral statistical table*

With the accepted risk of α, if Student's T belongs to one of the two shaded zones, we must reject H_0 and adopt the alternative hypothesis H_1.

Reading: Where dof = 10, the probability of obtaining a value of t > 2.228 is α = 0.05.

To illustrate the above, using Student's statistical table, we now present a small study regarding female students at the University of Geneva. "A researcher wants to study the behavior in terms of mean weekly expenditure of female UG students. His aim is to verify whether the mean weekly expenses are equal to 150 FS (considered to be the national average), within the acceptable risk level of 5%. In order to do so, he selects a random sample of 20 female students and obtains the following 20 responses":

The data collected from 20 female students are as follows, expressed in FS: 120, 150, 180, 200, 130, 150, 170, 160, 190, 100, 125, 145, 175, 200, 120, 130, 135, 165, 150, 180.

We wish to test the contradictory hypotheses:

– H_0: the daily expenditure of female students at the UG is in line with the national average;

– H_1: the daily expenditure of female students at the UG differs from the national average.

Solution: for dof = 20 – 1 = 19.

Mean: 153.75.

Standard deviation: 28.51.

Student's T, calculated value: 0.588.

Student's T 5%: 2.093.

External Probability / dof	0.90	0.50	0.30	0.20	0.10		0.02	0.01	0.001
1	0.158	1.000	1.963	3.078	6.314	12.706	31.821	63.657	636.619
2	0.142	0.816	1.386	1.886	2.920	4.303	6.965	9.925	31.598
3	0.137	0.765	1.250	1.638	2.353	3.182	4.541	5.841	12.924
4	0.134	0.741	1.190	1.533	2.132	2.776	3.747	4.604	8.610
5	0.132	0.727	1.156	1.476	2.015	2.571	3.365	4.032	6.869
6	0.131	0.718	1.134	1.440	1.943	2.447	3.143	3.707	5.959
7	0.130	0.711	1.119	1.415	1.895	2.365	2.998	3.499	5.408
8	0.130	0.706	1.108	1.397	1.860	2.306	2.896	3.355	5.041
9	0.129	0.703	1.100	1.383	1.833	2.262	2.821	3.250	4.781
10	0.129	0.700	1.093	1.372	1.812	2.228	2.764	3.169	4.587
11	0.129	0.697	1.088	1.363	1.796	2.201	2.718	3.106	4.437
12	0.128	0.695	1.083	1.356	1.782	2.179	2.681	3.055	4.318
13	0.128	0.694	1.079	1.350	1.771	2.160	2.650	3.012	4.221
14	0.128	0.692	1.076	1.345	1.761	2.145	2.624	2.977	4.140
15	0.128	0.691	1.074	1.341	1.753	2.131	2.602	2.947	4.073

16	0.128	0.690	1.071	1.337	1.746	2.120	2.583	2.921	4.015
17	0.128	0.689	1.069	1.333	1.740	2.110	2.567	2.898	3.965
18	0.127	0.688	1.067	1.330	1.734	2.101	2.552	2.878	3.922
19	0.127	0.688	1.066	1.328	1.729	2.093	2.539	2.861	3.883
20	0.127	0.687	1.064	1.325	1.725	2.086	2.528	2.845	3.850
21	0.127	0.686	1.063	1.323	1.721	2.080	2.518	2.831	3.819
22	0.127	0.686	1.061	1.321	1.717	2.074	2.508	2.819	3.792
23	0.127	0.685	1.060	1.319	1.714	2.069	2.500	2.807	3.767
24	0.127	0.685	1.059	1.318	1.711	2.064	2.492	2.797	3.745
25	0.127	0.684	1.058	1.316	1.708	2.060	2.485	2.787	3.725
26	0.127	0.684	1.058	1.315	1.706	2.056	2.479	2.779	3.707
27	0.127	0.684	1.057	1.314	1.703	2.052	2.473	2.771	3.690
28	0.127	0.683	1.056	1.313	1.701	2.048	2.467	2.763	3.674
29	0.127	0.683	1.055	1.311	1.699	2.045	2.462	2.756	3.659
30	0.127	0.683	1.055	1.310	1.697	2.042	2.457	2.750	3.646
∞	0.126	0.674	1.036	1.282	1.645	1.960	2.326	2.576	3.291

Table 3.5. *External bilateral statistical table for Student's T*

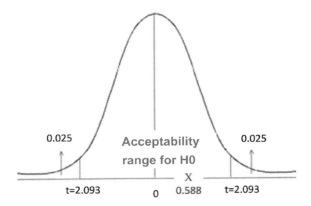

Figure 3.18. *University of Geneva female students:*
results and acceptability range for H_0

As the calculated Student's T value (0.588) is lower than the Student's T value for an accepted risk of 5% (2.093), we retain H_0 and thus can conclude that within the accepted risk of 5%, female students at the University of Geneva follow the national trend in terms of their weekly expenditure. The result is illustrated in Figure 3.18.

3.2.3. *Comparison of two observed means*

We often have cause to compare two samples. Those samples may be independent or matched. Remember that two samples are independent if they are made up of different individuals, and matched if it is the same individuals but measured at two different times, for example.

3.2.3.1. *Comparison of two means from independent samples*

To compare the means of two samples, we again need to adapt the definition of the truncated deviation or Student's T value depending on the size of the sample:

$$Z_k \text{ or } t = \frac{\text{Mean sample 1} - \text{Mean sample 2}}{\sqrt{\dfrac{\text{Var (pop or smpl) 1}}{\text{Population sample 1}} + \dfrac{\text{Var (pop or smpl) 2}}{\text{Population sample 2}}}}$$

The truncated deviation $(n > 30)$ thus defined obeys the TCND; at this level of discussion, it is a hypothesis, but it has been confirmed by numerous experimental publications and mathematical demonstrations. The same is true of the new way of expressing Student's T value (t < 30), which always obeys Student's law.

Here again, there are two situations that may arise: the variance of the population is known (or supposed to be known) or is unknown, whether for large or for small groups. The discussion below includes all these situations.

If the variances of the population are known, the variances used in the denominator are those of the population; if not, it is the (unbiased) variances of the samples.

When we are dealing with large groups (n > 30), the theoretical table which determines the value Z_T is the TCND table; in the case of small samples, it is the table for Student's law which can be used to evaluate t_T.

However, in this case, there are two constraints n1 and n2 (the populations of the two samples), which are imposed. Thus, the number of dof = n1 + n2 – 2.

3.2.3.1.1. Case of large samples (n > 30)

To deal with situations where we have a large number of samples, as the method remains the same, we shall limit our discussion here to two examples. After calculating the truncated deviation, we use the TCND table.

EXAMPLE 1.– The population variance is known and n > 30.

Children's reaction times: Consider two samples of children, shown either a word or a drawing. They are asked to name what they see as quickly as possible, and we measure the reaction times expressed in milliseconds. The results obtained are presented in Table 3.6.

	Sample 1 – Words	Sample 2 – Drawings
Population	51	43
Known standard deviation (ms)	110	140
Mean for verbal reactions (ms)	473.05	563.04

Table 3.6. Data table: children's reaction times

In this case:

$$Z = \frac{473.05 - 563.04}{\sqrt{\dfrac{110^2}{51} + \dfrac{140^2}{43}}} = -3.42$$

At the 5% risk of error, the TCND table gives a theoretical truncated deviation $Z_T = 1.96$.

As the distance Z between the two samples is greater than the theoretical distance for an acceptable risk of 5%, we can consider that the means of the reaction times are statistically different, and not attributable solely to the effect of sampling. Hence, the result observed is "significant".

EXAMPLE 2.– The variance of the population is unknown and n > 30.

Impregnation with mother's scent: A researcher wants to test the calming effect of their mother's smell on breastfeeding babies. To do so, he measures the amount of time the baby takes to fall asleep after breastfeeding depending on whether, beside them in their cot, there is a T-shirt imbued with their mother's smell or one impregnated with the smell of another woman having a child of the same age.

The variances (standard deviations) of the two variables "time taken to fall asleep in the presence of the mother's scent" and "time taken to fall asleep in the presence of a stranger's scent" are not known. Thus, we must calculate the two variances of the samples on the basis of the experimental data. The results are summarized in Table 3.7.

	Population 1 Mother's scent	Population 2 Stranger's scent
Populations	73	64
Mean minutes	8.62	12.43
Standard deviation sample	4.21	5.26

Table 3.7. *Data table: impregnation with mother's scent*

In this case:

$$Z_k = \frac{8.62 - 12.43}{\sqrt{\dfrac{4.21^2}{73} + \dfrac{5.26^2}{64}}} = -4.635$$

At a 5% risk of error, the table of the TCND gives a theoretical truncated gap of 1.96. The value found is beyond the 5% confidence range.

We can therefore affirm that the mean values of the "time taken to fall asleep" for the two samples are statistically different and not connected only to a sampling effect. Therefore, the result observed is significant.

3.2.3.1.2. Case of small samples (n < 30)

The method employed in the case of small samples is the same as in the previous case. The only difference is that instead of using the TCND table, we must use Student's statistical table.

3.2.3.2. *Comparison of two means from two matched samples: repeated measurements*

Remember that two matched samples are made up of the same individuals, or by individuals deemed to be "similar". For example, we are dealing with matched samples when we look at the evolution of a variable over time, measured for the same sample. Such is the case, for instance, if we look at the evolution of a class over the course of a year. Numerous checking tests are conducted on the basis of recognized indicators; often, in such circumstances, one would speak of repeated measurements. No longer is the aim to determine whether one or two samples belong to a given; rather, it is to detect (or fail to detect) internal variations in a sample. To do so, we take a reading for each individual i in the group for the same variable at two different times: 1 and 2. We obtain two series of values, which must then be compared in order to see whether there is a significant change between points 1 and 2.

Though the logic behind the method is very similar to that applied for two independent samples, there are some fundamental differences which must be noted.

In this case, the parameter used for the test is written as:

$$Z \text{ or } t = \frac{\text{Mean of the differences}}{\dfrac{\text{Standard deviation of the differences}}{\sqrt{\text{number of data pairs}}}}$$

Here, again, it has been shown that Z and t thus defined are distributed, respectively, according to the TCND for large populations and Student's law for small populations.

For each individual i, then, we have a pair of data points ($x1_i$ and $x2_i$). In this case, to construct Z or t, we must begin by constructing the variable "difference"$_i$i, $x1_i - x2_i$, for each individual i. The mean of the differences and the standard deviation of the differences are specified in the example below.

Subject	After autocratic teaching	After democratic teaching
1	5	8
2	12	14
3	10	11
4	9	15
5	8	9
6	7	12
7	12	12
8	8	13
9	13	15
10	10	13
11	14	15
12	11	13
13	8	12
14	11	13
15	15	14
16	13	11
17	10	12
18	11	13
19	13	14
20	16	17
Mean	10.8	12.80

Table 3.8. *[I/V] table: autocratic teaching versus democratic teaching*

EXAMPLE.– In the context of a training course for adults, the same group of 20 individuals in turn test two means of teaching at two different times. The first method is described as "autocratic", followed by the second, which is described as "participative" or "democratic". A 20-point questionnaire is put to the respondents after each of the experiments. This classic test, known as locus of control, is designed to force the trainees to explain their individual positions in the organization. It is the number of explanations deemed acceptable for each of the 20 points, which serves as an indicator. The results and the computational elements are outlined in the Table 3.8.

Indications for calculating Student's T:

$$\text{Mean of differences} = \frac{(5-8)+(12-14)+\cdots+(13-14)+(16-17)}{20} = \frac{-40}{20} = -2$$

$$\text{Standard deviation of differences} = \sqrt{\text{variance of differences}}$$

The variance of the differences is the sum, across all subjects, of the terms (difference-mean)^2 divided by the number of subjects -1 (unbiased variance).

Variance of differences =

$$\frac{[-3 - (-2)]^2 + [-2 - (-2)]^2 + \cdots + [-1 - (-2)]^2}{20 - 1} = \frac{74}{19}$$

$$\text{Standard deviation of differences} = \sqrt{\frac{74}{19}} = 1.97$$

Thus:

$$t = \frac{-2}{\frac{1.97}{\sqrt{20}}} = -4.54$$

Student's theoretical table for an acceptable risk threshold of 5% and for dof $= 20 - 1 = 19$ indicates a value of t_T, which is equal to 2.10. The T, calculated on the basis of the observations, falls outside of the confidence interval, so we must reject H_0 and adopt H_1, and thus conclude that "democratic" and "autocratic" teaching are significantly different.

3.2.4. *What we have learned*

Means tests and Student's T test are used when we are working with a quantitative (numerical) variable, recorded for one or two samples. At the very least, we must be able to calculate the mean of the variable and its standard deviation. Strictly, they must be used when the variable under study is distributed across the population in accordance with a normal distribution. However, it is commonplace to use these tests as long as the distribution is not too far removed from a normal distribution.

They can be used to check:

– whether a sample conforms to a norm, or to the population;

– whether or not two independent samples are identical;

– whether or not a sample taken at two different times has evolved. If so, we say that we are dealing with two matched samples.

We have looked at two cases: small samples ($n < 30$) and large samples ($n > 30$).

For large samples, we define a parameter Z, the truncated deviation, which obeys the TCND. For small samples, we define Student's T that obeys another statistical law, Student's law, which depends on the number of dof.

Z and t are constructed in such a way that they are a measurement of the distance between the sample and the norm, or between the two samples, or the same sample at two different times. Simply put, if Z and t are small, we adopt H_0 (the sample is compliant with the norm, the two independent samples are identical, the two matched samples have not evolved). If, on the other hand, the distance (Z or t) is large, then we reject H_0 and adopt H_1 (the sample does not obey the norm, the two independent samples are different, the two matched samples have evolved).

To decide whether the distance is small or large after deciding on the acceptable risk of error (often we choose a risk of 5%), we must refer either to the TCND table for Z, or to Student's double-entry table (accepted % of risk, dof).

3.2.5. *Implementation of tests: use of software*

The foregoing discussion has demonstrated the fundamentals and the logic to be followed in conducting a mean test. We have seen that it is possible to perform the calculations directly (mean, standard deviation, Z or t) and then consult the tables for the TCND or Student's statistical law to draw a conclusion as to whether H_0 should be accepted or rejected. We can also work with a spreadsheet such as Excel to facilitate the calculations, step by step, and potentially use macros. This task is sometimes lengthy and very painstaking, though very good from a learning point of view, because it forces users to go through all the different steps in the procedure.

In reality, there are numerous software packages available – some of them very simple, and others more elaborate – to aid in the task, but all of them require at least a certain amount of knowledge before they can be used with confidence. To dive straight in to using a piece of software is risky if we are not fully aware of the fundaments and aims of the tests implemented by the machine: what are their purposes? Upon what are they based? Are the usage conditions required? Is the test used appropriate for the situation at hand? Which concrete conclusions may we draw from the results? These and other such questions must be borne in mind.

All statistical software tools handle mean tests and Student's T test. Usually, the difference between large ($n > 30$) and small ($n < 30$) samples is not explicitly apparent. Only by Student's T test can it be discerned, because when $n > 30$, Student's statistical law becomes identical to the TCND. If we only need to perform mean or

Student's tests, it is possible to use very simple programs, e.g. Excel (using macros), JASP which is based on R, BioStat, etc.

There are also very highly evolved software tools (R, SPHINX, SPSS, MODALISA, SAS, XLSTA, etc.), but some of these require a significant degree of investment. Each has its own peculiarities, but all cater to the majority of situations we are likely to encounter when processing data in the human and social sciences, and thus in the field of education. R is indubitably the most complete and the most flexible tool available, but it is also the one which requires the most investment. XLSTAT is undeniably the simplest and most user-friendly, as it is directly built into Excel.

IMPORTANT POINT.– Software programs, in general, state the result of the tests by directly displaying a value: the P-value. This indicates the risk taken by rejecting H_0. For example, if the risk is 5%, then p = 0.05; if it is 10%, then p = 0.1; and if it is 1%, then p = 0.001. In general, if the P-value is lower than 0.05, we reject H_0 and adopt H_1.

This is where we shall leave our discussion of this topic, because beyond the broad outlines we have just described, each package has its own ins and outs that need to be mastered by the users, and also, they evolve or die out very quickly; yet it must not be forgotten that using a piece of software requires prior effort in learning not only the fundamental bases of the methods used, but also the way in which the software itself works.

3.3. Analysis of variance

3.3.1. *General points*

Having looked at a comparison between a sample and a norm, and between two samples, for a quantitative variable, it is natural that we should want to compare more than two samples. This is exactly the aim of tests based on examining the variance, which are commonly collectively referred to by the generic term "ANOVA" (analysis of variance). ANOVA tests can be considered a generalization of the means test and Student's T test, although the method used is noticeably different and, as we shall see, is based on other statistical laws.

More specifically, there are a range of different forms of ANOVA, which are distinguished by the number and nature of the variables taken into account. We can cite ANOVA (the original), ANCOVA, MANOVA and MANCOVA.

For the coming discussion, we shall limit ourselves to presenting ANOVA itself, which focuses on cases where a continuous quantitative variable is read on $K > 2$ samples. ANOVA is the basic component for all the other approaches. Our presentation of it here is fairly brief – only what is needed for readers to understand the bases of the method.

For its part, ANCOVA compares a continuous quantitative variable (such as a score on a test), recorded for multiple samples (different classes) and influenced by another quantitative variable (e.g. the amount of class time given over to studying the particular subject). MANOVA is a variant of ANOVA with two or more continuous quantitative variables read for $K > 2$ samples. MANCOVA compares two or more continuous quantitative variables read for $K > 2$ samples, with one or more qualitative variables categorizing the individuals in each sample.

Let us return now to look at the ANOVA test itself; it applies to quantitative variables that obey a normal distribution. As is the case with mean tests, it is a parametric test, and it is helpful to check that the distribution of the variables in question is indeed normal. If the hypothesis of normality is not satisfied, we could, for example, use the Kruskal–Wallis test, which is a non-parametric test and does not require the data to be normally distributed.

Hereafter, we discuss the example of ANOVA for independent samples and then examine the case of matched samples (repeated measurements).

3.3.2. *ANOVA for K > 2 independent samples*

We record a variable X for individuals divided into $K > 2$ samples k, which are made up of n_k individuals, and we wish to decide between the following two hypotheses:

– the null hypothesis H_0: The K samples are identical with respect to the variable X;

– the alternative hypothesis H_1: There is at least one distribution, across the K samples, whose mean departs significantly from the other means.

For example, we measure a variable X on 3 samples ($K = 3$; $k = 1, 2, 3$) of young children, grouped by age (ages 4, 5 and 6). We can imagine two different situations, represented by the distributions shown in Figure 3.19.

In the first figure, the differences observed are only slight, and may be interpreted as being attributable to variations within each sample.

In the second figure, the differences are greater, and seem more likely to be due to the fact that the samples are truly different.

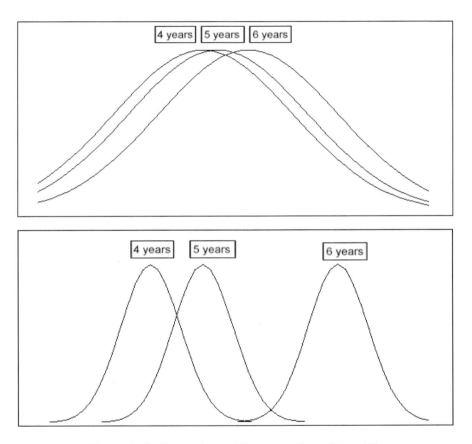

Figure 3.19. *Comparison of three samples – H_0 and H_1*

The ANOVA test is capable of finding the difference between the two situations. In the first case, we would conclude that the samples are equal (H_0), and in the second case, the samples are different (H_1).

The question that now arises is how to reach those conclusions.

3.3.2.1. *Posing of the problem on the basis of a cognitive psychology study*

In the context of research on the memorization of information in image and verbal forms, a researcher examines the influence of various types of media.

He presents 24 actions to five different groups (K = 5), with each group receiving a different visual information medium. The five media used are: a sentence describing the action carried out by a person, a drawing where we see the person performing that action, a color photo showing the same action, a series of three sequential photos illustrating the action, and a film clip showing the same behavior. The subjects are asked to recall the 24 actions presented. Each group is made up of 15 individuals (N = 75 and n_k = 15 for k = 1, 2, 3, 4, 5). However, with ANOVA, it is not necessary for all the samples to contain the same number of individuals.

This example is drawn from *Manuel de statistique pour psychologues* [GUÉ 97].

Table 3.9 represents the number of actions memorized for each of the five informational media.

Individuals	Sentence	Drawing	Photo	Three photos	Film
	5	9	9	10	8
	8	10	8	12	10
	6	9	11	11	12
	8	7	6	10	14
	7	10	9	8	11
	9	8	11	12	8
	6	11	8	9	10
	7	9	7	11	12
	5	7	9	8	9
	10	10	8	10	11
	6	11	10	13	13
	7	8	12	11	8
	8	12	8	10	11
	7	9	10	12	9
	4	8	7	9	10
Mean	6.87	9.20	8.87	10.40	10.40
Standard deviation	1.60	1.47	1.68	1.40	1.84

Table 3.9. *Data table: memorization as a function of the delivery medium*

The researcher wants to check the hypothesis: "With the accepted degree of risk of 5%, there is a difference between the recollective performances depending on the informational medium used".

Thus, hypothesis H_0 is that the five groups are equal. The null hypothesis holds that the medium used has no influence and, in this case, the hypothesis formulated by the researcher is rejected. In other words, this would mean that the differences observed between the means – 6.87-9.20-8.87-10.40-10.40, with a 5% risk of uncertainty – are attributable to a fluctuation in the sampling.

In the opposite situation, H_0 is rejected and H_1 – the hypothesis formulated by the researcher – is borne out.

NOTE.– ANOVA makes an overall ruling, and H_0 or H_1 will be applied to all five treatments. For example, if four treatments obey H_0 and just one obeys H_1, then ANOVA validates H_1 for all of them. Hence, it is sometimes worth continuing to work on a problem afterwards by conducting partial analyses.

NOTE.– Obviously, it is possible to answer the question at hand by testing the means (or conducting Student's tests) for the samples, examining them two by two. However, in this case, such an approach would mean 10 tests would have to be carried out, and the errors would also increase 10-fold.

The solution to this problem is proposed later on, after we have looked at the theoretical fundaments of ANOVA.

3.3.2.2. *The theoretical bases of ANOVA*

Let us examine a situation where K = 3, the different values that need to be taken into account to carry out an ANOVA are intended to show the amount of the differences due to what happens within each sample (intra variation) and the differences due to what actually sets the groups apart from one another (inter variations).

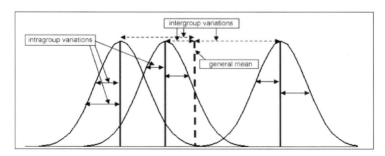

Figure 3.20. *Distance used to implement an ANOVA*

Consider a population in which we observe a variable X. We randomly select K (K > 2) samples within that population, each sample being made up of n^k individuals, and the total population tested being $N=\sum_{k=1}^{K} n^k$. For each individual i in each sample k, we record the values x_i^k of the random variable X, where $i = 1..., n^k$ and $k = 1..., K$. In this context, we can define the following values, in turn.

3.3.2.2.1. Means of samples

Sample mean: This is the mean of the values relating to a single sample of population n^k:

$$\overline{X}^k = \frac{1}{n^k} \sum_{i=1}^{n^k} x_i^k$$

3.3.2.2.2. General or intersample mean

The intersample mean is the mean of all the values in all the samples – thus, it is also the mean of the means of the samples, weighted by their respective populations n^k. Using the double sum, this can be written as:

$$\overline{X} = \frac{1}{N} \sum_{k=1}^{K} \sum_{i=1}^{n^k} X_i^k = \frac{1}{N} \sum_{k=1}^{K} n^k \overline{X}^k$$

Now, we need to introduce values to characterize the variations in each sample (intragroup variations) and the variations between the different samples (intergroup variations).

To characterize the different intragroup and intergroup variations, we define two values: SSE_{inter} and SSE_{intra} (sum of squared errors).

3.3.2.2.3. Characterization of intragroup variations

$$SSE_{intra} = \sum_{k=1}^{K} \sum_{i=1}^{n^k} (x_i^k - \overline{X}^k)^2$$

The intragroup variation expresses the sum, across all the samples k, of the variability within the samples around their respective mean values. It is not a reflection of the difference between the samples.

3.3.2.2.4. Characterization of intergroup variations

$$SSE_{inter} = \sum_{k=1}^{K} n^k (\overline{X}^k - \overline{X})^2$$

The intergroup variation expresses the differences between samples, which may be due to the different treatments undergone by the samples.

We can also define the quantity:

$$SSE_{total} = \sum_{k=1}^{K} \sum_{i=1}^{n^k} (x_i^k - \overline{X})^2$$

It expresses the sum of the variations around the general mean value of the K samples as though they formed one contiguous sample.

We can show that:

$$SSE_{total} = SSE_{inter} + SSE_{intra}$$

3.3.2.2.5. Inter variance and intra variance

In these conditions, we can define two unbiased variances: the "intergroup variance" and the "intragroup variance". It is these values upon which ANOVA is based:

$$V_{inter} = \frac{SSE_{inter}}{K-1} \text{ and } V_{intra} = \frac{SSE_{intra}}{N-K}$$

As seen in the previous chapters, the unbiased variances (or sample variances) are obtained by finding the ratio of the SSE to the number of dof. Without going into further detail on the subject of dof, we can state:

– for the calculation of V_{inter}, there is a constraint because the number K of samples is fixed ($dof_{inter} = K - 1$);

– for the calculation of V_{intra}, there are K constraints, because the K n^k are fixed ($dof_{intra} = N - K$).

3.3.2.2.6. Fisher's parameter

Now, we construct a parameter, F, which is the ratio between the inter- and intraunbiased variance. It is Fisher's parameter, which obeys the Fisher–Snedecor statistical distribution:

$$F = \frac{V_{inter}}{V_{intra}}$$

Thus, F is larger when the difference between the samples is greater; hence, the higher the value of F, the higher the likelihood of rejecting the null hypothesis. As is the case with mean tests, we still need to know beyond what point it is to be rejected.

3.3.2.2.7. The statistics behind ANOVA: the Fisher–Snedecor distribution

Although the variables observed on samples are random variables following a normal distribution (it is a parametric test), Fisher's parameter does not obey a normal distribution. In the way in which it is built, it obeys the Fisher–Snedecor statistical distribution, on the basis of which (much like we saw with the mean tests) it is possible to establish statistical tables that enable us, if we accept a certain percentage of risk, to say whether the K groups belong to the same population (H_0) or not (H_1).

For readers to whom it is of interest, the probability density of a Fisher–Snedecor distribution is written as follows, for a random variable observed x, which obeys a normal distribution:

$$f(x) = \frac{\left(\dfrac{d_1 x}{d_1 x + d_2}\right)^{d_1/2} \left(1 - \dfrac{d_1 x}{d_1 x + d_2}\right)^{d_2/2}}{x \mathrm{B}\left(d_1/2, d_2/2\right)}$$

where:

– d1 = K – 1;

– d2 = N – K.

Its graphic representation for various couples of dof is shown in Figure 3.21.

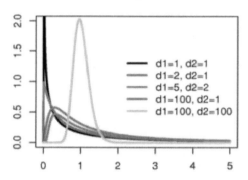

Figure 3.21. *Probability density for Fisher's statistical distribution for different dof*

Without going into detail, based on the probability density, tables have been established (Fisher–Snedecor tables). The approach is the same as that which was employed for determining the statistical tables for the TCND and Student's distribution. In the present case, we have two parameters, d1 and d2, which are, respectively, the dof due to the total population studied and to the number of samples in question. Thus, the tables include three parameters: the accepted uncertainty threshold and the two dof $d1 = K - 1$ and $d2 = N - K$.

Table 3.10 has two entries – d1 and d2 – and gives the value of F for a risk of 5%. If we choose a different value of acceptable risk, we would need to look at a different table, calculated specifically for that new level of acceptable risk:

– v_1: number of dof for the lesser of the two variances;

– v_2: number of dof for the greater of the two variances.

For x = 0.05:

v_2	1	2	3	4	5	6	8	12	24	∞
1	161.40	199.50	215.70	224.60	230.20	234.00	238.90	243.90	249.00	254.30
2	18.51	19.00	19.16	19.25	19.30	19.33	19.37	19.41	19.45	19.50
3	10.13	9.55	9.28	9.12	9.01	8.94	8.84	8.74	8.64	8.53
4	7.71	6.94	6.59	6.39	6.26	6.16	6.04	5.91	5.77	5.63
5	6.61	5.79	5.41	5.19	5.05	4.95	4.82	4.68	4.53	4.36
6	5.99	5.14	4.76	4.53	4.39	4.28	4.15	4.00	3.84	3.67
7	5.99	4.74	4.35	4.12	3.97	3.87	3.73	3.57	3.41	3.23
8	5.32	4.46	4.07	3.84	3.69	3.58	3.44	3.28	3.12	2.93
9	5.12	4.26	3.86	3.63	3.48	3.37	3.23	3.07	2.90	2.71
10	4.96	4.10	3.71	3.84	3.33	3.22	3.07	2.91	2.74	2.54
11	4.84	3.98	3.59	3.36	3.20	3.09	2.95	2.79	2.61	2.40
12	4.75	3.88	3.49	3.26	3.11	3.00	2.85	2.69	2.50	2.30
13	4.67	3.80	3.41	3.18	3.02	2.92	2.77	2.60	2.42	2.21
14	4.60	3.74	3.34	3.11	2.96	2.85	2.70	2.53	2.35	2.13
15	4.54	3.68	3.29	3.06	2.90	2.79	2.64	2.48	2.29	2.07
16	4.49	3.63	3.24	3.01	2.85	2.74	2.59	2.42	2.24	2.01
17	4.45	3.59	3.20	2.96	2.81	2.70	2.55	2.38	2.19	1.96
18	4.41	3.55	3.16	2.93	2.77	2.66	2.51	2.34	2.15	1.92
19	4.38	3.52	3.13	2.90	2.74	2.63	2.48	2.31	2.11	1.88
20	4.35	3.49	3.10	2.87	2.71	2.60	2.45	2.28	2.08	1.84
21	4.32	3.47	3.07	2.84	2.68	2.57	2.42	2.25	2.05	1.81
22	4.30	3.44	3.05	2.82	2.66	2.55	2.40	2.23	2.03	1.78
23	4.28	3.42	3.03	2.80	2.64	2.53	2.38	2.20	2.00	1.76
24	4.26	3.40	3.01	2.78	2.62	2.51	2.36	2.18	1.98	1.73
25	4.24	3.38	2.99	2.76	2.60	2.49	2.34	2.16	1.96	1.71
26	4.22	3.37	2.98	2.74	2.59	2.47	2.32	2.15	1.95	1.69
27	4.21	3.35	2.96	2.73	2.57	2.46	2.30	2.13	1.93	1.67
28	4.20	3.34	2.95	2.71	2.56	2.44	2.29	2.12	1.92	1.65
29	4.18	3.33	2.93	2.70	2.54	2.43	2.28	2.10	1.90	1.64
30	4.17	3.32	2.92	2.69	2.53	2.42	2.27	2.09	1.89	1.62
40	4.08	3.23	2.84	2.61	2.45	2.34	2.18	2.00	1.79	1.51
60	4.00	3.15	2.76	2.52	2.37	2.25	2.10	1.92	1.70	1.39
120	3.92	3.07	2.68	2.45	2.29	2.17	2.01	1.83	1.61	1.25
∞	3.84	2.99	2.60	2.37	2.21	2.09	1.94	1.75	1.52	1.00

Table 3.10. *Fisher–Snedecor table*

Example of how to interpret the F table

For $v_1 = 5$, $v_2 = 20$, the calculated value of F must be greater than 2.71 for the regression coefficient to be deemed significant, with a 5% risk of error.

3.3.2.3. *Solution of recall problem*

Now, let us look again at the problem of recall performances presented in section 3.3.2.1. To begin with, for educational purposes, we shall present the "manual calculation", before going on to use the software tool BioStat directly.

3.3.2.3.1. "Manual" calculation

We used Excel to help in the various stages of the calculation. To do so, we constructed a calculation spreadsheet to determine, in turn, SSE_{inter} and SSE_{intra}, followed by V_{inter} and V_{intra} and finally the experimental Fisher parameter F.

It is possible to verify that we obtain, for $d1 = K - 1 = 4$ and for $d2 = N - K = 70$:

$$SSE_{inter} = 126.30; \quad SSE_{intra} = 185.07; \quad V_{inter} = 31.60; \quad V_{intra} = 2.64$$

and finally, the Fisher number found experimentally:

$$F_{exp} = 11.97$$

We still need to use the table to find the theoretical value of Fisher's parameter for an accepted risk of 5%. Reading from the table, we find:

$$F_{5\%} = 2.51$$

As $F_{exp} > F_{5\%}$, we must reject H_0 at the 5% risk of error, and accept the hypothesis that the recall performances are different. Yet, as the value found experimentally is much greater than the value in the table at 5%, the risk is certainly considerably lower. This can be confirmed by the calculation using BioStat.

3.3.2.3.2. Calculation using BioStat software

The calculation can be performed by numerous software packages. For example, below, we present the results obtained using BioStat, which is based on the open-source tool R. It is open access and easy to use to perform confirmatory tests.

On the homepage, we select the test we want to perform: ANOVA for [K > 2 independent samples and only one variable (Friedman–Fisher test)].

It returns the following result – results of ANOVA test:

– observed statistics Qobs: 11.944884726225;

– P-value: 1.8740674688154E-7.

We can read that the P-value = 1.8740674688154E-7, which confirms that the risk incurred by rejecting H_0 is much lower than 5% and, in addition, we find the same value of Fisher's parameter as found experimentally: F_{exp} = Qobs: 11.944884726225.

Generally, software tools will verify the normality and homogeneity of the variances of the distribution. Here, we content ourselves with the supposition that these conditions are sufficiently satisfied.

3.3.2.4. Another very simple example

Three groups of students (A(6), B(8), C(7)) are evaluated following a math test. Their results are shown in Table 3.11. H_0 states that the three groups are equivalent.

A	B	C
10	8	10
11	11	13
11	11	14
12	13	14
13	14	15
15	15	16
	16	16
	16	

Table 3.11. Data table: comparison of the three samples A, B, C

BioStat returns the following result – results of ANOVA test:

– observed statistics Qobs: 1.1895043731778;

– P-value: 0.3271937841627.

At the risk of 5%, we must preserve H_0; indeed, the P-value = 0.3271937841627 indicates that there is over a 32% chance of committing an error. Hence, we hold that statistically, the three groups are not different.

3.3.3. *ANOVA for K > 2 matched samples: repeated measurement ANOVA*

We now present the case of ANOVA for matched samples; we also speak of repeated measurements. We shall approach the subject using an example, the results for which will be calculated directly using BioStat, without presenting the theoretical modifications to be made to the case of independent samples. The software takes these modifications into account.

A researcher is studying the effectiveness of relaxation techniques to control headaches. As part of the experiment, he has recruited nine people suffering from regular headaches, asking them to record the frequency and duration of their migraines. Following the first 4 weeks of base readings, with no exercises done, the subjects undergo relaxation therapy for a period of 6 weeks.

For our example, we shall analyze the data corresponding to the last 2 weeks of base readings (weeks 1 and 2) and the last 3 weeks of relaxation exercises (weeks 3–5). The dependent variable is the duration (hours/week) of the migraines for each of these 5 weeks.

The results of the experiment are as follows:

Subject	Week 1	Week 2	Week 3	Week 4	Week 5
1	21	22	8	6	6
2	20	19	10	4	4
3	17	15	5	4	5
4	25	30	13	12	17
5	30	27	13	8	6
6	19	27	8	7	4

Table 3.12. *Data table: relaxation therapy*

In BioStat, we begin by selecting, on the homepage, the test for [repeated ANOVA for K > 2 for matched samples with a single variable (Friedman–Fisher test)].

We are asked to state the number of samples (K = 5) and the number of individuals (9). We are then shown a page in which to enter the data for each of the matched samples.

In this case:

– H_0: the results obtained over the 5 weeks are identical, so the relaxation therapy is ineffective in treating the subjects' headaches;

– H_1: there is at least 1 week in which the results are different, so the relaxation therapy does have an effect.

Test results

– Observed statistics Qobs: 31.545454545455;

– *P*-value: 2.3691647714391E-6.

The return confirms what was already apparent from looking at the table: the samples are very different (*P*-value: 2.3691647714391E-6). This means that the risk of error in rejecting H_0 is insignificant.

In addition to the repeated ANOVA results, the last 3 weeks with relaxation therapy exhibit much lower frequencies of occurrence than the last 2 weeks without treatment. Hence, we can also say that the relaxation therapy is effective.

3.4. Bivariate analysis: Bravais–Pearson correlation test

3.4.1. *General points*

Consider two variables X and Y having the components x_i and y_i, read for a sample of n individuals extracted from a population of N individuals.

Variable/individuals	I_1	.....	I_i	.....	I_n
X	x_1	....	x_i	....	x_n
Y	y_1	....	y_i	....	y_n

Table 3.13. *Generic bivariate table*

Remember that Pearson's coefficient of linear correlation between the two variables X and Y is written as:

$$\text{Cor}(X, Y) = \frac{1}{n}\sum_{i=1}^{n} (x_i - \overline{X})(y_i - \overline{Y})/S(X)S(Y)$$

S(X) and S(Y) are the respective standard deviations of the two variables defined by:

$$S^2(X) = \text{Var}(X) = \frac{1}{n}\sum_{i=1}^{n}(x_i - \overline{X})^2$$

$$S^2(Y) = \text{Var}(Y) = \frac{1}{n}\sum_{i=1}^{n}(y_i - \overline{Y})^2$$

We have seen that if the linear relation between the two variables is perfect, the correlation coefficient is equal to ± 1. Its absolute value decreases when the link becomes less strong, and it tends toward 0 when the two variables are independent.

Having calculated the correlation coefficient on a sample, we may wish to find out whether the value obtained can be extended to apply to the whole population and, more specifically, what the level of risk of error is in performing that generalization. That risk is heavily dependent on the number of individuals in the sample. For example, we shall see that for a correlation coefficient of +0.6 established on a sample of 10 people, the link is not significant at the threshold of 5%. In this case, there is nothing to suggest that the result would be the same were we to take a different sample of 10 people from the population. On the other hand, a correlation coefficient of +0.2 established on a sample of 200 people is significant at the threshold of 5%. In this case, though the measured link is weak, it is unlikely to be due to random chance.

Hence, we can see that there are two problems at play: the value of the link between the two variables measured on the sample and the fact that the link is proven, i.e. that it is not dependent on the sample taken.

3.4.2. Bravais–Pearson test

The Bravais–Pearson test informs us about the significance of a correlation coefficient calculated on a sample.

This test is very easy to perform. We begin by calculating the linear correlation coefficient on the basis of the values observed experimentally, and then compare it to the theoretical values given by the Bravais–Pearson table (Table 3.14), which expresses the probability of obtaining the link between the two variables by chance. Here, we shall not go into detail about how to construct the table, but we can say that the principle is the same as that which leads to the construction of the tables for the TCND, Student's distribution and the Fisher–Snedecor distribution.

The table gives us the value of the correlation occurring by chance, for a given acceptable level of risk (a) and for a given number of dof (v). It can also be read as the probability (a) of obtaining a given value of the correlation coefficient, for a given number of dof (v), solely by the influence of random chance.

In order for the experimental correlation obtained to be significant – i.e. in order for it not to be attributable to random chance in the sample selection, with an accepted risk of error a – the correlation coefficient calculated on the basis of the observations must exceed the theoretical value given in the table at the accepted uncertainty threshold a and for a value of the dof equal to v = n – p – 1 (n: the number of observations, p: the number of relations in question). In the case of a simple correlation, as is the case in the examples presented here, we have p = 1, so v = n – 2.

v/a	0.10	0.05	0.02	v/a	0.10	0.05	0.02
1	0.9877	0.9969	0.9995	16	0.4000	0.4683	0.5425
2	0.9000	0.9500	0.980	17	0.3887	0.4555	0.5285
3	0.8054	0.8783	0.9343	18	0.3783	0.4438	0.5155
4	0.7293	0.8114	0.8822	19	0.3687	0.4329	0.5034
5	0.6694	0.7545	0.8329	20	0.3598	0.4227	0.4921
6	0.6215	0.7067	0.7887	25	0.3233	0.3809	0.4451
7	0.5822	0.6664	0.7498	30	0.2960	0.3494	0.4093
8	0.5494	0.6319	0.7155	35	0.2746	0.3246	0.3810
9	0.5214	0.6021	0.6851	40	0.2573	0.3044	0.3578
10	0.4973	0.5750	0.6581	45	0.2428	0.2875	0.3384
11	0.4762	0.5529	0.6339	50	0.2306	0.2732	0.3218
12	0.4575	0.5324	0.6120	60	0.2108	0.2500	0.2948
13	0.4409	0.5139	0.5923	70	0.1954	0.2319	0.2737
14	0.4259	0.4973	0.5742	80	0.1829	0.2172	0.2565
15	0.4124	0.4821	0.5577	90	0.1726	0.2050	0.2422
				100	0.1638	0.1946	0.2301

Table 3.14. *Bravais–Pearson table*

The complete method to conduct the test is as follows:

– express the hypotheses: H_0: there is no linear relation between the two variables X and Y; H_1: there is a significant link between the two variables;

– set a threshold for the risk of error in rejecting H_0 (generally a = 0.05, which is 5%);

– calculate the absolute value of the "observed" correlation coefficient Cor (X, Y);

– from the table for (a, v), read the "theoretical" value of the correlation coefficient.

The hypothesis H_0 is kept if $Cor_{observed} < Cor_{theoretical}$, and in this case, the observed correlation is not proven.

The hypothesis H_0 is rejected if $Cor_{observed} > Cor_{theoretical}$. In this case, we adopt H_1 and the link between the two variables is proven.

In addition, if $Cor_{observed} > 0$ as X increases, then Y increases. On the other hand, if $Cor_{observed} < 0$, as X increases, Y decreases.

3.4.3. *Pitfalls in using linear tests*

The correlation test enables us to accept or reject a link between the variables. The link shown by the Bravais–Pearson test is a linear link. However, the variables may be strongly linked to one another, but by a nonlinear link. To encourage caution, below, we present some frequent examples of biased correlations.

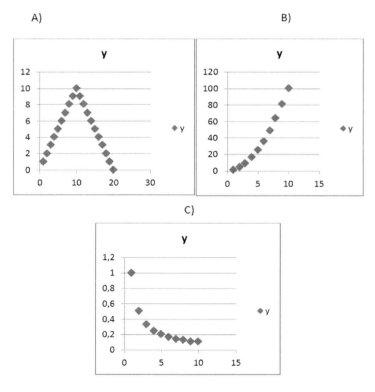

Figure 3.22. *Examples of strong but nonlinear relations*

A) Cor (X, Y) = –0.14870813

The link is non-significant, and we keep H_0; there is no linear link. However, we are dealing with two straight lines.

B) Cor (X, Y) = 0.97455863

The link is significant, and we reject H_0; there is a proven linear link. Yet what the plot actually shows is a parabola.

C) Cor (X, Y) = –0.80863064

The link is significant, and we reject H_0; there is a proven linear link. Yet the curve shown is actually a hyperbola.

These three examples show that it is essential to always construct a graphic representation of the point cloud before drawing a conclusion. In case A, we would conclude that there are two linear links, though the test suggests that there is none. In cases B and C, although the test concludes that a linear link does exist, logic would lead us to search for a nonlinear link. There are tests which can verify the nonlinear link between data for theoretical functions (parabolas, hyperbolas, etc.), but they are beyond the remit of this book.

3.4.4. *Example of calculation*

The following example is drawn from *Manuel de statistique pour psychologues* [GUÉ 97].

Researchers wished to find out whether there was a link between long-term semantic memory and achievement at school. To investigate, they developed a multiple-choice questionnaire with 800 questions, which they put to 20 pupils at the end of their second year of secondary school (referred to in France as 5^e – 5 years away from taking final exams). This test measures the level of vocabulary acquisition in all taught disciplines. The level of acquisition, represented by the score on the MCQ (variable 1), is compared to the overall mean for the year (variable 2) obtained by each pupil at the end of the year. The results are shown in Table 3.15.

To begin with, as prescribed, using Excel to plot the point cloud corresponding to the data, we ensure that there is no biased dependency. The representation obtained shows the straight line which most closely conforms to the point cloud. This line accounts for 51.88% of the mean grade obtained by the pupils (this idea will be explored in detail in Chapter 5).

Pupils	Grade on MCQ	Overall mean for the year
1	603	18.05
2	264	4.58
3	537	13.33
4	347	9.67
5	463	12.24
6	562	16.18
7	520	14.11
8	314	7.54
9	397	12.56
10	504	10.37
11	331	9.85
12	357	11.21
13	568	12.34
14	454	10.43
15	471	8.21
16	438	9.23
17	389	6 .45
18	514	10.1
19	488	16.54
20	435	14.58

Table 3.15. *Data table: link between semantic memory and school grades*

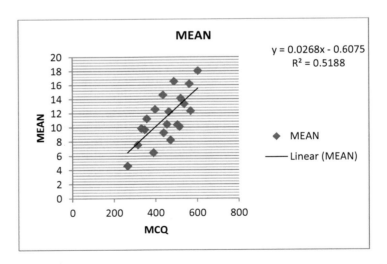

Figure 3.23. *Point cloud: link between semantic memory and school grades*

3.4.4.1. *Manual (or almost manual) calculation with Excel*

In this case, the contrasting hypotheses are:

– H_0: the observed link is not proven; it may depend on the sampling;

– H_1: the observed link is proven.

We use Excel for this purpose. Once the data have been input, we can obtain the value of the correlation coefficient observed by the following path: Formulas → More functions → Statistical, and, from the dropdown menu, select "CORREL" (correlation coefficient). The result obtained is as follows:

$$Cor_{observed} (Mean, MCQ) = 0.72$$

The link is significant, but is it proven? In other words, can it be deemed to be independent of the sample, within the accepted level of risk of 5%?

To answer this question, we must refer to the Bravais–Pearson table and read off the theoretical value for dof = $n - 2 = 20 - 2 = 18$ and an accepted risk of 5% (a = 0.05).

From the table, we read:

$$Cor_{theoretical} = 0.4438$$

The theoretical value, read from the statistical table, is lower than the value obtained from the experimental values, and in this case, at the risk of 5%, we must reject H_0; thus, the link is proven.

Hence, we can say that the researcher has proven that a strong link exists between long-term semantic memory and performances at school.

3.4.4.2. *Calculation using BioStat software*

There are numerous software tools that can perform this calculation directly. Once again, we have chosen to use the open-source program BioStat.

It returns the following result – test results are as follows:

– method: *Pearson's product-moment correlation*; alternative: *two-sided*;

– observed statistics Qobs: 4.4049113015214;

– P-value: 0.00034173166536933;

– ρ: 0.7202 Confidence interval at 95% [0.4077; 0.8817];

– dof: 18.

The P-value for the test is 0.00034173166536933.

In particular, here, we find the value of the correlation coefficient calculated on the basis of the experimental data for the sample (here, ρ = 0.7202), which gives a P-value = 0.00034. Thus, there is a 0.034% chance of making a mistake in rejecting H_0.

3.5. Confirmatory tests for qualitative variables: χ^2 and frequency comparison

3.5.1. *General points*

Unlike the means comparison tests, ANOVA or the Bravais–Pearson test that we have seen in the previous sections, χ^2 tests pertain to situations where we are dealing with qualitative variables having multiple modalities, or with quantitative variables but grouped into classes (modalities). In any case, they are based on population tables or contingency tables where each modality of the variable has a corresponding given population.

χ^2 tests are non-parametric tests that do not impose conditions on the distribution of the variables within the population. Thus, they are simpler to use than are parametric tests.

Even though the method is always based on the same parameter, χ^2, we shall see later on that there can be considered to be three types of χ^2 tests, each with a different objective:

– fitting tests, which look at how well the observed distribution in the sample fits with a known distribution;

– independence tests for two variables, which look at the link that may exist between two variables measured on a given sample;

– homogeneity tests for multiple samples, which look at the equality between two or more samples with respect to the same variable, measured in each of the samples.

In all cases, the χ^2 test is based on the "difference", the "distance" between the observed and theoretical population distributions. Technically, the difference between the three types of tests is only in the formatting of the population tables, the nature of the theoretical populations and the resulting null hypothesis (H_0).

We shall begin by presenting the general principles of χ^2 tests using a classic example: that of a "loaded die". Next, we shall look at each of the three types of tests in turn using simple examples.

3.5.2. Presentation of a χ^2 test: the "loaded die"

A die is said to be "loaded" if it is unevenly weighted (unbalanced); in this case, a particular face will come up more frequently than any of the others in a series of throws. The example presented here falls into the category of fitting tests. After stating the problem, we then discuss how to perform a χ^2 test, and finally, close the section with a complete numerical simulation of this example.

3.5.2.1. Statement of the problem

We perform a certain number (n) of experiments (here, throwing the die). We observe the variable X: "face obtained". The variable X has six modalities [1, 2, 3, 4, 5, 6]. For throw i, the variable X is written as x_i; its value is one 1 and five 0s. The 1 corresponds to the number of the face which came up.

The null hypothesis H_0 is that the die is not loaded, so the contrary hypothesis H_1 is that the die is loaded.

In order to decide between H_0 and H_1, we compare the observed population to the theoretical population that shows that, if the die is not loaded, when n is high, the population of each modality tends toward n/6.

The results of the experiment can be presented in a table, which has the following form:

	1	2	3	4	5	6
x1	0	0	1	0	0	0
...	...	...	...	...	...	...
xi	1	0	0	0	0	0
...	...	...	...	...	...	...
x_n	0	0	0	0	1	0
Total observed probabilities	n 1	n 2	n 3	n 4	n 5	n 6
Theoretical probability: p_i	1/6	1/6	1/6	1/6	1/6	1/6
Theoretical populations: t_i	n/6	n/6	n/6	n/6	n/6	n/6

Table 3.16. *Data table [I/V]: loaded die problem*

3.5.2.2. How to perform the χ^2 test

The first step in performing a χ^2 test is to define a "distance" between the populations observed for each of the modalities (n_i) and the theoretical populations (n/6) corresponding to the null hypothesis H_0: "the die is not loaded".

The first idea would be to base the distance on the numerical differences ($n_i - t_i$). In this case, logic would dictate that the distance between the two populations be expressed by:

$$\sum_{i=1}^{6}(n_i - t_i)^2 = (n_1 - t_1)^2 + (n_2 - t_2)^2 + (n_3 - t_3)^2 + (n_4 - t_4)^2 + (n_5 - t_5)^2 + (n_6 - t_6)^2$$

We take the sum of squared errors, rather than the errors themselves, because otherwise, the negative values of $(n_i - t_i)$ would cancel out the positive ones.

However, Pearson proposed a different definition to express that distance:

$$\chi^2 = \sum_{i=1}^{6} \frac{(n_i - t_i)^2}{t_i}$$

The choice of this parameter, once again, is neither arbitrary nor without impact. Indeed, Pearson established that the χ^2 function thus formed obeyed a particular statistical law which, today, is known as Pearson's statistical law or the χ^2 statistical law.

For example, looking at Student's T tests, the χ^2 acts as Student's T and the χ^2 statistical distribution plays the role of Student's statistical distribution.

For clarity's sake, note that the χ^2 statistical distribution is written as:

$$F(\chi^2) = C(dof)\, \chi^{2\left(\frac{dof}{2}-1\right)} e^{-\chi 2/2}$$

It expresses a probability density. C (dof) is a constant that depends on the number of dof. We shall see later on that in the case of the die, dof = 5.

The above formula can be used to plot a curve for each value of the number of dof (represented as n in Figure 3.24). When dof is high, it can be shown that Pearson's distribution tends toward the TCND.

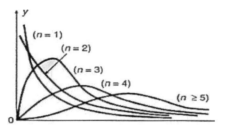

Figure 3.24. χ^2 statistical distributions for different numbers of dof

3.5.2.2.1. Determination of dof

Consider a distribution of a random variable with K modalities; one might think that the number of dof is equal to K, but this is absolutely not true, as the total population (N) is imposed, which creates a link (a constraint) between the terms. For example, for K = 6, if the populations of five modalities are known, then the population of the sixth is strictly necessary (imposed). Therefore, the number of dof is reduced by 1, so dof = K – 1. For the example of the die, dof = 6 – 1 = 5.

3.5.2.2.2. χ^2 statistical table

Based on Pearson's law, by integration, we establish the theoretical statistical table known as the χ^2 table. For each value of the dof, we perform the same operation as when constructing the TCND table.

Figure 3.25, for dof = 5, shows that for a value of χ^2 = 11.07, the black surface represents 5% of the total surface area (gray + black). This means that a value of χ^2 > 11.07 has less than a 5% chance of occurring in a series of random throws.

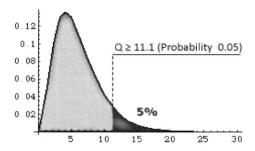

Figure 3.25. *Statistical curve of χ^2 for dof = 5*

Table 3.17, for each value of the dof (v), gives us the probability (α) of χ^2 taking a value greater than a given value.

v\α	0.90	0.50	0.30	0.20	0.10	0.05	0.02	0.01	0.001
1	0.016	0.455	1.074	1.642	2.706	3.841	5.412	6.635	10.827
2	0.211	1.386	2.408	3.219	4.605	5.991	7.824	9.210	13.815
3	0.584	2.366	3.665	4.642	6.251	7.815	9.837	11.345	16.266
4	1.064	3.357	4.878	5.989	7.779	9.488	11.668	13.277	18.467
5	1.610	4.351	6.064	7.289	9.236	11.070	13.388	15.086	20.515
6	2.204	5.348	7.231	8.558	10.645	12.592	15.033	16.812	22.457
7	2.833	6.346	8.383	9.803	12.017	14.067	16.622	18.475	24.322
8	3.490	7.344	9.524	11.030	13.362	15.507	18.168	20.090	26.125
9	4.168	8.343	10.656	12.242	14.684	16.919	19.679	21.666	27.877
10	4.865	9.342	11.781	13.442	15.987	18.307	21.161	23.209	29.588
11	5.578	10.341	12.899	14.631	17.275	19.675	22.618	24.725	31.264
12	6.304	11.340	14.011	15.812	18.549	21.026	24.054	26.217	32.909
13	7.042	12.340	15.119	16.985	19.812	22.362	25.472	27.688	34.528
14	7.790	13.339	16.222	18.151	21.064	23.685	26.873	29.141	36.123
15	8.547	14.339	17.322	19.311	22.307	24.996	28.259	30.578	37.697
16	9.312	15.338	18.418	20.465	23.542	26.296	29.633	32.000	39.252
17	10.085	16.338	19.511	21.615	24.769	27.587	30.995	33.409	40.790
18	10.865	17.338	20.601	22.760	25.989	28.869	32.346	34.805	42.312
19	11.651	18.338	21.689	23.900	27.204	30.144	33.687	36.191	43.820
20	12.443	19.337	22.775	25.038	28.412	31.410	35.020	37.566	45.315

Table 3.17. *χ^2 statistical table*

EXAMPLE.– We read that if dof = 5, the probability that the theoretical χ^2 will take a value greater than 11.070 is 0.05.

Choosing between hypotheses H_0 and H_1: As the accepted uncertainty threshold is generally a risk of 0.05 (5%), if the observed χ^2 is lower than the theoretical χ^2, for a 5% risk and a given number of dof, read from the table, we stick with hypothesis H_0, because the difference (distance) between the observed distribution and the expected theoretical distribution is not sufficiently great (significant). If, on the other hand, the observed χ^2 is greater than the theoretical χ^2, we reject H_0 and accept the alternative hypothesis H_1. We choose H_1, because there is too high a chance for the distribution observed to be explained by a random fluctuation in sampling around the theoretical distribution.

3.5.2.3. Complete simulation of the loaded die test

The die is thrown 200 times. The frequency with which each face appears is shown in Table 3.18.

	1	2	3	4	5	6	Total
Observed populations: n_i	21	39	26	43	27	44	200
Theoretical populations: t_i	33.33	33.33	33.33	33.33	33.33	33.33	200

Table 3.18. *Population table: loaded die simulation*

We compare the populations (n_i) for each of the faces of the die, obtained during the experiment, against the theoretical population (t_i) indicating that the die is not loaded. The latter expresses equiprobability between each of the faces, and thus $t_i = \frac{200}{6} = 33.33$.

We begin by calculating the χ^2 observed for the populations obtained during the experiment (21, 39, 26, 43, 27, 44) and the theoretical populations:

$$\chi^2 = \frac{(21-33.33)^2}{33.33} + \frac{(39-33.33)^2}{33.33} + \frac{(26-33.33)^2}{33.33} + \frac{(43-33.33)^2}{33.33} + \frac{(27-33.33)^2}{33.33} + \frac{(44-33.33)^2}{33.33} = 14.56$$

The number of dof $= 6 - 1 = 5$. The acceptable degree of uncertainty is taken as equal to 0.05 (5%).

For dof $= 5$ and an uncertainty threshold of 5%, we consult the table to find the theoretical value of the $\chi^2_{5\%} = 11.07$.

As the observed χ^2 is higher than $\chi^2_{5\%}$, we reject H_0 and accept H_1. There is too low a chance that the distribution observed is attributable to a fluctuation in the sampling. Thus, we can conclude that the die is loaded. Indeed, it seems to display more 4s and 6s, and to a lesser extent, 2s, than any of the odd-numbered faces.

NOTE.– Had we set an acceptable uncertainty threshold of 2%, we would still have concluded that the die is loaded, because in that case, the theoretical value of the $\chi^2_{2\%} = 13.388$ is still lower than the observed χ^2.

3.5.3. Fitting χ^2 test: general formulation

3.5.3.1. Presentation

With the loaded die, we have already seen an example of the fitting χ^2. There now follows a general presentation of it using an appropriate formalism that may prove useful for future exploits.

Generally speaking, we observe a qualitative variable X, which has k modalities A_i ($i = 1, ..., k$), recorded on a sample of n individuals. The observed populations for each modality are written as n_i, where $i = 1,..., k$.

We want to know whether the populations observed on the sample obey a theoretical distribution whose populations are given by the relation $t_i = nxp_i$, where p_i is the probability of obtaining the modality i in a random draw. In the example of the "loaded die", the theoretical probability law was the equiprobability law, but in other instances, it may be the normal distribution or any other statistical distribution.

After collecting the data, we can draw up the following generic population table:

Modalities of the observed variable X	A_1	A_2	.....	A_i	.....	A_k	
Observed populations: n_i	n_1	n_2	.....	n_i	.....	n_k	$n = \sum_{i=1}^{K} n_i$
Theoretical probability: p_i	p_1	p_2	.....	p_i	.....	p_K	$\sum_{i=1}^{K} p_i = 1$
Theoretical populations: $t_i = np_i$	t_1	t_2	.....	t_i	.....	t_K	$n = \sum_{i=1}^{K} t_i$

Table 3.19. Generic data table: fitting χ^2

To answer the question at hand, we begin by calculating the parameter χ^2:

$$\chi^2 = \sum_{i=1}^{k} \frac{(n_i - t_i)^2}{t_i}$$

It expresses the distance between the observed distribution (n_i) and the theoretical distribution (t_i). If the χ^2 were equal to zero, the two distributions would be perfectly identical. The larger the value of the observed χ^2, the further the observed distribution is from the theoretical distribution.

To apply a χ^2 test in the proper conditions, the following rules must be respected:

– the population n of the sample must be greater than 50 ($n \geq 50$);

– the theoretical population of each modality must be greater than or equal to 5 ($t_i \geq 5$).

When one of the observed populations is less than 10, Yates' correction needs to be introduced into the χ^2 calculation:

$$\text{corrected } \chi^2 = \Sigma \, (|n_i - t_i| - 0.5)^2 / \text{theoretical population}$$

3.5.3.2. Example: soft toys, children and a trader

Let us now return to an example that was mentioned in an earlier section, but for which the result was, at the time, given without any reasoned discussion. Now, we are able to discuss the reasoning behind that result and the calculations that justify it.

The CEO of a toy factory wants to know whether children are more attracted to a soft toy in the form of a rabbit, a tortoise or an elephant. To find out, he commissions a study in which a sample of 54 2-year-old children is observed.

To answer the question, the study compares the children's choice of toy to a theoretical choice whereby they have no preference. In this case, $t_i = 54/3 = 18$.

The following population table is obtained:

	Rabbit	Tortoise	Elephant
Children's selection	10	23	21
Theoretical populations	18	18	18

Table 3.20. *Data table: soft toy problem*

The hypothesis H_0 holds that there is no preferred choice, while H_1 states the opposite.

By calculating the observed χ^2, we find:

$$\chi^2 = [(10 - 18)^2/18] + [(23 - 18)^2/18] + [(21 - 18)^2/18] = 5.44$$

In our case, dof = 3 − 1 = 2, so in the χ^2 statistical table, for an accepted risk of 5%, we read the value of 5.99.

The value of the observed χ^2 is less than the theoretical value for the accepted risk of 5%. Thus, we cannot conclude that the children show a preference in their selection. Hence, it is the null hypothesis H_0 which must be preserved.

However, the observed χ^2 is near to the theoretical χ^2 for an acceptable risk of 5%. A simple linear interpolation, based on the values in the χ^2 table, shows that the observed value (5.44) corresponds to the theoretical value for an acceptable risk of 7%. Thus, the risk incurred by rejecting the null hypothesis is 7%. The statisticians have done their job; it is now up to the CEO to decide whether or not that level of risk is acceptable.

3.5.3.3. *Fitting to a normal distribution (or to any other law)*

In the above examples, the aim was to verify whether the observed sample could be considered to obey an equiprobability law. However, the χ^2 is capable of verifying the fitting to all statistical laws and, in particular, verifying the normality of a distribution.

3.5.4. χ^2 tests of the independence of two variables

In the foregoing discussion, for the fitting χ^2, the aim was to compare, for the same variable, the observed population and the population that would be obtained if the distribution obeyed a given statistical law.

Now, we shall look at the link between two variables observed on the same sample; we also speak of the independence of the two observed variables. The populations of the two variables form a contingency table.

The method consists of using the χ^2 parameter to assess the distance between the observed contingency table, which is constructed from the data obtained in the experiment, and a theoretical contingency table that needs to be determined. The populations of the theoretical table express a lack of any difference between the two variables – in other words, they are independent.

The theoretical table is not easy to determine, so in the following discussion, we begin by considering the case of two variables that each have only two modalities, before going on to discuss the general case of two variables having n and p modalities.

3.5.4.1. *Case of two variables, each with two modalities (2 × 2 table)*

A Master's student sets out to investigate the following question:

"Is there a difference between the preferences of each member of a couple and the sex they want their first child to be?" This problem relates to two variables: X: the parent's gender and Y: the gender they want their child to be.

To find an answer, the student asks 100 childless young couples, obtaining the results in the following contingency table:

Child's gender/parent's gender	Man	Woman
Boy	45	57
Girl	55	43

Table 3.21. *Data table: independence test (child's gender/parent's gender)*

H_0 states that the choice of child's gender does not depend on the parent's gender.

The contradictory hypothesis H_1 states that the choice of child's gender does depend on the parent's gender.

Reading the table, at first glance, we may have the impression that there is a certain amount of difference. Indeed, it expresses the fact that out of 100 men, 45 would prefer to have a son and 55 a daughter, while out of 100 women, 57 would prefer to have a boy and 43 a girl. Yet can this difference actually be found statistically? Can we conclude that men's preferences are different from those of women?

In order to answer this question, we need to evaluate the distance that exists between the observed results, as shown in the table, and the theoretical table which shows no difference between men's and women's choices. Despite what one might initially think without too much reflection, the theoretical table is not one which contains 50 of each gender of parent.

Indeed, the table below indicates that overall (M+W), the preference leans a little more toward a son than a daughter. To fill in the four cells with 50 would be to ignore this overall difference, whereas we must, at all costs, take account of this imbalance, because the question at hand is whether or not men and women make the same choice.

Child's/parent's gender	Man	Woman	Sum rows
Boy	45	57	102
Girl	55	43	98
Sum columns	100	100	200

Table 3.22. *Data table with the margins: independence test (child's gender/parent's gender)*

The table showing that men and women make the same choice is presented in Table 3.23.

Child's/parent's gender	Man	Woman	Total rows
Boy	51	51	102
Girl	49	49	98
Total columns	100	100	200

Table 3.23. *Theoretical table: independence test (child's gender/parent's gender)*

Now, for each cell, we can calculate a partial χ^2 (Table 3.24). It has a value of 0 if the observed and theoretical populations are identical, and grows as the differences between the observed and theoretical populations become greater. We obtain a table of partial χ^2 values (Table 3.24).

Child/parent's gender	Man	Woman
Boy	$\dfrac{(45-51)^2}{51} = 0.71$	$\dfrac{(57-51)^2}{51} = 0.71$
Girl	$\dfrac{(55-49)^2}{49} = 0.73$	$\dfrac{(43-49)^2}{49} = 0.73$

Table 3.24. *Table of partial χ^2 values: independence test (child's gender/parent's gender)*

Total $\chi^2 = 0.71 + 0.71 + 0.73 + 0.73 = 2.88$

We can show that the total χ^2 as defined obeys the χ^2 statistical law. Hence, we can continue to use the χ^2 statistical table.

In our case, we have two variables (desired child's gender, parent's gender). We have $2 \times 2 = 4$ populations, but if the total population, for each variable, is fixed, each of them is subject to a constraint, so dof $= (2 - 1)(2 - 1) = 1$.

For a dof of 1, for an acceptable risk of 5%, the χ^2 table gives us a threshold value for $\chi^2 = 3.84$.

CONCLUSION.– The χ^2 observed (2.88) is lower than the threshold χ^2 at 5%. Therefore, we must stick with hypothesis H_0. This means that at a 5% risk of error, men's and women's choices are no different.

We could also say that the choice of child's gender is independent of the parent's gender. For this reason, we say that the variables are independent and this test is described as an independence test.

CRUCIALLY IMPORTANT POINT.– (Regarding the compiling of the theoretical table). For the establishment of the theoretical contingency table, which shows that the choices of men and women are perfectly identical, we can see that:

$$51 = \frac{100 \times 102}{200} \qquad 49 = \frac{100 \times 98}{200}$$

In our example, with two modalities for each of the two variables, we can see that for each cell in the theoretical table, expressing the independence of the two variables, we have:

$$\text{Theoretical population} = \frac{\text{Total row} \times \text{Total column}}{\text{Total number of observations}}$$

This observed relation can be generalized to apply to more complex tables with $(n \times p)$ modalities. It will be used in the following sections.

3.5.4.2. *Case of two variables having more than two modalities (n×p)*

We shall approach this situation, which is a generalization of the case of two variables having only two modalities each, using an example that pertains to two variables with four and three modalities, respectively.

We wish to find out whether there is a link between radio listening habits and the place of listening in the three largest cities in France.

To do this, we question residents of Paris, Lyon and Marseille about their habits in terms of listening to four different radio stations. In total, 200 people responded.

Cross-referencing these two variables, "City" and "Radios playing", gives us the following contingency table:

	Paris	Lyon	Marseille	$\sum$ Rows
Radio 1	18	18	11	47
Radio 2	12	15	18	45
Radio 3	32	20	23	75
Radio 4	15	12	6	33
$\sum$ Columns	77	65	58	200

Table 3.25. *Data table: radio listening habits in Paris, Lyon and Marseille*

H_0 holds that "radio listening habits are independent of the city" and of course, H_1 holds that "radio listening habits depend on the city".

The acceptable error threshold is set at 5%.

3.5.4.2.1. Manual calculation

The calculation can be performed manually, as with example (2 × 2) in the previous section. For this, we begin by calculating the theoretical table, filling in each cell using the relation introduced in the previous section that, as we have seen, can be applied in the general case with n×p modalities.

$$\text{Theoretical population} = \frac{\text{Total row x Total column}}{\text{Total number of observations}}$$

For example, for cell 1/1 (Paris/Radio1), this gives:

$$\text{Theoretical population}_{1/1} = 47 \times 77/200 = 18.095$$

The full theoretical table is shown as Table 3.26.

We can therefore calculate 12 partial χ^2 values and, by summing them together, we obtain $\chi^2 = 7.61$.

3.5.4.2.2. Calculation of the number of dof in general

If we are dealing with two variables, respectively, having p and q modalities, the number of populations is equal to $p \times q$. However, the number of dof, i.e. the number of independent populations, is equal to $(p - 1) \times (q - 1)$. Indeed, the populations associated with column p can be obtained by difference; the same is true for the populations associated with row q.

In our example, we have dof $= (4 - 1) \times (3 - 1)$, which is 6.

In the cell corresponding to column 0.05 and row 6, we find the value of the theoretical threshold $\chi^2 = 12.59$.

Given that the calculated χ^2 is below this value, we cannot reject the null hypothesis H_0. Despite the differences shown in the table, there is not enough evidence to state, within a 5% risk of error, that the habits differ from one city to another. Thus, radio listening habits are found to be independent of the three cities studied.

3.5.4.2.3. Calculation using the software BioStat

After indicating that we want to perform a χ^2 test of independence and inputting the contingency table of the data collected during the experiment, BioStat returns the result in the following form:

– test results;

– method: Pearson's χ^2 test;

– observed statistic Qobs: 7.6111851420329;

– P-value: 0.2679945786302.

The P-value returned by the software tells us that there is a 26.799% chance of error if we reject H_0. This risk is too high, and therefore we retain the hypothesis H_0.

The software also generates the population table, which shows that there is no difference in listeners' habits for the three cities.

	Y1	Y2	Y3
X1	18.095	15.275	13.63
X2	17.325	14.625	13.05
X3	28.875	24.375	21.75
X4	12.705	10.725	9.57

Table 3.26. *Theoretical population table: radio listening habits in Paris, Lyon and Marseille*

3.5.4.3. *Case of matched samples – McNemar's χ^2*

As we have already seen, we are dealing with matched samples when we take data readings at different times on the same sample; generally, the aim is to assess the impact of actions or events occurring between those times. The tests prescribed for independent samples cannot be used in this case, as they may mask phenomena connected to the matching of the samples.

Below, we present McNemar's test, which can be used to compare two variables, each of which has two modalities.

If the two variables have more than two modalities, there is an extension of that test: the Stuart–Maxwell test, which we shall not present here as it is rather complex.

To test the effectiveness of a training session on a particular sample, we can define two variables: "test before" and "test after", which express the totals of the population results for two tests, undergone before and after the training session. These two variables have two modalities, "yes" and "no", depending on whether or not the result in the test was deemed satisfactory (Table 3.27).

Test: before/after	Yes before	No before
Yes after	A	B
No after	C	D

Table 3.27. *Generic table: McNemar's χ^2 test*

– A: populations passing the test both before and after;

– B: populations failing the test before but passing the test after;

– C: populations passing the test before but failing the test after;

– D: populations failing the test both before and after.

We must estimate the difference between those who failed before but passed after (B), and those who passed before but failed after (C). Those whose results have not changed (pass or fail, A and D) are not taken into account here.

To do this, we define the quantity:

McNemar's $\chi^2 = \dfrac{(B-C)^2}{B+C}$

We can show that McNemar's χ^2, with the null hypothesis H_0, which holds that the variables are the same "before" and "after", obeys the χ^2 law with 1 dof.

There is a variant of this distance, the Yates correction: $(|B - C| - 1)^2 / (B + C)$ for small populations.

EXAMPLE.– Training for independence (autonomy).

In the context of a scheme to integrate people having a minor mental handicap, a program is devised to help them acquire or increase the degree of their independence in terms of getting around (taking the bus, asking for directions, etc.). A questionnaire can be used to evaluate their level of autonomy, and is put to them before and after a training program. The results of the assessments are as follows:

Test after/test before	Autonomous before	Non-autonomous before
Autonomous after	30	50
Non-autonomous after	13	25

Table 3.28. Data table: McNemar's test, strengthening of autonomy

$$\text{McNemar's chi}^2 = \frac{(50-13)^2}{50+13} = 21.73$$

As dof = 1, if we set the standard risk of error at 5%, the χ^2 table indicates the value 3.84. The calculated value is significantly greater. Thus, we must reject the hypothesis H_0: the group's autonomy is identical before and after training, and accept H_1: the group's autonomy is different after training.

In addition, we can read from the table that for dof = 1 and at a 0.1% risk of error, the value is 10.83. In this case again, the calculated value is greater than the read value. We can conclude that we must accept H_1 and that the risk of error is less than 0.1%.

3.5.5. Sample equality tests

In this section, we look at a variable X having q modalities that we measure across p samples.

The question posed is: are the samples under observation equal? (H_0). In this case, any differences that may be observed are due to fluctuations in sampling (background noise). If not, the samples will be deemed different with respect to the variable X (H_1).

Even if the problem at hand is different, to solve it, we need to look again at the example solved in section 3.5.3.2, which deals with the problem of the independence of two variables (X, Y), measured on the same sample. Indeed, in the case of interest to us here, we can always consider that the first variable is the variable being tested X, with q modalities, and the second variable Y is simply the samples with p modalities.

To carry out the test, as was the case in section 3.5.3.2, we compare the table of observed data to the "theoretical" table, which expresses the hypothetical case that the samples are strictly equal. The method used to draw up the theoretical table is the same as that outlined in the previous section. On the assumption that readers understand the principle of the approach, we shall take the opportunity here to supplement that understanding with a general presentation of the data table and the theoretical table.

3.5.5.1. *Expression of the data table and the theoretical table generally*

This general presentation of the observed contingency table and the theoretical table could have been given in the context of the independence test, but to simplify the presentation, we found it preferable to use examples in that case.

It is not absolutely essential for readers to have knowledge of this section; after all, it did not stop us from solving the problems posed in the previous section. However, it is helpful to read it, as it will familiarize readers with the mathematical formalism upon which software packages are built.

The contingency table below is identical in form to the one which we saw, in the previous section, for two variables, respectively, having p and q modalities, but now, the variable studied X has q modalities and the variable Y has p modalities that are, respectively, the populations of the variable X for each sample.

X/Y	Modality 1	....	Modality j	....	Modality q	Total
Sample 1	n_1^1		n_1^j		n_1^q	n_1
....						
Sample i	n_i^1		n_i^j		n_i^q	n_i
....						
Sample p	n_p^1		n_p^j		n_p^q	n_p
Total	$n_.^1$		$n_.^j$		$n_.^q$	$n_.=N$

Table 3.29. *Generic table: χ^2 test for equality of samples*

In Table 3.29, n_i^j is the population of row i and of column j; n_i is the sum of populations of row i; n^j is the sum of populations of column j; n. is the total population of the contingency table.

3.5.5.2. *Theoretical contingency table*

The theoretical table contains the populations that express that all the samples observed are identical (we also say that they are "equal").

The theoretical table is constructed in the same way as the theoretical table for the independence of two variables. Hence, in each cell is a theoretical population equal to the product of the total row and column, all divided by the total population.

With the mathematical formalism introduced, the theoretical table is presented in Table 3.30.

	Modality 1	....	Modality j	....	Modality q	Sum rows
Sample 1	$\dfrac{n_1 x n^1.}{N}$		$\dfrac{n_1 x n^j.}{N}$		$\dfrac{n_1 x n^q}{N}$	n_1
....						
Sample i	$\dfrac{n_i x n^1.}{N}$		$\dfrac{n_i x n^j.}{N}$		$\dfrac{n_i x n^q}{N}$	n_i
....						
Sample p	$\dfrac{n_p x n^1.}{N}$		$\dfrac{n_p x n^j.}{N}$		$\dfrac{n_p x n^q}{N}$	n_p
Sum columns	$n^1.$		$n^j.$		$n^q.$	N

Table 3.30. *Generic theoretical table: χ^2 test for sample equality*

The distance between the observed table and the theoretical table is measured using χ^2, which is calculated by summing together the partial χ^2 values. We can write it as:

$$\chi^2 = \sum_{i=1}^{p} \sum_{j=1}^{q} \frac{(n_i^j - t_i^j)^2}{t_i^j}$$

We set:

$$t_i^j = \frac{n_i \times n^j}{N}$$

In addition, $dof = (p - 1) \times (q - 1)$ by virtue of the general rule stated in the previous sections.

Now, the observed χ^2 thus defined can be compared to the theoretical threshold value of χ^2, read from the table for $dof = (p - 1) \times (q - 1)$ and the accepted threshold of uncertainty (generally 5%).

If the χ^2 observed is lower than the theoretical threshold value of χ^2, the null hypothesis H_0 is adopted. In this case, the differences observed are due to fluctuations in the sampling within the same population.

If the χ^2 observed is higher than the threshold χ^2, then H_0 is rejected with the accepted level of risk of error. This means that the samples belong to populations having different distributions for the variable X in question.

A little mathematical support (for those readers who have stuck with us) is given by double summation.

Consider, for example, a two-way entry table (4×3) containing 12 terms, each with a known value.

A_1^1	A_1^2	A_1^3	A_1^4
A_2^1	A_2^2	A_2^3	A_2^4
A_3^1	A_3^2	A_3^3	A_3^4

Table 3.31. *Two-way table with two indices*

The generic term is written as A_i^j, where $i = 1, 2, 3$ and $j = 1, 2, 3, 4$. We wish to find the double sum:

$$S = \sum_{i=1}^{3} \sum_{j=1}^{4} A_i^j$$

To do this, we begin by calculating one of the two sums – summation on j, for example:

$$\sum_{j=1}^{4} A_i^j = A_i^1 + A_i^2 + A_i^3 + A_i^4$$

We now find the second sum on i:

$$\sum_{i=1}^{3}(A_i^1 + A_i^2 + A_i^3 + A_i^4) = (A_1^1 + A_1^2 + A_1^3 + A_1^4)+(A_2^1 + A_2^2 + A_2^3 + A_2^4)$$
$$+(A_3^1 + A_3^2 + A_3^3 + A_3^4) = S$$

The double sum produces the sum of all the terms in the table. We could have begun by finding the sum on i and ended by finding the sum on j.

EXAMPLE.– In the context of an ongoing research project (a Franco-Greek collaboration), a group of researchers wishes to test the effectiveness of a teaching course, given to primary school students, intended to instill in them an understanding of the properties of light propagation through analyzing the position of the shadows cast by different items.

After the lesson, the researchers administer an identical test to the students at two different schools in Marseille, the aim being to assess their perception of light propagation. The test splits the students into three groups: A (sufficient); B (lacking explanation); and C (insufficient). In total, 108 pupils were surveyed: 60 in school 1 and 48 in school 2. The results of the test are summarized in Table 3.32.

The example presented here takes account of two schools, but it is perfectly possible to take account of more than two schools, pursuing exactly the same method.

Assessments	A	B	C	Total row
School 1	18	15	27	60
School 2	21	13	14	48
Total column	39	28	41	108

Table 3.32. *Data table: χ^2 of equality of samples, properties of light propagation*

The question posed is: "Do the two schools belong to the same population after the training course?" Note that the same test, conducted prior to the course, concluded that the two schools did not belong to the same population.

The calculation can be performed manually quite easily; it would be a good exercise. However, here, we present the result returned by the software BioStat:

– Test results:

- method: Pearson's χ^2 test;

- statistics observed Qobs: 3.2017723130528;

- *P*-value: 0.201717685326.

The theoretical table is presented in Table 3.33.

	Y1	Y2	Y3
X1	21.667	15.556	22.778
X2	17.333	12.444	18.222

Table 3.33. *Table of expected populations under H_0*

The *P*-value returned is 0.201717685326. Thus, there is a chance of slightly more than 20% of error if we reject H_0. Therefore, we stick with H_0 and can state that the two classes are statistically identical with the accepted degree of risk of 5%.

– Sensitivity of the test:

- another simulation: to demonstrate the sensitivity of the χ^2 test, we examine an imaginary situation where the tests for the two classes yielded the following results.

Assessments	A	B	C	Total row
School 1	18	15	27	60
School 2	24	15	9	48
Total column	39	28	41	108

Table 3.34. *Fictitious data table: χ^2 of equality of samples, properties of propagation of light*

– Results of test:

- method: *Pearson's χ^2 test*;

- statistics observed Qobs: 8.6303571428571;

- *P*-value: 0.013364162815393.

– Theoretical table:

- table of populations expected with H_0 (Table 3.35).

	Y1	Y2	Y3
X1	23.333	16.667	20
X2	18.667	13.333	16

Table 3.35. *Theoretical table*

The *P*-value returned is 0.013364162815393. Thus, the chance of error if we reject H_0 is scarcely more than 1%. Thus, we reject H_0 and choose the alternative hypothesis H_1. In this case, we can state that the two classes are statistically different with the accepted degree of risk of 5%.

3.5.6. *Intensity of the link between variables: Cramer's V*

The χ^2 test tells us whether two variables (and more generally, the rows and columns) are dependent or independent. However, the χ^2 value and the *P*-value tell us nothing about the intensity of the link between the two variables. This is due to the fact that the χ^2 value depends on the number of individuals, the number of rows and the number of columns. Hence, the value of χ^2 cannot be compared from one situation to the next. It only gives us a binary indication, with an X% risk of error, whether there is a link between the variables (H_1) or not (H_0).

Cramer's V measures the intensity of that link; it is defined as follows: it is the square root of the ratio between the calculated χ^2 and the maximum value of χ^2 which corresponds to a "total" link between the two variables. We can show that the maximum value that can be reached by χ^2 is the product of the total population by the minimum value between the number of rows -1 and the number of columns -1.

$$\chi^2{}_{max} = \text{Total population} \times \text{Min(number of rows} - 1, \text{number of columns} - 1)$$

Thus:

$$V = \sqrt{\frac{\chi^2}{\chi^2{}_{max}}}$$

Cramer's V does not depend on the total population, or on the dimensions of the table. Thus, it can be compared from one situation to another. It lies between 0 and 1; the closer it is to 1, the stronger the link between the variables. If V = 0, the independence is "total"; if $V = 1$, the dependence is "absolute", meaning that the variables are identical.

For illustrative purposes, let us look again at the examples encountered in the previous sections.

EXAMPLE 1.– "Is there a difference between the members of a couple and the sex they want their first child to be?" (section 3.5.4.1).

The calculated χ^2 was 2.88 and, with a 5% risk of error, the conclusion was reached that the choices made by men and women were identical, i.e. that the variables were independent.

In this case, $\chi^2_{max} = (2 - 1) \times N$, where $N = 200$.

Thus, $V = \sqrt{\dfrac{2.88}{200}} = 0.12$, which measures the weakness of the link between the two variables.

EXAMPLE 2.– "Radio listening habits in large cities" (section 3.5.4.2).

At a 5% risk of error, it was concluded that it could not be categorically stated that the habits were different. Cramer's V calculation gives us $V = \sqrt{\dfrac{7.61}{200 \times (2-1)}} = 0.195$, which again indicates a weak link. However, as we can compare tables of differing dimensions, we can nonetheless say that it is higher than in the case of the previous example regarding parents' preference as to the sex of their firstborn child.

4

Multivariate Analyses

In Chapter 2, we presented elementary descriptive statistics that studies variables one by one (mean, variance, histograms, etc.), and also examines the links that can exist between variables taken two by two (correlation, point clouds, curves, etc.). In this chapter, we will further highlight the links that may exist between variables by considering the case where more than two variables are taken into account.

We will begin in the first section with the presentation of multivariate analyses, by discussing the principal component analysis (PCA) which examines the case of $N > 2$ quantitative variables. PCA was introduced in 1972 by the French mathematician and philosopher Jean-Paul Benzeckri. Since then, the approach has led to further developments, and in particular, factorial component analysis (FCA) and factorial multiple correspondence analysis (FMCA), which deal with the case of qualitative variables. This is the subject discussed in the second section.

Multivariate analyses involve complex mathematical developments that are restricted to high-level initiates. They are found in PCA and that is why we make a detailed but very progressive presentation avoiding, as much as possible, to enter into overly theoretical considerations. With regard to FCA and FMCA, they are direct or indirect adaptations of the PCA, and for this reason the presentation of their bases will be more succinct.

Carrying out a multivariate analysis requires the use of advanced software such as SPHINX, SPSS, Modalisa, XLSTAT and SAS. As already mentioned, we will not dwell on the presentation of software because they are fast changing. In any case, the appropriation of one of these software requires an inescapable personal investment, but once the tool is mastered, it becomes very easy to use. It suffices to simply enter the data directly or transfer them from the data table, and the software then does all the work, but to understand the information it returns, we must know the basis of the method. The "open" software R can be added to the list of above-mentioned software. It allows specific adaptations, and in this sense it is more efficient, but its use requires a very significant investment, which in the end is very beneficial.

For this part, the references we have used include [BUS 09, BAC 10b], as well as many Internet sources not often referenced.

4.1. Principal component analysis

4.1.1. *Overview*

Since the mathematical bases of the PCA are complex and not accessible to a layperson, we offer an original presentation that is at the same time progressive and as clear as possible. It is intended to provide an understanding of the bases of PCA without going into too much mathematical detail. To this end, in the following sections, we will limit ourselves to bivariate problems (two variables), and highlight elements that are simple to observe and understand and that we will find in PCA proper. In the next stage, we will examine the case of trivariate problems (three variables) where we present all aspects of PCA but which still has the advantage of allowing visual representations. Finally, we will present situations with four variables or more. In this case, graphic representations, which support understanding, are no longer possible. We have to use our intuition and a minimum of abstraction.

4.1.2. *Bivariate approach*

We will start by addressing bivariate problems (also referred to as 2D), which have the advantage of enabling a simple visualization that facilitates the analysis of results. In this case, we do not talk of PCA, but we can highlight several fundamental elements that are found in PCA, which will need to be expanded to three then P dimensions.

In the case of 2D, two variables (X1 and X2) can be drawn from individual n. In the section devoted to elementary descriptive statistics, we have seen that in the "initial" plane, X1 on the x-axis and X2 on the y-axis, each individual, I_i, is represented by a point of coordinates $x1_i$ and $x2_i$. Let us see what we can learn from such representation.

4.1.2.1. *Representation of individuals in the initial plane*

Two variables, students' marks in two subjects, are taken from 12 students; we will work successively on two very simple examples:

– math and physics marks;

– math and history–geography marks.

4.1.2.1.1. X1 = math and X2 = physics

The marks taken are shown in Table 4.1.

I/V	Math	Physics
Student No. 1	10	10
Student No. 2	15	14
Student No. 3	8	8
Student No. 4	9	9
Student No. 5	19	18
Student No. 6	2	3
Student No. 7	14	14
Student No. 8	5	6
Student No. 9	4	5
Student No. 10	8	8
Student No. 11	2	3
Student No. 12	1	4
Average	8.08	8.5
Standard deviation	5.45	4.59

Table 4.1. *[I/V] data table: math and physics marks*

In Figure 4.1, in the plane, "math" on the x-axis and "physics" on the y-axis, each student is represented by a point that corresponds to the marks obtained by each student in math and physics.

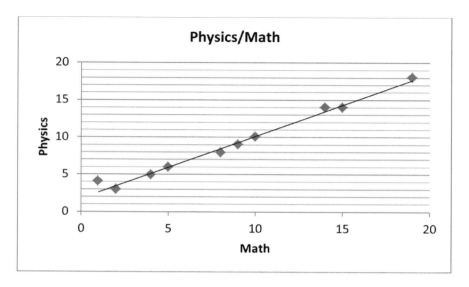

Figure 4.1. *Point cloud: math/physics*

The graphical representation shows that there is a linear link between mathematics and physics marks. What we learn from it is that if you are good at math, you are good at physics and if you are poor at math, you are poor at physics. The line was calculated using the least squares method. It is the line closest to the point cloud and it minimizes the Euclidean distance of the right points. As we will see later, its extension to P dimensions plays a very significant role in the PCA.

4.1.2.1.2. X1 = math and X2 = HG

Table 4.2 contains the marks obtained by students in mathematics and history–geography.

In the Figure 4.2, each student is represented, in the plane, by a point on the x-axis "math" and y-axis "HG", that is the marks obtained by each student in math and history–geography, respectively.

From a point cloud, we can always calculate using the least squares method the "closest" line, in the Euclidian sense, of the point cloud. But in the case of HG/math, we see that student representative points are very scattered around the line closest to the plot, and we can no longer say that if you are good at math, you are good at HG or that if you are poor at math, you are poor at HG. At most, there is a trend.

I/V	Math	HG
Student No. 1	10	8
Student No. 2	15	4
Student No. 3	8	4
Student No. 4	9	12
Student No. 5	19	13
Student No. 6	2	15
Student No. 7	14	14
Student No. 8	5	6
Student No. 9	4	7
Student No. 10	8	3
Student No. 11	2	2
Student No. 12	1	4
Average	8.08	7.67
Standard deviation	5.45	4.46

Table 4.2. *[I/V] data table: math and HG marks*

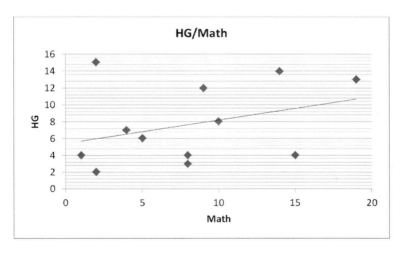

Figure 4.2. *Point cloud: math/HG*

4.1.2.2. Standard scores

In the previous examples, the variables were of the same nature and had the same "units", but it is not always the case. X1 and X2 units can be very different and the representative points very poorly distributed in the plane because of a problem of scales and/or intercept. To center the results and to compensate for the scale effects of X1 and X2 variables, we work with the standard scores (z-scores) that were already seen when defining the standard normal distribution. In this part, we note the z-scores $\widehat{X1}$ and $\widehat{X2}$ and for the individual I_i, the principal components are written as:

$$\widehat{X_{1i}} = \frac{x_{1i} - \overline{X1}}{S(X1)} \qquad \widehat{X_{2i}} = \frac{x_{2i} - \overline{X2}}{S(X2)}$$

where $\overline{X}$ is the mean of the variable on the sample and $S(X)$ its standard deviation.

If we come back to the case X1 = math and X2 = HG, we obtain an Excel spreadsheet.

I/V	Math	HG	$\widehat{\text{Maths}}$	$\widehat{\text{HG}}$
Student No. 1	10	8	0.352293578	0.073991031
Student No. 2	15	4	1.269724771	−0.822869955
Student No. 3	8	4	−0.014678899	−0.822869955
Student No. 4	9	12	0.168807339	0.970852018
Student No. 5	19	13	2.003669725	1.195067265
Student No. 6	2	15	−1.11559633	1.643497758
Student No. 7	14	14	1.086238532	1.419282511
Student No. 8	5	6	−0.565137615	−0.374439462
Student No. 9	4	7	−0.748623853	−0.150224215
Student No. 10	8	3	−0.014678899	−1.047085202
Student No. 11	2	2	−1.11559633	−1.271300448
Student No. 12	1	4	−1.299082569	−0.822869955
Average	8.08	7.67	0.000611621	−0.000747384
Standard deviation	5.45	4.46	1.000307458	0.999931851

Table 4.3. [I/V] data table: math and HG with z-scores

We recall some z-score properties:

– the means of the z-scores are zero;

– the standard deviations are always equal to 1;

– we can illustrate that Cor (math, HG) = Cor ($\widehat{\text{Math}}$, $\widehat{\text{HG}}$). This is illustrated as such: "the correlation coefficient of two variables is equal to the correlation coefficient of standard scores";

– with z-scores, the line closest to the point cloud passes through the intercept and the points are equitably distributed among the four quadrants.

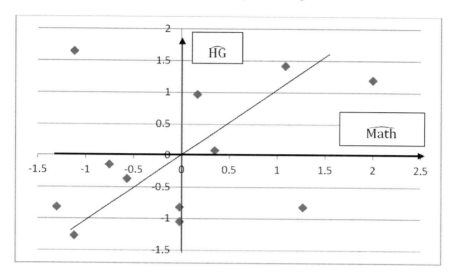

Figure 4.3. *Point cloud in the math/HG standard plane*

In PCA, the variables used are always the standard scores, but when carrying out a PCA with a software, variables are entered in raw form and the software transforms them automatically into standard scores.

4.1.2.3. F1 and F2 factorial axes

After transforming the initial variables (X1 and X2) into z-scores ($\widehat{X1}$ and $\widehat{X2}$), we calculate, using the least squares method, the line closest to the point cloud in the plane of z-scores ($\widehat{X1}$ and $\widehat{X2}$). This line is called "first factorial axis F1"; the "second factorial axis F2" is the axis that passes through the intercept and that is deduced from the F1 axis by +90° rotation.

In Figure 4.4, the two factorial axes F1 and F2 are represented, they define a plane called factorial plane, and also axes relative to initial standard scores $\widehat{X1}$ and $\widehat{X2}$.

We show, in 2D case only, that when we are dealing with z-scores, the angle α that constitutes axis $\widehat{X1}$ with axis F1 is always equal to $\pi/4 = 45°$.

In addition, an individual (I_i in the figure) has as components ($\widehat{x_{1i}}$ and $\widehat{x_{2i}}$) in the initial coordinate system and (f_{1i} and f_{2i}) in the factorial coordinate system. The latter, called principal or factorial components, can be expressed in terms of initial z-scores.

A simple geometric calculation shows that the link between the coordinates is:

$$f_{1i} = \widehat{x_{1i}} \cos \pi/4 + \widehat{x_{2i}} \sin \pi/4 = 0.707\, \widehat{x_{1i}} + 0.707\, \widehat{x_{2i}}$$

$$f_{2i} = \widehat{x_{1i}} - \pi/4 + \widehat{x2_i} \sin \pi/4 = -0.707\, \widehat{x_{1i}} + 0.707\, \widehat{x_{2i}}$$

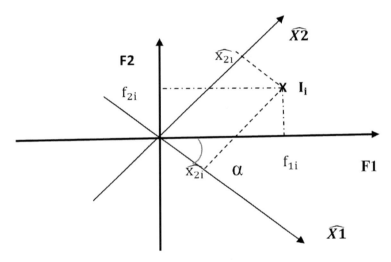

Figure 4.4. *Coordinates of a point in the initial and principal axes*

Thus, by knowing the initial z-score components of a point I_i we can calculate its factorial components. When carrying out a PCA, the software return these values, which play a significant role in PCA analysis.

4.1.2.4. *Percentage of information contained by each principal axis*

Each of the F1 and F2 axes is said to contain a percentage of the initial information contained in the point cloud. The closer the axis is to the plot, the more its percentage of representativity. If all individuals belong to the F1 axis, the latter would contain 100% of the information. In all cases, in 2D, the sum of the two F1 and F2 percentages is equal to 100%, because the two axes define a plane that contains all the points, and therefore all the information.

Calculation of the percentage of information contained in an axis and/or a plane is the result of a complex mathematical calculation, which we believe is not necessary to present. However, when calculating a PCA, the percentage of information contained by the principal axes is systematically calculated and returned by the software used. It is even the first variables that are returned by the software.

4.1.2.5. *Meaning of the quadrants of the factorial plane: representation of individuals*

We have just seen that in the F1 and F2 factorial plane, the components of individuals are expressed in terms of the initial standard components.

For the case X1 = Math and X2 = HG, we can have:

$$f1 = 0.707. \widehat{Math} + 0.707.\widehat{HG}$$

$$f2 = -0.707. \widehat{Math} + 0.707.\widehat{HG}$$

The following observations can be made:

– the more f1 increases, the more students are generally "good";

– when f2 is positive, they are better at HG, and when f2 = 0, they have the same level in HG and math. When f2 is negative, they are better at math.

We can therefore give meaning to each quadrant:

– first quadrant "Students good but better at HG";

– second quadrant "Students not good but better at HG";

– third quadrant "Students not good but better at math";

– fourth quadrant "Students good but better at math".

This analysis makes it possible to give meaning to individual groups depending on whether they belong to either of the quadrants (see Figure 4.5). It is this characteristic that often justifies the implementation of a PCA.

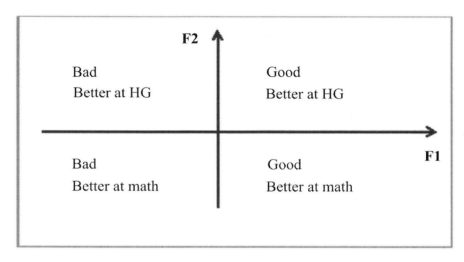

Figure 4.5. *Factorial plane: meaning of quadrants, math/HG*

4.1.2.6. *Representation of X1 and X2 variables*

After positioning the individuals, defining the factorial axes, and giving meaning to each quadrant of the factorial plane, we will present another important element of the PCA: representation of the initial variables X1 and X2 in the factorial plane (F1, F2).

For each individual I_i, the initial variable X1 has component x_{1i} and the factorial variables F1 and F2, respectively, have components f_{1i} and f_{2i}. We start by calculating the correlation coefficients Cor (X1, F1) and Cor (X1, F2), and then we position the coordinate point (Cor (X1, F1), Cor (X1, F2)) in the plane (F1, F2). The representation of the variable X1, in the factorial plane, is thus a vector resulting from the intercept and whose end is the point defined. The same approach leads to the representation of X2 in the factorial plane.

Let us now see how it works for the two situations that we have considered (math, physics) then (math and HG).

X1 = Math and X2 = Physics

Below is the complete table that contains the initial math and physics variables with the corresponding z-scores and components in the factorial plane.

I/V	Math	Physics	$\widehat{\text{Maths}}$	$\widehat{\text{Physics}}$	F1	F2
Student No. 1	10	10	0.3657964	0.34005894	0.49903973	−0.01819639
Student No. 2	15	14	1.3200313	1.24688279	1.81480826	−0.05171599
Student No. 3	8	8	−0.01589755	−0.11335298	−0.09138013	−0.06890099
Student No. 4	9	9	0.17494943	0.11335298	0.2038298	−0.04354869
Student No. 5	19	18	2.08341921	2.15370664	2.99564798	0.04969321
Student No. 6	2	3	−1.16097943	−1.24688279	−1.70235859	−0.06072268
Student No. 7	14	14	1.12918432	−1.24688279	1.67987945	0.08321282
Student No. 8	5	6	−0.58843849	−0.56676491	−0.8167288	0.01532322
Student No. 9	4	5	−0.77928547	−0.79347087	−1.11193873	−0.01002908
Student No. 10	8	8	−0.01589755	−0.11335298	−0.09138013	−0.06890099
Student No. 11	2	3	−1.16097943	−1.24688279	−1.70235859	−0.06073368
Student No. 12	1	4	−1.35182641	−1.02017683	−1.67700629	0.23447625

Table 4.4. *Initial math and physics variables:*
standard scores s, factorial components

Calculation of the correlation coefficients for each of the variables leads to:

Cor (Math, F1) = 0.9983   Cor (Math, F2) = –0.05768

Cor (Physics, F1) = 0.9983   Cor (Physics, F2) = 0.05768

Math and physics vectors can then be positioned in the factorial plane F1 and F2 (Figure 4.6).

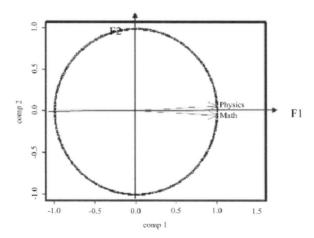

Figure 4.6. *Circle of correlations: representation of physics and math variables*

The remarks below rely on mathematical bases, but the meaning and consequences have to be known in order to analyze the results of a PCA. The different software return this information, which has to be interpreted.

– The ends of the vectors representing the variables are on a unit circle radius. This is always the case in 2D because the plane contains 100% of the information contained in the initial plot.

– Two variables are close; they form an angle close to zero. Also, they are almost confused with the F1 axis. This means that the F1 axis contains most of the information contained in the initial plot. The information contained in the F2 axis is insignificant in this case.

– The cosine of the angle between two variables gives their correlation. In this case, it is close to +1. This explains the fact that math and physics variables are closely related.

X1 = Math and X2 = HG

Table 4.5 presents the math and HG variables with the corresponding z-scores and components in the factorial plane.

I/V	Math	HG	$\widehat{Maths}$	$\widehat{HG}$	F1	F2
Student No. 1	10	8	0.352293578	0.073991031	0.301383219	–0.196759901
Student No. 2	15	4	1.269724771	–0.822869955	0.315926355	–1.479464471
Student No. 3	8	4	–0.014678899	–0.822869955	–0.59214704	–0.571391077
Student No. 4	9	12	0.168807229	0.970852018	0.805739165	0.567045588
Student No. 5	19	13	2.003669725	1.195067265	2.261507052	–0.571681939
Student No. 6	2	15	–1.11559633	1.643497758	0.37322631	1.95067952
Student No. 7	14	14	1.086238532	1.419282511	1.771403377	0.235462093
Student No. 8	5	6	–0.565137615	–0.374439462	–0.664280993	0.134823594
Student No. 9	4	7	–0.748623853	–0.150224215	–0.635485584	0.423068544
Student No. 10	8	3	–0.014678899	–1.047085202	–0.750667219	–0.729911256
Student No. 11	2	2	–1.11559633	–1.271300448	–1.687536022	–0.110082811
Student No. 12	1	4	–1.299082569	–0.822869955	–1.500220434	0.336682318

Table 4.5. *Initial math and HG variables: standard scores, factorial components*

Calculation of the correlation coefficients for each of the variables leads to:

Cor (Math, F1) = 0.8186   Cor (Math, F2) = –0.5743

Cor (HG, F1) = 0.8186   Cor (HG, F2) = 0.5743

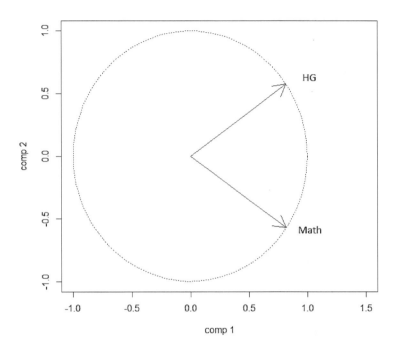

Figure 4.7. *Circle of correlations:*
representation of math and HG variables

– The ends of the vectors representing the variables are on a unit circle radius. This is always the case in 2D because the plane contains 100% of the information contained in the initial plot.

– Two variables are clearly different. The information contained in the initial plot is evenly distributed on the F1 and F2 axes.

– The position of the variables gives information about the meaning of the quadrants.

4.1.3. *PCA 3D*

4.1.3.1. *Overview of the principles of the PCA 3D*

We will now discuss what a PCA is really all about, but we limit ourselves to the case of three initial variables X1, X2 and X3. The advantage of the three-dimensional (3D) situation is that it allows a description of the approach alongside a graphical representation that enhances understanding (Figure 4.8).

With regard to the approach, the procedure is similar to that of the 2D case. Thus, three variables (X1, X2 and X3) are first transformed into standard scores. In the orthonormal trirectangular coordinate system $\widehat{X1}$, $\widehat{X2}$ and $\widehat{X3}$, the representative points of each individual, such as I_i of coordinates $\widehat{x_{1i}}$, $\widehat{x_{2i}}$ and $\widehat{x_{3i}}$, form a point cloud in the 3D space.

But in this case, using the least squares method, we look for the two orthogonal axes F1 and F2 that define the plane closest to the point cloud. The plane defined is the first factorial plane. Finally, we construct a third axis F3 that completes the principal coordinate system such as to obtain a direct coordinate system.

We project all representative points of individuals, such as I_i on the principal plane (F1, F2).

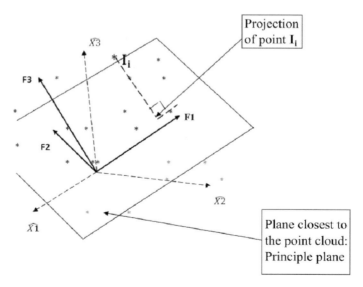

Figure 4.8. *3D representation: initial axes, principal axes and principal plane*

If we consider that the cloud constituted by projections of points on the plane (F1, F2) leads to a good representation of the initial cloud in 3D, we can study the projections of points, in this plane, in place of the cloud in the 3D space. In this case, we reduce the number of dimensions, we move from a 3D to a 2D problem. This is the basic principle of the PCA: "reducing the number of dimensions of the problem". This reduction is of good quality when the principal plane is close to the initial point cloud. In this case, it retains much of the information contained in the initial point cloud.

The study carried out in the plane (F1, F2) has many points in common with what we have already seen in the 2D case. But in this case, we can no longer say that the plane (F1, F2) contains 100% of the information contained in the initial point cloud, since part of the information was lost because of the projection exercise. Moreover, in this case, for each point, such as I_i, the two components f_{1i} and f_{2i} of the point projected in the factorial plane are a function of the three components $\widehat{x_{1i}}$, $\widehat{x_{2i}}$ and $\widehat{x_{3i}}$ of the three variables $\widehat{X1}, \widehat{X2}$ and $\widehat{X3}$.

It is difficult to consider carrying out a PCA without using any software. In the following sections, in order to provide a first illustration of what a PCA processed from a software is, we examine a very simple 3D problem. In this example, we use the XLSTAT software, which integrates directly into Excel.

4.1.3.2. *Example (math, physics, HG)*

We take up the previously examined case of 12 students of a class. We took mathematics, physics and history–geography marks (Tables 4.1 and 4.2). But now, instead of carrying out a separate study of the links between math and physics marks, on the one hand, and math and HG, on the other hand, we will examine the links that can exist globally between the three variables.

We provide a summary of the stages that are systematically involved in carrying out a PCA including data entry, characterization of variables, launching of PCA and analysis of results. For more details, XLSTAT tutorials can be viewed directly online on the Internet.

– Data table input

With XLSTAT software, we work directly on the spreadsheet by opening the XLSAT ribbon that is added to the classical Excel ribbon. The data table used is the one that was developed in Excel.

I/V	Math	Physics	HG
S1	10	10	8
S2	15	14	4
S3	8	8	4
S4	9	9	12
S5	19	18	13
S6	2	3	15
S7	14	14	14
S8	5	6	6
S9	4	5	7
S10	8	8	3
S11	2	3	2
S12	1	4	4

Table 4.6. *[I/V] data table: math, physics, HG*

– Launching the PCA

We open "data analysis", then choose "principal components analysis" and select the columns corresponding to the variables to be processed.

– Characterization of variables or tables-launching calculation

In XLSTAT, the nature of the table presented to it should be indicated, [I/V] or contingency table. All that remains is to launch calculation.

– Analyzing results returned by the software

All the software return results that relate to most of the variables, which were presented previously.

All results returned by the software are not presented here. We limit ourselves to those that enable a simple interpretation related to the above. We have included some comments alongside the results to enable a better understanding of their meaning. For more information, we can view the XLSTAT tutorial dedicated to PCA.

– Pearson correlation matrix

Variables	Math	Physics	HG
Math	1	0.993	0.340
Physics	0.993	1	0.350
HG	0.340	0.350	1

Table 4.7. *Correlation matrix*

The cross-tabulated table shows the correlation coefficients between the initial variables. We note a correlation coefficient close to 1 between math and physics and a much weaker link between HG and math and HG and physics.

Explained variance: % information contained in each factorial axes – cumulative %.

	F1	F2	F3
Variability (%)	73.102	26.678	0.220
Cumulative (%)	73.102	99.780	100.000

Table 4.8. *Explained variance*

We observe the % of information of the initial cloud contained in each factorial axis (variability [%]).

The last row gives the cumulative %, so we see that the first factorial plane (F1, F2) contains 99.780% of the information contained in the initial cloud. This means that the representation of the cloud in the first factorial plane is remarkable. We will be able to work in the plane (F1, F2) with confidence and, given the little information contained in F3 axis, we can ignore (F1, F3) and (F2, F3) factorial planes.

– Contribution of initial variables to factor variables

	F1	F2	F3
Math	0.654	−0.273	−0.706
Physics	0.655	−0.262	0.708
HG	0.379	0.925	−0.008

Table 4.9. *Contribution of initial variables to factor variables*

Table 4.9 presents the contribution of initial variables to each factorial component. If we consider only the plane (F1, F2):

$$f_{1i} = 0.654\text{xMath}_i + 0.655\text{xPhysics}_i + 0.379\text{xHG}_i$$

$$f_{2i} = -0.273\text{xMath}_i - 0.262\text{xPhysics}_i + 0.925\text{xHG}_i$$

As for the 2D case of sections 4.1.2.1, 4.1.2.2 and 4.1.2.5, this makes it possible to give meaning to each of the quadrants of the factorial plane.

We see that for the F1 axis, f_1 increases when each of the initial variables increase, so the larger that f_1 is, the better students generally are. For the F2 axis, since the contributions of math and physics variables are negative while that of HG is positive, we can say that the more we move toward the large and >0 f_2 the better students are at history. On the contrary, the more we move toward the large and <0 f_2 the better students are at math and physics. By combining these remarks, meaning can be given to the four quadrants. This allows the categorization of students as a first approximation.

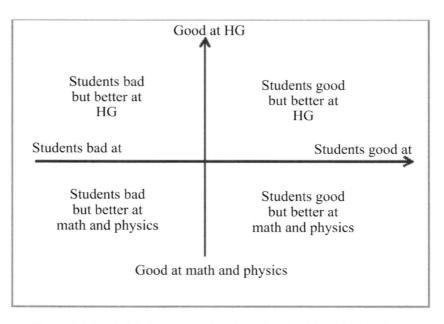

Figure 4.9. *Factorial plane: meaning of quadrants of the principal plane*

	F1	F2	F3
Math	0.968	−0.245	−0.057
Physics	0.970	−0.235	0.058
HG	0.561	0.828	−0.001

Table 4.10. *Correlation coefficients between initial variables and factorial variables*

Table 4.10 gives the correlation coefficients between initial components and factorial components. These correlations form the coordinates of the end of vectors representative of initial variables in the factorial plane (F1, F2).

– Representation of variables

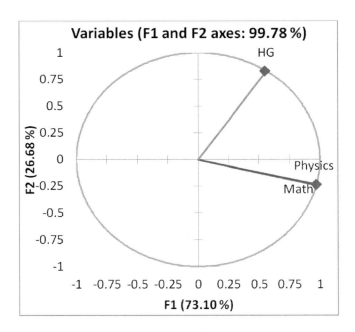

Figure 4.10. *Circle of correlations: representation of math, physics and HG variables*

We note that the first factorial axis F1 contains 73.102% of the information contained in the initial 3D cloud and the second axis 26.678%. Thus, the factorial plane (F1, F2) contains 99.780% of the initial information.

The three math, physics and HG variables are well represented and this can be seen, because the ends of vectors that represent them are very close to the correlation circle of radius 1.

The physics and math variables are almost confused; this shows that they are highly correlated. On the other hand, the HG variable forms a close to 90° angle with math and physics. This shows that the HG variable is weakly correlated with the math and physics variables.

We note that the positioning and orientation of "initial variable" vectors give information on the meaning of the quadrants.

– Representation of individuals

Observation	F1	F2	F3
Obs1	0.472	−0.113	−0.017
Obs2	1.303	−1.422	−0.040
Obs3	−0.393	−0.728	−0.060
Obs4	0.549	0.825	−0.049
Obs5	3.117	0.017	0.044
Obs6	−0.891	2.141	−0.074
Obs7	2.032	0.704	0.072
Obs8	−0.868	−0.049	0.016
Obs9	−1.045	0.266	−0.010
Obs10	−0.478	−0.936	−0.058
Obs11	−1.995	−0.557	−0.051
Obs12	−1.802	−0.149	0.229

Table 4.11. *Coordinates of individuals on factorial axes*

In Table 4.11, we find the coordinates of "student points" in the 3D factor space. In particular, this enables their representation in the plane (F1, F2).

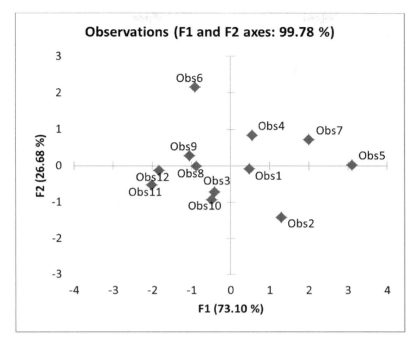

Figure 4.11. *Representation of individuals in the first factorial plane*

The points represent students' projections on the factorial plane (F1, F2).

In accordance with what we have seen above, the more we move toward increasing F1 the more students are "good". The more we move toward increasing and positive F2 the more students are good at HG. The more we move toward increasing and negative F2 the more students are good at science, that is, in math and physics. There are more "poor" (7) than "good" students (5) and there are more students better at math and physics (7) than students good at HG (5), but many are at the threshold.

With most software, individuals can be categorized (Obs). For example, if we introduce the categorical variable "GENDER", we can distinguish girls and boys by a play of colors.

– Squared cosine of observations

	$\text{Cos}^2(1)$	$\text{Cos}^2(2)$
Obs 1	0.945	0.054
Obs 2	0.456	0.543
Obs 3	0.224	0.771
Obs 4	0.306	0.691
Obs 5	1.000	0.000
Obs 6	0.148	0.851
Obs 7	0.892	0.107
Obs 8	0.997	0.003
Obs 9	0.939	0.061
Obs 10	0.206	0.791
Obs 11	0.927	0.072
Obs 12	0.978	0.006

Table 4.12. *Table of squared cosines of observations*

$\cos^2(1)$ and $\cos^2(2)$: Expresses the quality of the representation of each student on each F1 of F2 factorial axis, respectively. In other words, is the student properly projected on the (F1, F2) plane?

The two quantities are added, axis by axis, to give the "quality" of the projection on the factorial plane. For example, for student no. 8 $(0.997 + 0.003 = 1)$, his/her representation is perfect. For student no. 12 $(0.978 + 0.006 = 0.984)$, the representation is also very good but some little information was lost during the projection exercise.

4.1.4. *4D examples*

We are still in a very simple school case but now with four variables (Math, Physics, French, and English). In this case, we have to move from a four-dimensional (4D) space to a 2D plane. The image we have given in 3D, with the projection of points, is not so simple, so we have to use abstraction and our imagination.

Thus, Table 4.13 shows the marks obtained by nine students in four subjects.

Students	Math	Physics	French	Engineering
S1	6	6	5	5.5
S2	8	8	8	8
S3	6	7	11	9.5
S4	14.5	14.5	15.5	15
S5	14	14	12	12.5
S6	11	10	5.5	7
S7	5.5	7	14	11.5
S8	13	12.5	8.5	9.5
S9	9	9.5	12.5	12

Table 4.13. *[I/V] 4D data table*

The XLSTAT software returns the following main results: they are only accompanied by some comments that complement those of the preceding 3D example. They enable the understanding of what differentiates the 4D case from the 3D case. For the rest, it suffices to use the comments of the previous example.

– *Pearson correlation matrix*

Variables	Math	Physics	French	Engineering
Math	*1*	0.983	0.227	0.508
Physics	0.983	*1*	0.397	0.652
French	0.227	0.397	*1*	0.951
Engineering	0.508	0.652	0.951	*1*

Table 4.14. *Table of cross correlation coefficients between variables*

Explained variance: % information contained in each factorial axis – cumulative %.

	F1	F2	F3	F4
Variability (%)	71.892	27.992	0.089	0.026
Cumulative (%)	71.892	99.884	99.974	100.000

Table 4.15. *Table of explained variances by the four principal axes and cumulative explained variances*

In 4D, we have four factorial axes. The first two contain 71.892% and 27.992% of the information contained in the initial 4D cloud. Thus, the first factorial plane (F1, F2) contains 99.884% of the information of the initial cloud, which is remarkable.

We will be able to work in the (F1, F2) plane with confidence and, given the little information contained in F3 and F4 axes, all the other factorial planes could be ignored.

– Contribution of initial variables to factor variables

	F1	F2	F3	F4
Math	0.478	−0.552	0.203	0.652
Physics	0.532	−0.407	−0.441	−0.597
French	0.444	0.621	−0.532	0.365
Engineering	0.540	0.379	0.693	−0.290

Table 4.16. *Contribution of initial variables to factor values*

Table 4.16 shows the contribution of initial variables to each factorial component; thus for the first two factorial variables, we have:

$$f_{1i} = 0.478 \times Math_i + 0.532 \times PHYS_i + 0.444 \times FREN_i + 0.540 \times ENG_i$$

$$f_{2i} = -0.552 \times Math_i - 0.407 \times PHYS_i + 0.621 \times FREN_i + 0.379 \times ENG_i$$

This, in particular, gives meaning to each of the quadrants of the factorial plane.

We see that for the F1 axis, f1 increases when each of the initial variables increase, so the larger f1 is the better students are. For the F2 axis, the contributions of MATH and PHYS variables are negative, while the contributions of FREN and ENG variables are positive. Thus, if f2 is positive, the students are better at arts subjects, and if f2 is negative, they are better at science subjects.

We can then give meaning to the different quadrants of the first factorial plane (F1, F2); the procedure leads to the diagram below (Figure 4.12), similar to the 3D case.

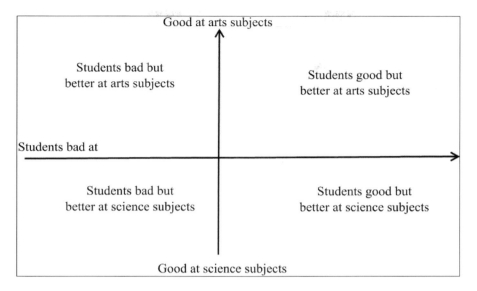

Figure 4.12. *Meaning of quadrants*

– Coordinates of variables – correlations between variables and factors

	F1	F2	F3	F4
Math	0.811	−0.584	0.012	0.021
Physics	0.902	−0.430	−0.026	−0.019
French	0.753	0.657	−0.032	0.012
Engineering	0.915	0.401	0.041	−0.009

Table 4.17. *Table of initial variables/factorial axes correlations*

– Circle of correlations

Since the (F1, F2) factorial plane contains nearly 100% of the initial cloud information, it is normal for the four variables to be perfectly represented and with their respective ends practically on the correlation circle.

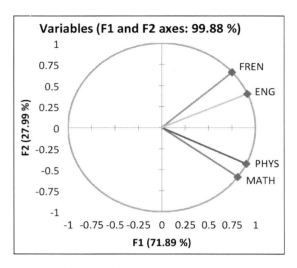

Figure 4.13. *Circle of correlations*

– Representation of individuals (observations)

Observation	F1	F2	F3	F4
Obs1	−2.743	-0.427	0.023	−0.023
Obs2	−1.241	−0.153	0.004	0.022
Obs3	−1.031	1.049	−0.058	−0.004
Obs4	3.138	0.186	0.011	0.047
Obs5	2.051	−0.628	−0.025	−0.060
Obs6	−0.971	−1.498	0.026	0.043
Obs7	−0.335	1.937	−0.055	0.009
Obs8	0.620	−1.291	−0.066	−0.012
Obs9	0.510	0.824	0.139	−0.023

Table 4.18. *Coordinates of individuals on factorial axes*

The coordinates are obtained with the relationships resulting from Table 4.16 "Contribution of initial variables to the coordinates of factorial variables:"

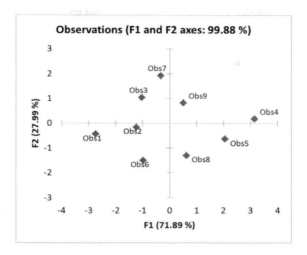

Figure 4.14. *Representation of individuals in the first factorial plane*

– *Squared cosines of observations*

	F1	F2	F3	F4
Obs1	0.976	0.024	0.000	0.000
Obs2	0.985	0.015	0.000	0.000
Obs3	0.490	0.508	0.002	0.000
Obs4	0.996	0.003	0.000	0.000
Obs5	0.914	0.086	0.000	0.001
Obs6	0.296	0.703	0.000	0.001
Obs7	0.029	0.970	0.001	0.000
Obs8	0.187	0.811	0.002	0.000
Obs9	0.271	0.708	0.020	0.001

Table 4.19. *Table of squared cosines*

4.1.5. Another example: study of "graduation from school" in nine European countries

Previously, to simplify the presentations, we adopted situations where the first factorial plane almost perfectly represented the point cloud for all the variables. Here, we present a more realistic situation where it is no longer the case.

This concerns a research work in sociology that studied "The graduation of young people from school to the world of work" in nine European countries (Eurostat 2000). The full version of the work is presented in the book *Analyse factorielle simple en sociologie* [BUS 09], but as far as we are concerned, we have used XLSTAT software to exploit the data.

The nine countries studied include Austria, Belgium, Spain, Finland, France, Greece, Hungary, Italy and Sweden. These are the nine individuals from which five variables were taken.

The five variables selected include:

– V11: average age of graduation of young people from school;

– V12: average age of obtaining a primary or secondary school diploma;

– V13: average age of obtaining a degree at the undergraduate or graduate level;

– V31: percentage of parents having obtained a level of primary or secondary school education;

– V33: percentage of parents having obtained education at the undergraduate and graduate level.

The data result from surveys of a large number of people in each country. We will carry out the CPA and present the main results; only a few comments will be added. Table 4.20 presents the data collected.

Var. Country	V11	V12	V13	V31	V33
Austria	19.9	18	24.7	27	19
Belgium	20.6	18.3	22.8	45	26
Spain	19.1	15.2	22.5	80	10
Finland	21.6	16.9	25.3	21	36
France	20.8	17.9	23.2	51	15
Greece	19.4	14.5	23.3	66	9
Hungary	18.3	14.9	23.1	26	13
Italy	18.4	14.6	25	68	6
Sweden	23.9	22.6	26.4	26	36

Table 4.20. *[I/V] data table for the nine countries*

– *Pearson correlation matrix*

Variables	V11	V12	V13	V31	V33
V11	1	0.912	0.611	−0.502	0.873
V12	0.912	1	0.556	−0.540	0.777
V13	0.611	0.556	1	−0.513	0.577
V31	−0.502	−0.540	−0.513	1	−0.736
V33	0.873	0.777	0.577	−0.736	1

Table 4.21. *Cross-correlation coefficients between variables*

Explained variance: % information contained in each factorial axis – cumulative %.

	F1	F2	F3	F4	F5
Variability (%)	73.356	12.086	10.377	3.512	0.670
Cumulative (%)	73.356	85.442	95.819	99.330	100.000

Table 4.22. *Explained variances by each factorial axis and cumulative percentage*

The factorial plane (F1, F2) contains 85.442% of the information contained by the cloud in its five-dimensional space. This result is remarkable. We also note that the second factorial plane (F1, F3) contains 83.733% of this information. This plane should equally be studied, though we limit ourselves to the presentation of results in the first factorial plane.

– *Contribution of initial variables to coordinates of factor variables*

	F1	F2	F3	F4	F5
V11	0.483	0.441	−0.030	−0.196	0.730
V12	0.469	0.417	−0.111	0.665	−0.389
V13	0.390	−0.247	0.883	−0.018	−0.078
V31	−0.395	0.754	0.357	−0.285	−0.256
V33	0.488	−0.029	−0.281	−0.661	−0.495

Table 4.23. *Initial/factorial variable relationships*

– Coordinates of variables – correlations between variables and factors

	F1	F2	F3	F4	F5
V11	0.926	0.343	−0.021	−0.082	0.134
V12	0.898	0.325	−0.080	0.279	−0.071
V13	0.747	−0.192	0.636	−0.008	−0.014
V31	−0.757	0.586	0.257	−0.120	−0.047
V33	0.935	−0.023	−0.202	−0.277	−0.090

Table 4.24. *Table of correlations between initial and factorial variables*

– Circle of correlations

In this case, part of the information was lost during projection exercises, although the factorial plane (F1, F2) contains 85.44% of the initial cloud information, even though the variables are no longer perfectly represented, particularly V13 and V33.

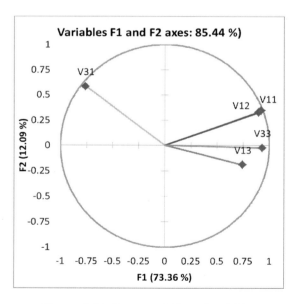

Figure 4.15. *Representation of variables*

– Representation of individuals

Observation	F1	F2	F3	F4	F5
Obs1 (Austria)	0.663	−0.720	0.100	0.551	−0.117
Obs2 (Belgium)	0.316	0.522	−1.119	−0.104	−0.288
Obs3 (Spain)	−2.201	0.978	−0.136	−0.255	-0.130
Obs4 (Finland)	2.022	−0.839	−0.015	−0.924	0.053
Obs5 (France)	−0.196	0.679	−0.434	0.356	0.273
Obs6 (Greece)	−1.780	0.275	0.230	−0.236	0.282
Obs7 (Hungary)	−1.137	−1.379	−0.703	0.309	0.060
Obs8 (Italy)	−1.705	−0.222	1.538	0.042	−0.162
Obs9 (Sweden)	4.017	0.706	0.539	0.261	0.030

Table 4.25. *Representation of countries in the first factorial plane*

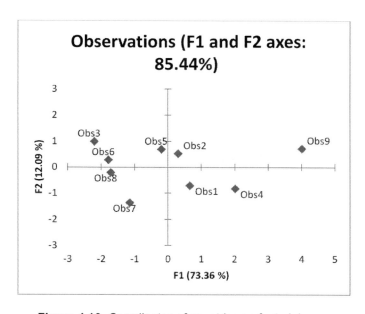

Figure 4.16. *Coordinates of countries on factorial axes*

– Squared cosines of observations

	F1	F2	F3	F4	F5
Obs1	0.342	0.404	0.008	0.236	0.011
Obs2	0.058	0.159	0.728	0.006	0.048
Obs3	0.821	0.162	0.003	0.011	0.003
Obs4	0.724	0.125	0.000	0.151	0.000
Obs5	0.043	0.519	0.212	0.143	0.084
Obs6	0.923	0.022	0.015	0.016	0.023
Obs7	0.341	0.502	0.130	0.025	0.001
Obs8	0.544	0.009	0.442	0.000	0.005
Obs9	0.950	0.029	0.017	0.004	0.000

Table 4.26. *Table of squared cosines*

The example reveals the following:

The table shows that countries 1, 3, 4, 6, 7 and 9 are well projected on the F1/F2 plane, but this is not the case for points 2 and 5, which are properly projected instead on the F2/F3 plane, or for point 8, which was properly projected on the F1/F3 plane.

Without questioning the method, this example shows a situation where the interpretation of data loses strength because of the loss of information due to successive projections. In particular, would it perhaps be appropriate to examine planes other than the F1/F2 plane?

As the number of variables increases, the number of factorial axes also increases. The information contained in the initial cloud is distributed over all the axes and, consequently, that contained in the first factorial plane decreases. This makes the interpretation of the results more inaccurate and therefore more delicate. So if we have to consider a large number of variables, it is advised not to take all of them into account from the start, but rather to work while gradually increasing their number, each step brings its own lot of what can be learned. There is no established rule in this respect; it is only through a proper implementation of the method that we can make the best use of results by consulting all the results returned by the software.

4.2. Factorial correspondence analyses

4.2.1. *Overview*

After presenting, using PCA, the multivariate approaches for numerical (quantitative) variables, we will discuss in this section the multivariate approaches for dummy (qualitative) variables.

First, we will present the factorial correspondence analysis (FCA), which focuses on the links that exist between the modalities of two dummy variables. The term "correspondence" is to dummy variables what the term "correlation" is to numerical variables. The FCA is a multivariate approach, although it only deals with two variables, because the method used is an adaptation of those used for multivariate approaches. FCA is based on a contingency table (see section 2.1.3.3) that compares the numbers of modalities of the two variables.

Subsequently, to study the links that exist between $P > 2$ dummy variables, we will discuss the multiple factorial correspondence analysis (MFCA). It is based on Burt tables or complete disjunctive tables that we will present later. However, it should be noted that for many software programs, you just enter the individual/ variable [I/V] table and the program develops Burt or complete disjunctive tables.

As will be seen later, both approaches (FCA and MFCA) rely on the bases of the PCA. Also the theoretical bases will not be presented in detail, especially as we focus mainly on users' needs.

4.2.2. *Factorial correspondence analysis*

4.2.2.1. *What is the purpose of FCA*

We attempt to discover what FCA is all about from an example inspired by a Master 1 ESA course at the Université de l'Orléans (Internet source):

In a sample of 592 women, eye and hair color were simultaneously noted. The contingency table compares the numbers of the two variables "eye color" with four modalities [brown], [hazel], [green], [blue] and "hair color" with four modalities [brown], [chestnut], [red], [blond]. Thus, for example, out of a total of 71 red-haired women, 14 have green eyes.

The results presented were developed with the XLSTAT software.

Contingency table:

	Brown	Chestnut	Red	Blond	Sum
Brown	68	119	26	7	220
Hazel	15	54	14	10	93
Green	5	29	14	16	64
Blue	20	84	17	94	215
Sum	108	286	71	127	592

Table 4.27. *Contingency table: eye/hair color*

Two questions are asked: Is there a link between the women's eye and hair color, and what is the nature of this link?

To answer the first question, we have to know whether the two variables are independent (H_0) or not (H_1). We already know how to answer such a question with the χ^2 test of independence (section 3.5.4).

χ^2 (observed value)	138.290
χ^2 (critical value)	16.919
Ddl	9
P-value	<0.0001
Alpha	0.05

Table 4.28. χ^2 *test of the contingency table*

From the test, we note that H_0 has to be rejected without hesitation and therefore admit that, overall, there is a link between the two variables. But we want to take the analysis further, and know the types of links, that is, the "closest" and most "distant" modalities of variables.

4.2.2.2. *Row profile and column profile tables*

Before presenting what PCA is all about, strictly speaking, it is interesting to transform the contingency table in order to directly collect valuable information. Although the case presented is simple, the numbers of rows and columns are different, and its reading is not obvious. For this purpose, the contingency table is transformed into two tables, row and column profile tables that systematically accompany the FCA results analysis. In very simple cases, most of the information can be collected from it, and sometimes the FCA may not be useful unless we wish to have a graphical representation of the results.

In Table 4.29, we divide the numbers of each row by the total of numbers of the row. Thus, the column "sum" contains only 1.

	Brown	Chestnut	Red	Blond	Sum
Brown	0.309	0.541	0.118	0.032	1
Hazel	0.161	0.581	0.151	0.108	1
Green	0.078	0.453	0.219	0.250	1
Blue	0.093	0.391	0.079	0.437	1
Average	0.160	0.491	0.142	0.207	1

Table 4.29. *Table of row profiles*

The table can be easily read when written in this form. For example, 58.1% of women with hazel eyes have chestnut hair while 43.7% of women with blue eyes have blond hair. Another reading (averages row) shows that 49.1% of women have chestnut hair.

In Table 4.30, we divide the numbers of each column by the total of numbers of the columns. Thus, the "sum" row contains only 1.

	Brown	Chestnut	Red	Blond	Average
Brown	0.630	0.416	0.366	0.055	0.367
Hazel	0.139	0.189	0.197	0.079	0.151
Green	0.046	0.101	0.197	0.126	0.118
Blue	0.185	0.294	0.239	0.740	0.365
Sum	1	1	1	1	1

Table 4.30. *Table of column profiles*

A reading of the table shows that 18.9% of women with chestnut hair have hazel eyes and 36.6% of women with red hair have brown eyes.

4.2.2.3. *Theoretical bases of the FCA*

As mentioned above, the theoretical bases will not be presented in detail. However, most of the bases of PCA have to be integrated in order to understand what FCA is, and especially, what can be obtained from it.

For FCA to be carried out, two successive PCAs need to be performed. For the first PCA, we consider the modalities of the "eye color" variable (the rows) as individuals and the modalities of the "hair color" variable (the columns) as numerical variables. For the second PCA, we reverse the roles and consider the modalities of the "hair color" variable as individuals and the modalities of the "eye color" variable as numerical variables.

However, there is a difference between the classical PCA presented in the previous section and the two PCAs used to carry out FCA. To search for the principal axes, which optimize the distance from the point cloud to the axes, instead of using the Euclidean distance, we use another distance, "the χ^2 distance" which balances the weight of the rows and columns. We will not discuss this subject further. Moreover, for FCA, unlike PCA, we are not interested in the representation of variables that would not have meaning, because here the concept of variable is only a computational artifice.

Finally, regarding the factorial axes, they are numbered $N - 1$ in which N is the number of modalities of the variable that possesses the least.

Ultimately, we show that since the two PCAs rely on the same contingency table, the calculated factorial axes are identical and the factorial planes are therefore the same. Thus, the results of the two PCAs can be superimposed. This is the feature that makes the method relevant.

4.2.2.4. *Reading the graph analysis returned by the XLSTAT software*

After entering the contingency table in the XLSTAT software, the software returns tables and graphs. For more information on using the XLSTAT software to carry out FCA, you can directly view the online tutorial.

Below, we present the graph that summarizes the results returned by the software, it shows the position of the different modalities $(4 + 4)$ of the two variables projected in the first factorial plane.

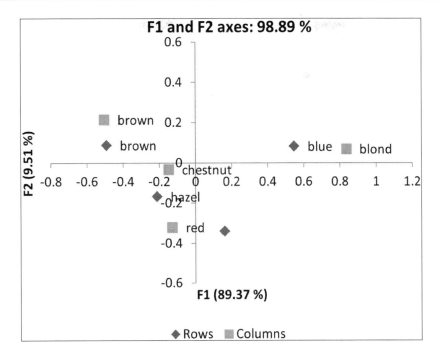

Figure 4.17. *Representation of modalities in the first factorial plane*

Just as with PCA, the quality of FCA is based on the quality of the projections of the cloud points on the first factorial plane and therefore on the percentage of information it contains. In the case considered, the first factorial plane contains 98.89% of information, so we can say that the representation is very good and therefore works with confidence.

Most of the results are contained on the graph that has to be read and interpreted in terms of the proximity between the different modalities of each of the two variables but also the modalities of the two variables as a whole. In general, a close distance indicates a similarity and, conversely, a large distance indicates a dissimilarity.

For example, if we consider the proximity of the modalities of the "eye color" variable, we see that blue and brown eyes are the most distant. This means, we will observe in what follows that their profiles with regard to hair color are different. On the other hand, hazel and brown eyes are closer and therefore their profiles, regarding hair color, should be similar.

Concerning hair color, we note that blond and brown hair are the most distant and therefore their profiles with regard to eye color should be very different. In contrast, brown and chestnut hair, which are closer, should have comparable profiles.

If we now observe the closeness between the modalities of the two variables, we see that blue eyes and blond hair are close, which suggests that many blond hair women have blue eyes and vice versa. We also observe a closeness between the modalities "red" for hair and "green" for eyes. It is the same with "red" and "hazel". However, given the distance, we may assume that few women with blue eyes have brown hair.

4.2.2.5. Interpreting the different tables

A simple reading of the graph provides information, but we have to make sure that this correlates well with the reality. Indeed, the graph gives a projected image of the different points and if the quality of the projection of a specific point is not of good quality, the graph does not accurately portray the reality.

For this, in support of the graph, the XLSTAT software returns various tables. We present only those necessary for our analysis:

– distances between the modalities of the "eye color" variable:

	Brown	Hazel	Green	Blue
Brown	0	0.398	0.784	1.040
Hazel	0.398	0	0.453	0.806
Green	0.784	0.453	0	0.579
Blue	1.040	0.806	0.579	0

Table 4.31. χ^2 distance: eye color modalities

For example, for brown and blue eyes, which are the most distant on the graph, it can be observed on the table that these two modalities are indeed the most distant. As for brown and hazel eyes, we observe that they are the closest:

– distances between the modalities of the "hair color" variable:

	Brown	Chestnut	Red	Blond
Brown	0	0.446	0.654	1.348
Chestnut	0.446	0	0.316	0.991
Red	0.654	0.316	0	1.043
Blond	1.348	0.991	1.043	0

Table 4.32. χ^2 distances: hair color

We observe that blond and brown hair are indeed the most distant while brown and chestnut hair are the closest:

– meaning of the distances between the modalities of the same variable: we will, now, observe that if two modalities of the same variable are close on the graph, then their respective profiles regarding the other variable are close, and that the more distant the two modalities are, the more different are their profiles. To this end, we will use the two tables already presented, row and column profiles, which are systematically returned by the software. Below we present extracts to highlight the meaning of distances between the modalities of the same variable.

In the case of blue and brown eyes, which are the two most distant modalities, we can observe that their profiles, with regard to the "hair color" variable, are very different.

	Brown	Chestnut	Red	Blond	Sum
Brown	0.309	0.541	0.118	0.032	1
Blue	0.093	0.391	0.079	0.437	1

Table 4.33. Extract from row I profile

On the other hand, for brown and hazel eyes, which are the closest modalities, their profiles are closer.

	Brown	Chestnut	Red	Blond	Sum
Brown	0.309	0.541	0.118	0.032	1
Hazel	0.161	0.581	0.151	0.108	1

Table 4.34. Extract from row II profile

The same observation can also be made for hair color using the column profiles table:

– meaning of the distances between the modalities of the "eye color" and "hair color" variables: for example, we observed on the graph that blue eyes were close to blond hair and that on the contrary blue eyes were very distant from brown hair. Again, we can give meaning to this closeness and distance by using the "row" and "column" profile tables.

On the "row profiles" table, we can read that a large proportion of blue-eyed individuals has blond hair (43.7%) and specifically on the "column profiles" table, a large proportion of blond hair individuals has blue eyes (74%). These values explain their closeness.

In contrast, blue eyes are distant from brown hair, which is confirmed by the fact that only 9.3% of women with blue eyes have brown hair and, conversely, only 18.5% of brown-haired women have blue eyes.

4.2.2.6. Another example: the distribution of farmlands in the Midi-Pyrénées region

We will now present a more complex situation, which examines the types of agricultural holdings in the eight departments of the Midi-Pyrénées region. This example is inspired by Baccini [BAC 10b]. This involves highlighting the similarities and differences between the departments and sizes of agricultural holdings. For this, an FCA was carried out from Table 4.35, which compares the numbers of the two variables: "Departments of the Pyrénées-Languedoc region" with eight modalities and "Size of agricultural holdings" with six modalities. Sizes ranging from "less than 5 ha" (INF05) to "greater than 50 ha" (SUP50) and S1020, for example, indicate land ranging between 10 and 20 ha.

We can read, for example, that there are 1,260 agricultural holdings with an area ranging between 5 and 10 ha in Aveyron.

	INF05	S0510	S1020	S2035	S3550	SUP50
Ariè.	870	330	730	680	470	890
Aver.	820	1,260	2,460	3,330	2,170	2,960
HG	2,290	1,070	1,420	1,830	1,260	2,330
Gers	1,650	890	1,350	2,540	2,090	3,230
Lot	1,940	1,130	1,750	1,660	770	1,140
HP	2,110	1,170	1,640	1,500	550	430
Tarn	1,770	820	1,260	2,010	1,680	2,090
TG	1,740	920	1,560	2,210	990	1,240

Table 4.35. *Contingency table: department/agricultural holdings size data*

Just as in the previous example, we carried out the FCA using the XLSTAT software. Although it is difficult to provide a standard plan of exploitation of the results, because each studied case has its own specific features, we attempt to present a procedure to interpret the results. Our analysis is not exhaustive; it only aims at drawing attention to situations that we may encounter. Again, we will not use all the data returned by the software, but only those that we consider necessary to provide responses to the questions that arise.

First, we check that the two variables are not independent. To this end, the XLSTAT software returns the result of a χ^2 test of independence.

χ^2 (observed value)	5,375.488
χ^2 (critical value)	49.802
Ddl	35
P-value	<0.0001
Alpha	0.05

Table 4.36. χ^2 test of the contingency table

Interpretation of the test:

– H_0: the rows and columns of the table are independent;

– H_a: there is a link between the rows and columns of the table;

– since the calculated P-value is below alpha significance level = 0.05, the null hypothesis H_0 should be rejected, and the alternative hypothesis H_a retained;

– the risk of rejecting the null hypothesis H_0 when it is true is less than 0.01%.

If the test assumed the H_0 hypothesis, meaning that the two variables were independent, that is, without a proven link, there would be no point in carrying out an FCA because it will only confirm this absence of a link.

We must make sure that the first factorial plane is of quality. That is, it contains a significant portion of the initial cloud information.

Table 4.37 shows the five factorial axes, the percentage of the initial cloud information that they contain and the cumulative percentage.

	F1	F2	F3	F4	F5
Inertia (%)	74.708	20.245	3.252	1.059	0.736
Cumulative %	74.708	94.953	98.206	99.264	100.000

Table 4.37. *Information contained in the factorial axes: cumulative %*

The first factorial plane (F1, F2) contains 94.953% of the information of the initial cloud. This means that the projection of points has slightly degraded the information. The other axes contain very little information, so the other factorial planes are not significant and as such, we will limit our analysis to the first factorial plane.

We can observe the graph that contains the projections of the different modalities.

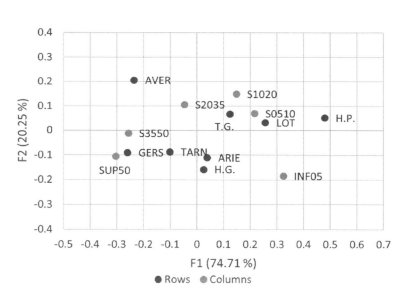

Figure 4.18. *Representation of modalities in the first factorial plane*

As in the previous case, we observe the closeness and distances between the modalities of a variable or the modalities of each of the two variables.

– Quality of projections: squared cosines

Although globally the principal plane contains 94.95% of the information, we must question the quality of the projection of each modality. Just as in the case of a classical CPA, we obtain information on this subject from the "squared cosine". But for an FCA, there are two squared cosine tables. To carry out an FCA, we perform two PCAs during which the two variables alternatively play the role of individuals or quantitative variables. Thus, these are the two representations that should be tested.

Without going into detail on the "squared cosine" tables, we recall that they provide, for each individual, the quantity of information contained on each of the factorial axes. The sum on the five axes is always equal to 1.

– Squared cosine "rows:" individuals are the departments

	F1	F2	F3	F4	F5
Ariè.	0.046	0.404	0.320	0.083	0.147
Aver.	0.564	0.427	0.008	0.001	0.000
HG	0.020	0.883	0.064	0.000	0.033
Gers	0.890	0.104	0.004	0.000	0.002
Lot	0.951	0.015	0.033	0.001	0.000
HP	0.982	0.012	0.002	0.005	0.000
Tarn	0.439	0.315	0.172	0.032	0.042
TG	0.536	0.165	0.173	0.123	0.003

Table 4.38. *Table of squared cosines of rows*

For example, we can observe that the representation on the first factorial plane of Aver. departments (0.99 = 0.564 + 0.427), Gers (0.99) and HP (0.99) is excellent; the same goes for HG (0.90) and Lot (0.96) departments. On the other hand, for Tarn (0.75) and TG (0.70) departments, the quality is average and for Ariè. (0.45), the quality is poor. These elements must be taken into account before any conclusions are drawn.

– Squared cosines of columns: individuals are the lands

	F1	F2	F3	F4	F5
INF05	0.752	0.244	0.003	0.001	0.000
S0510	0.819	0.086	0.010	0.051	0.033
S1020	0.448	0.462	0.071	0.001	0.018
S2035	0.128	0.638	0.172	0.048	0.014
S3550	0.920	0.002	0.042	0.025	0.011
SUP50	0.868	0.100	0.029	0.001	0.001

Table 4.39. *Table of squared cosines of columns*

Regarding the quality of the representation of farm lands on the first factorial plane, all have scores between 0.99 and 0.90, except S2035 (0.77).

We now attempt a quick analysis of the graph.

Some observations can be made that are suggestive of questions.

– The dimensions of the lands are strictly ordered in the opposite direction of the axis of increasing F1. As we move to the right, the farmlands become smaller and smaller. Can it be concluded that the same goes for the department profiles? That is, the more a department is located on the right, the more its distribution is rich in small holdings.

– Some departments are close such as (Ariè., HG) or (TG, Lot). Does the observation show that these "close" departments have comparable land distribution profiles?

– Some departments are distant such as (Aver., HP) or (Gers, HP). Does the observation show that these "distant" departments have different land distribution profiles?

– Some departments are close to farmlands such as (Gers, SUP50) or (TG, S0510). Does this closeness have meaning?

– Some departments are distant from farmlands (HP, SUP50) or (HP, 35-50). Do these distances have meaning?

The answers to the questions raised are found by examining the table of row or column profiles.

	INF05	S0510	S1020	S2035	S3550	SUP50	Sum
Ariè.	0.219	0.083	0.184	0.171	0.118	0.224	1
Aver.	0.063	0.097	0.189	0.256	0.167	0.228	1
HG	0.225	0.105	0.139	0.179	0.124	0.228	1
Gers	0.140	0.076	0.115	0.216	0.178	0.275	1
Lot	0.231	0.135	0.209	0.198	0.092	0.136	1
HP	0.285	0.158	0.222	0.203	0.074	0.058	1
Tarn	0.184	0.085	0.131	0.209	0.174	0.217	1
TG	0.201	0.106	0.180	0.255	0.114	0.143	1
Average	0.194	0.106	0.171	0.211	0.130	0.189	1

Table 4.40. *Table of row profiles*

If, in the figure, we take the departments from left to right, namely Gers, Aver., Tarn, HG, Ariè., TG, Lot and HP, we can observe, in Table 4.40, that those which are more to the right, HP, Lot, TG, in this order, are made up primarily of small farms, while those that are more to the left, Gers, Aver., Tarn, consist mainly of large farms, still in the right order. Thus, the order of the departments has close links with the size of the farms.

Still examining the table of row profiles, we see that close departments, for example (TG, Lot), have distribution profiles of the number of farms with a specific size that are similar.

Conversely, for the "distant" departments (Aver., HP) or (Gers, HP), we observe that their profiles are very different.

For the departments and close farms, for example (Gers, SUP50), we want to make sure that the closeness has meaning. For this, we have to study the row and column profiles tables, the latter of which is represented in Table 4.41.

	INF05	S0510	S1020	S2035	S3550	SUP50	Average
Ariè.	0.066	0.043	0.060	0.043	0.047	0.062	0.054
Aver.	0.062	0.166	0.202	0.211	0.217	0.207	0.178
HG	0.174	0.141	0.117	0.116	0.126	0.163	0.139
Gers	0.125	0.117	0.111	0.161	0.209	0.226	0.158
Lot	0.147	0.149	0.144	0.105	0.077	0.080	0.117
HP	0.160	0.154	0.135	0.095	0.055	0.030	0.105
Tarn	0.134	0.108	0.104	0.128	0.168	0.146	0.131
TG	0.132	0.121	0.128	0.140	0.099	0.087	0.118
Sum	1	1	1	1	1	1	1

Table 4.41. *Table of column profiles*

Regarding the close link (Gers, SUP50), we read on the row profile that there are 27.5% of holdings in Gers with a size greater than 50 ha; this is the modality with the highest score. A reading of the column profile shows that 22.6% of SUP50 holdings are in Gers; again, this is the highest score. It is clear that Gers is the department in which we find most holdings of SUP50 size.

Finally, there are departments that are distant from the farmlands (HP, SUP50). In this case, it is observed that in the Hautes-Pyrénées, there are only 5.8% of holdings >50 ha and only 3% of farmlands >50 ha are found in the Hautes-Pyrénées.

In the examples that we have considered, the closeness between departments, between farmlands or between departments and farmlands that appear on the graph are confirmed by the review of different tables. This seems normal, because the modalities concerned are all correctly represented in the first factorial plane, which has retained nearly 95% of the initial information.

Conclusion: The interpretation of the graph should be complemented by the data of the different tables (contributions to the axes, contribution to χ^2, squared cosines, etc.). The row and column profiles must first be examined because they contain most of the information. Finally, we have to be cautious when the modalities observed are poorly represented in the factorial plane, in this case, simple observation of the graph could lead to wrong conclusions.

4.2.3. *Factorial multiple correspondence analysis*

4.2.3.1. *Overview*

We have just presented the FCA, often described as simple or binary, the purpose of which is to highlight the links between the modalities of two qualitative variables. Often, when processing surveys or questionnaires, more than two qualitative variables are taken into account and it is natural to attempt establishing links between the modalities of $P > 2$ qualitative variables. The FCA cannot address these situations, so we have to use another approach: the FMCA.

There are two methods for carrying out an FMCA. The first consists of performing an FCA on the Burt table and the second is applying a PCA to a complete disjunctive table. To this end, it is necessary, following use of the software, to enter the Burt table or the complete disjunctive table or, more simply, to directly enter the Individuals/Variables [I/V] table, the software transforms it into the Burt or complete disjunctive table. These two tables are defined in the subsequent sections. Carrying out an FMCA requires the implementation either of an FCA or PCA, whose theoretical bases have already been presented.

The way the results of an FMCA are interpreted is identical to that of an FCA. However, some tables used for the FCA are no longer valid and, in view of the larger number of variables, the interpretation of results is more delicate. A good mastery of the FMCA requires more practicing of the method than mathematical knowledge.

Below, after presenting Burt and complete disjunctives tables, we will present an example of a very simple toy made with XLSTAT software, which enables the use of a complete disjunctive table.

4.2.3.2. Burt table

We imagined a "fictional" survey conducted in a high school; it is based on success in the baccalaureate (bac). The number of individuals involved is 220 and three variables are taken into account: bac series with three modalities (L, SES, S); gender with two modalities (G, B); age of graduation with three modalities (18 and below, 19, 20 and above).

First, the data are collected in an [I/V] table that contains 220 rows and three columns, one for each of the variables. From this table, we can develop three contingency tables that combine the three variables taken in pairs: (gender, bac series); (gender, graduation age); (bac series, graduation age). Below are the three contingency tables that we developed.

	H	F	Total
L	25	35	60
SES	45	55	100
S	35	25	60
Total	105	115	220

	H	F	Total
18	40	60	100
19	50	40	90
20	15	15	30
Total	105	115	220

	L	SES	S	Total
18	20	50	30	100
19	30	35	25	90
20	10	15	5	30
Total	60	100	60	220

Table 4.42. *Contingency table: gender/bac series, gender/graduation age, bac series/graduation age*

When there are more than three variables, there are more than three contingency tables. For example, if there were four variables, we would have six contingency tables.

From the three tables, we can develop the corresponding Burt table by comparing all the modalities in rows and columns as shown below.

	H	F	L	SES	S	18	19	20
H	105	0	25	45	35	40	50	15
F	0	115	35	55	25	60	40	15
L	25	35	60	0	0	20	30	10
SES	45	55	0	100	0	50	35	15
S	35	25	0	0	60	30	25	5
18	40	60	20	50	30	100	0	0
19	50	40	30	35	25	0	90	0
20	15	15	10	15	5	0	0	30

Table 4.43. *Burt table: gender/bac series/graduation age*

It then suffices to enter this table in the software by following the instructions given by the corresponding tutorial and to analyze the results as in the case of an FCA. But we have to be careful because as has already been mentioned, the analysis is sometimes difficult and requires practice.

4.2.3.3. *Complete disjunctive table*

A complete disjunctive table is an [I/V] table, which has as many rows as individuals and as many columns as the modalities for all variables. Each of the boxes, which compares an individual and a modality of a variable, contains either 1 when the modality corresponds to the individual or 0 if otherwise.

A complete disjunctive table can be very large. This is why we have taken a very simple case, "toy", with the purpose to both illustrate the development of the table and to then carry out the corresponding FMCA.

In a tasting of eight wines, each wine is considered as an individual. Three variables are taken into account to characterize each wine: "Origin" with two modalities Bordeaux and Rhône; "Color" with three modalities red, white and rosé; and "appreciation" with four modalities bad, average, good and very good. The tasting result is represented in the complete disjunctive table below:

I/V	Red	White	Rosé	Bordeaux	Rhône	Bad	Average	Good	Very good
11	0	1	0	1	0	0	0	0	1
12	0	1	0	1	0	0	0	1	0
13	0	1	0	0	1	1	0	0	0
14	0	0	1	0	1	0	0	1	0
15	1	0	0	1	0	0	1	0	0
16	0	0	1	1	0	0	1	0	0
17	0	0	1	0	1	1	0	0	0
18	1	0	0	0	1	0	0		0

Table 4.44. *[I/V] complete disjunctive table*

We can read, for example, that wine I5 is red Bordeaux and its appreciation is "average".

4.2.3.4. *Example: wine tasting*

For our school case presented above, we carry out the FMCA of the complete disjunctive table with the XLSTAT software. We will simply analyze the graph returned by the software and characterize each of the quadrants. The software works from the disjunctive table and carries out a PCA of the table, and thus on the graph, we find the individuals (wines) alongside the modalities.

We will, in this very simple case, try to see whether there is a real link between the modalities displayed on the graph and the individuals close to these modalities.

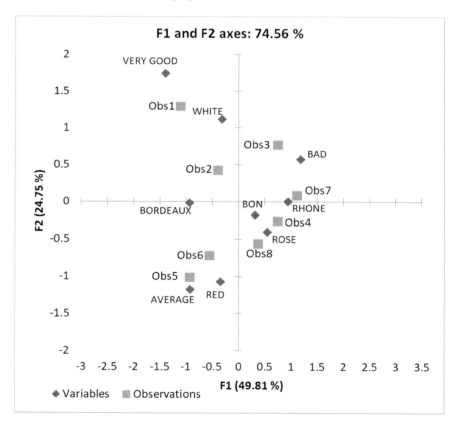

Figure 4.19. *Graphical representation in the first factorial plane: origin and nature of wine/wine quality*

4.2.3.4.1. Some observations

The first factorial plane contains 74.56% of the information contained in the initial cloud, which is correct, but caution still has to be observed.

– We distinguish on the one hand the individuals (wines) and modalities of the variables. We can observe that Bordeaux wines are all on the left and Rhône wines on the right. The origin of the wines seems to be contained in the F1 axis.

– The first quadrant contains the modalities "bad" and Rhône and obs3 and obs7 are Rhône wines, which have obtained the appreciation "bad".

– The second quadrant is characterized by the modalities "Bordeaux", "very good" and "white". Obs1 and obs2 are white Bordeaux wines but only Obs1 had the appreciation "very good".

– The third quadrant contains the modalities "Bordeaux", "red", "average". Obs5 and obs7 are Bordeaux wines, obs5 is red wine but obs6 is rosé wine. Yet, both were appreciated as average.

– Finally, the fourth quadrant contains the modalities Rhône, "rosé" and "good". Both wines, obs4 and obs8, are Rhône wines that were appreciated as good. Meanwhile, only obs4 is rosé wine.

We can conclude that there are links between the positions of modalities and individuals, but there are some poorly represented modalities. Thus, simply reading the graph can lead to partially erroneous interpretations. This gives us reason to be cautious and confirms that the analysis of an FMCA is delicate and requires experience.

5

Statistical Modeling

A population comprising N individuals is characterized by variables $q+1$. The purpose of statistical modeling is to show the relation between a variable (Y) known as an explained variable and other variables q known as explanatory variables. The relation takes the form of Y function $= f(X)$ when we have a single explanatory variable and it becomes generalized in the case of explanatory variables q. Such a relation makes it possible to predict the value of Y corresponding to the different values of explanatory variables. This is how we have a model from which the name statistical modeling originates.

The statistical modeling approach generally comprises three steps: determining the link (of the function), assessing the accuracy of the prediction (confidence interval) and determining the explicativity of the model.

If the population is large, the link between the variables cannot be established by working directly on the population, so we start by working on a representative sample, and then, using mathematical developments, we establish conditions for the extension of the law to the entire population.

The determined law is not an exact law if one has to consider the uncertainties and errors when collecting samples as well as those that occur during the passing of the sample to the population. Thus, it is necessary to evaluate the accuracy of the prediction by introducing the notion of confidence interval.

Finally, the existence of a law between the explained variable and explanatory variables s does not tell us if the explanatory variables selected explain all the variations of the explained variable. Should other variables be introduced? Can some be ignored? This is the last step that should be taken.

Statistical modeling can address situations with variables of different natures. The most frequent case is where the explained variable and explanatory variables are numerical variables. However, it is possible to have one or more nominal explanatory variables. The case of the nominal explained variable is seldom addressed: it is referred to as logistic regression.

Statistical modeling makes it possible to take linear or nonlinear dependencies into account, classify the variables, multilevel approach or take into account interactions between explanatory variables.

These different situations will be explained in the six sections of this chapter, but not all of them will be analyzed; for the completion of the approach, we recommend reading this specialized book, *Modélisation statistique appliquée aux sciences sociales* by Pascal Bressoux at De Boeck (2010), which is our main reference for this section.

5.1. Simple bivariate linear modeling

5.1.1. *Problem statement*

We start with the simplest case: bivariate linear modeling. Most of the notions in the approach that we will describe are generalized to more complex situations that will be discussed later. Also, an in-depth reading of this section is strongly recommended.

That is, a population of N individuals, usually N large. We want to know if there is a linear relation between two quantitative variables, X and Y, which characterize the individuals that make up the population. The sought relation is of conventional generic form:

$$\hat{Y} = \alpha X + \beta$$

α and β are the linear coefficients of the straight line (slope and y-intercept), $\hat{Y}$ is the value predicted by the law for a given value of the variable X. The relation written in this form shows that the two variables do not play the same role. Y is the explained variable while X is the explanatory variable. When such a law can be established, it does not describe the exact link between X and Y for all individuals of the population. For an individual i from whom the values Xi and Yi were taken, we will have the following relation:

$$Yi = \alpha Xi + \beta + \varepsilon i,$$

where εi is a random error term. Simultaneously, it is based on the fact that the variables collected from individuals are random in nature, but also on the fact that the values of α and β are not rigorously determined; they are, as shall be demonstrated later, simply estimated, because it is not possible to collect data on the entire population, and one must be contented to work on a supposedly representative sample. The choice of the sample itself is random and if another sample was chosen, then the results obtained would certainly be different.

After showing how to calculate the regression equation for the population (section 5.1.2), we explain how to evaluate the accuracy of the model (section 5.1.3), and finally we raise the question of its explicativity (section 5.1.4).

5.1.2. Determining the regression line in the population

Here, $\hat{Y} = \alpha X + \beta$ or $Yi = \alpha Xi + \beta + \varepsilon i$ sought a linear equation linking the two variables X and Y within the population. The parameters α and β are not known and we do not have any information about the random error terms εi. In addition, we only have data from a sample, so the process begins with determining the regression line that best expresses the link between the two variables at the sample level. Hypotheses will be formulated to enable an estimate of the regression line parameters for the population.

5.1.2.1. Determining the equation of the regression line in the sample

We begin by determining the equation of the straight line (D) closest to the point cloud associated with the individuals in the sample. This presentation may also be useful when the study is limited to the observation of a sample.

A data table for the selected sample is presented in Table 5.1.

Individuals	X	Y
1.	X1	Y1
.....	.....	.....
i	Xi	Xi
.....	.....	.....
n	Xn	Yn

Table 5.1. *Bivariate generic table [I/V]*

In a plane (X, Y), each individual (Mi) can be represented by coordinates (Xi, Yi). The set of individuals form a point cloud that is representative of the sample. The straight line (D) closest to the point clouds is the equation being calculated.

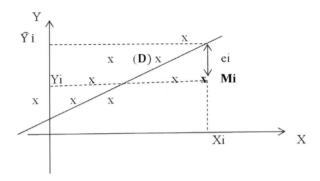

Figure 5.1. *Point clouds and regression line for a sample*

The points of the clouds, even if they are close, except otherwise, do not belong to the line. For this purpose, we define for each individual, Mi (Yi, Xi) the quantity $ei = \hat{Y}i - Yi$, algebraic vertical distance from point Mi on the line (D), where $\hat{Y}i$ is, for the sample, the value of Y "predicted" by the equation of (D) when the variable X is equal to Xi.

The equation of the sought line has the form: $\hat{Y} = aX + b$ or $Yi = aXi + b + ei$ for an individual point i.

In order to avoid confusion between the sample and population, we write the linear coefficients as a and b and error terms as ei, with Latin letters, whereas for the population, we have and will continue to use the Greek letters α, β and ε.

To calculate the equation of (D), we use the least squares method that looks for the values of a and b that minimize the quantity RSS = $\sum_{i=1}^{n} e_i^2$ (residual sum of squares (RSS)), which adds the squares of the vertical distances of the points of the cloud on the line (D). The fact that the term RSS is minimum assures us that (D) is the line closest to the point clouds. RSS is a measurement of the quality of the representation , if RSS = 0, all the points are on line (D) and the representation is perfect and at most RSS is large and at the most the quality degrades.

Here the distance to the right is not the Euclidean distance (normal to the right) but the vertical distance from the point to the right. In this case, the line closest to the point clouds is the one that minimizes the vertical distance to the line, and thus optimizes the quality of the prediction of Y.

5.1.2.1.1. For those interested

To determine a and b, we have to solve the system of two equations with two unknowns, $\frac{\partial RSS}{\partial a} = 0$ and $\frac{\partial RSS}{\partial b} = 0$; the first indicates that the derivative of RSS, with respect to the slope (a), of the line is zero and the second shows that the derivative of RSS, with respect to the ordinate at the origin (b), is zero. Thus, the two equations are verified if and only if the two coefficients a and b are such that the RSS is minimal.

For all

After some calculations, the least squares method gives us the linear coefficients of the line closest to the point clouds:

$$a = \frac{Cov(X,Y)}{Var(X)} \qquad b = \overline{Y} - \frac{Cov(X,Y)}{Var(X)}\overline{X}$$

For the values recorded on the sample, we can recognize: the variance of X, covariance of X and Y and mean values $\overline{X}$ and $\overline{Y}$ variables X and Y. In order not to weigh down the presentation, much emphasis has not been laid on the calculation of these terms, because all software and spreadsheets directly provide the values of linear coefficients of the line, which are assorted to other valuable information as we shall demonstrate.

EXAMPLE.– We have presented two fictitious situations to illustrate the approach. The objective is to determine the link between students' grades in mathematics and physics, on the one hand, and mathematics and history–geography on the other hand. As we shall see, the first link is of quality while the second is not.

The variables (mean grade in math, physics and HG) are collected on students in a class of 12 grade 10 students, which is supposed to be representative of the 10th grade student population of the academy.

In both cases, the grade in mathematics (Y) is the variable to be explained, while the grade in physics, on the one hand, and the grade in history–geography, on the other hand, are the explanatory variables (X).

– *"Mathematics/physics" case*

Students	Physics	Math
1	10	10
2	14	15
3	8	8
4	9	9
5	18	19
6	3	2
7	14	14
8	6	5
9	5	4
10	8	8
11	3	2
12	4	1

Table 5.2. *Data table [I/V] – physics/math*

When observing the students' cloud in plane X, Y, we realize that the points are properly distributed around a line. The Excel spreadsheet returns the equation of the line closest to the point clouds and its representation in the plane (X, Y).

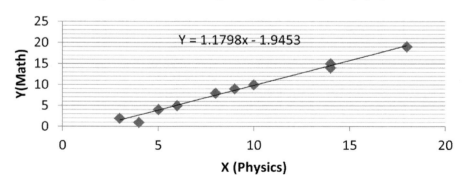

Figure 5.2. *Math/physics regression line for sample*

a and *b* can also be directly calculated by directly using the calculation functions of the Excel spreadsheet, and the following will be obtained:

$\overline{Y} = 8.5$ $\overline{X} = 8.08$

$\text{Var}(X) = 23$ $\text{Cov}(X, Y) = 27.1363$

thus:

$$a = \frac{27.1363}{23} = 1.1798 \qquad b = 8.5 - 1.1798 \times 8.08 = -1.9453$$

We find the equation of the line closest to the point clouds for the math/physics cases as returned by the Excel spreadsheet.

$\widehat{Math} = -1.9453 + 1.1798 \times \text{physics}$

– *"Mathematics/history–geography" case*

Students	HG	Math
1	8	10
2	4	15
3	4	8
4	12	9
5	13	19
6	15	2
7	14	14
8	6	5
9	7	4
10	3	8
11	2	2
12	4	1

Table 5.3. *Data table [IV]: HG/math*

Observation of the point clouds shows a great dispersion of the points. In this, it is not possible to say that there is a linear dependence, but at most, there is a trend.

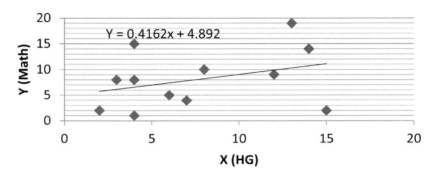

Figure 5.3. *Math/HG regression line for sample*

However, despite the dispersion of points, one can always determine the equation of the line closest to a point cloud.

The equation of the line as returned by Excel is: $\widehat{\text{Math}} = 0.4162 \times \text{HG} + 4.8925$.

5.1.2.2. *From sample to population: α and β estimate, sampling statistics*

We have seen how to determine the equation of the linear regression line between two variables X and Y for a given sample. If another sample had been selected, other values would have been obtained for coefficients a and b. But what we are interested in now is to know what values to give the linear coefficients α and β for the population.

This type of problem is addressed by sampling statistic; we shall present the outlines without going into any further details, just what is needed to understand the logic of its theoretical foundations.

Based on sampling statistics, it is assumed that n samples (1, ..., k, ..., n) can be extracted randomly from the entire population. For a specific sample k, there are regression equations:

$$\widehat{Y^k} = a^k X + b^k \text{ or } Y_i^k = a^k X_i + b^k + e_{xi}^k$$

The indexed variables k are random, according to sampling statistic, that is, they differ from one sample to another, but we consider that X is fixed, we are the ones choosing it, and so X is not random. This justifies the change in writing for the error term that appears here as being associated with a given value of Xi and a sample k. Under these conditions, the following random variables can be defined in the sense of sampling statistics:

$A = (a^1, ..., a^k, ..., a^n)$

$B = (b^1, ..., b^k, ..., b^n)$

And for a fixed value of Xi: $E_{Xi} = (e_{xi}^1, ..., e_{xi}^k, ..., e_{xi}^n)$.

For the entire population, we have $\hat{Y} = \alpha X + \beta$, where $\hat{Y}$ is the predicted (explained) value of Y for a given value of X; we can also say that it is the most probable value. This can be seen for each individual i of the population by the relation Yi = αXi + β + εi, where Yi and Xi are the variables that were taken from each individual. The term εi = $\hat{Y}$ − Yi is the random term related to the ignorance of all active variables and history of the individual *i*. The problem is that at this stage, α and β are unknown but we will see that an estimate can be given under certain conditions. For this purpose, we define, within the context of sampling statistics, a new notion, mathematical expectation. For example, the mathematical expectation of A denoted by E(A) is the expected mean of terms a^k over a number *n* of samples tending to infinity.

It is mathematically proven that if *n* is very large, then E (A) = α and also E (B) = β. This means that if one calculates regression lines n, one for each sample k, and if n was infinitely large, then the average value of a^k would tend to α, and likewise, the average value of b^k would tend to β. Moreover, it is established that the sampling variances of A (Var (A)) and B (Var (B)) tend to 0 when N tends to infinity. *It is said that any couple* (a^k, b^k) *constitutes a convergent unbiased estimate of α and β.* More concretely, this means that the values of *ak* and *bk* revolve around the unknown target values α and β.

For those who might face some difficulties in understanding, all the above can be summarized by saying that under these conditions, we can use a and b calculated based on the sample to estimate α and β.

But if we can choose the estimation α = a and β = b, we will have to support this choice, the question that arises: if I choose the two specific values *a* and *b*, then what is the quality (accuracy) of representation for the population?

5.1.3. *Quality of representation: confidence and prediction interval*

5.1.3.1. *Proven existence of the regression line*

The uncertainties inherent in data as well as the process compel us to check the quality, and first of all the existence of the regression line applied to the entire population.

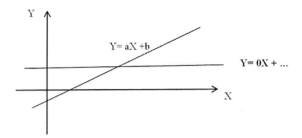

Figure 5.4. *Existence of the regression line in the population*

To assess the quality of the representation obtained by estimating α and β using linear coefficients *a* and *b*, we begin by performing a statistical test to decide between the following contradictory hypotheses:

– H_0: the slope of the line is zero;

– H_1: the slope of the line is equal to *a*.

If the slope of the line is zero (H_0), it is horizontal and, whatever the value of X, Y always maintains the same value. X has no influence on Y and in this case there is no possible regression line in the population. In the opposite case (H1), if the existence of the slope a $\neq$ 0 is proven, there is certainly a regression line.

Software programs return the confirmatory test result to decide between H_0 and H_1. Some perform the Student's test by comparing the slope a to zero, which corresponds to the case of a horizontal line. The XLSTAT software that we used returned, for its part, the results of a Fisher's test (F) to account for the existence of the representation.

As for the two examples that serve as a guide, we obtained the following:

– *For the math/physics case*

Analysis of variance (math):

Source	ddl	Sum of squares	Mean squares	F	Pr > F
Model	1	352.183	352.183	743.965	<0.0001
Error	10	4.734	0.473		
Adjusted total	11	356.917			

Table 5.4. *Results returned by the XLSTAT software: math variance*

With the conclusion:

"Given the *P*-value associated with the statistic F calculated in the variance analysis table, and given the 5% level of significance chosen, the information provided by the explanatory variables is significantly better compared to what the only mean of the dependent variable would explain".

The test used clearly states that, given a *P*-value <0.0001, we reject H_0 and adopt H_1. So it validates the existence of a quality regression line that links math grades and physics grades.

– For the math/HG case

Analysis of variance (math)					
Source	ddl	Sum of squares	Mean squares	F	Pr > F
Model	1	41.343	41.343	1.310	0.279
Error	10	315.574	31.557		
Adjusted total	11	356.917			

Table 5.5. *Results returned by the XLSTAT software: math/HG variance*

With the following comment:

"Given the *P*-value associated with the F statistic calculated in the variance analysis table, and given the 5% level of significance chosen, the explanatory variables do not provide information to the model compared to what the only mean of the dependent variable would provide. The fact that the variables do not provide meaningful information to the model can be interpreted in different ways: either the variables do not contribute to the explanation of the model, or Co variables that are combined with the already existing variables are lacking, or the shape of the model is not correct, or the data are vitiated by errors".

In other words, it is asserted that given the *P*-value = 0.279, we must maintain hypothesis H_0, thus the existence of the regression line is not proven.

However, the fact that the regression line is proven or not at the population level does not fully inform us of the accuracy that can be expected of the representation within the population. For this purpose and based on what follows, we propose that this problem be addressed by using the notions of confidence interval and prediction interval.

5.1.3.2. *Accuracy of regression line: confidence interval*

The confidence interval is a measurement of the accuracy of predictions provided by the regression line; it is represented as $\Delta (X_0)$. Thus, the most likely value (mean value) of Y for the value X_0 of the explanatory variable belongs to the interval $\Delta(X_0)$ of the mean value predicted by the regression line:

$$Y \in [aX_0 + b] \mp \Delta(X_0)$$

This means that the actual value of Y is given with an uncertainty range of $\mp\Delta(X_0)$ on the predicted value of variable Y.

Determining confidence interval: Complex mathematical bases are used to determine the confidence interval. We shall only present the starting point of the method and the framework of the hypotheses formulated. At the center of the problem is the "random error variable", according to sampling statistics, for the given value of Xi. It consists, for each of the random samples, of the error terms for the given value of Xi.

Hypotheses on the "random error variable" are formulated as follows:

– the sampling mean of random errors is zero;

– the sampling variance of random errors is constant;

– the covariance of sampling errors for two values (Xi and Xj) is zero;

– for each value of Xi, the random variable E_{ε^2/x_i} follows a normal distribution with mean zero and σ^2 N $(0, \sigma^2)$.

It is this last hypothesis that concludes the model. Considering these hypotheses, a heavy and complex calculation during which it was necessary to express, in particular, Var (A), Var (B), Cov (A, B) according to the explanatory variable Xi, the following relation was obtained:

$$\Delta (X_0) = t_{\theta/2} \, s_e \sqrt{(X_0 - \bar{X})^2 / \sum_1^n (X_i - \bar{X})^2 + 1/n},$$

where n is the sample size, $\bar{X}$ is the mean of Xi values taken from the sample, $t_{\theta/2}$ is Student's t at (n – 2) degrees of freedom for an accepted risk of θ and $s_e = \sqrt{SCR/(n-2)}$, where RSS is the RSS defined previously.

The value of $t_{\theta/2}$ is read directly from Student's statistical table and it depends on the percentage of risk accepted. Generally, the accepted risk is 0.05 and in this case $t_{\theta/2} = 1.96$. If the accepted risk is different, then the value of $t_{\theta/2}$ is no longer the same.

The relation that defines the confidence interval shows that if the sample size n increases, then the interval decreases. On the contrary, the confidence interval increases if the RSS recorded from the sample increases.

The following figure illustrates that if we accept a risk of being misled to less importance (3% instead of 5%), then the confidence interval increases. At least one wishes to take higher risk when the interval is large.

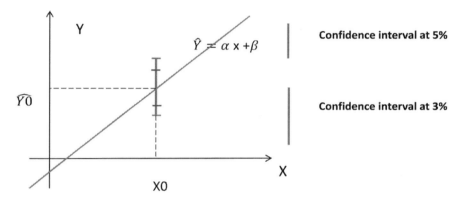

Figure 5.5. *Confidence interval at 5% and 3%. For a color version of this figure, see www.iste.co.uk/larini/education.zip*

– Prediction interval

Confidence interval expresses the confidence one can have in the regression line that provides an estimate of the mean of distribution of Y. It is also possible to look for the uncertainty related to a single case, that is estimating accuracy for a single observation. In this case, it is referred to as the prediction interval and the sought value of Y is no longer the most likely mean value, so it has its own fluctuations and these are added to those already taken into account when calculating the confidence interval.

The following is obtained under these conditions:

$$Y \in [aX_0 + b] \mp \Delta'(X_0)$$

with:

$$\Delta'(X_0) = t_{\theta/2}\, s_e \sqrt{1 + (X_0 - \bar{X})^2 / \sum_1^n (X_i - \bar{X})^2 + 1/n}$$

For example, let us go back to our two previously contemplated situations on the link between math and physics grades, on the one hand, and mathematics and history–geography grades, on the other hand. We present for these two cases the main figure returned by the XLSTAT software. First, there are the representative points of each of the individuals, but also the regression line (Model (Math), the confidence interval band at 5% (referred to as "conf. int. (mean 95%)" and that of the interval prediction at 5% referred to as "conf. int. (Obs 95%)". Here the term confidence interval is used both for the prediction of the mean value and for the value relative to an observation.

In the "math/physics" case for a given physics grade value, the most likely value of the math grade is within the band delimited by two dotted curves. For specific information, it lies within the band delimited by the curves in continuous lines, which is always wider than that relating to the confidence interval. The same applies to the "mathematics/history–geography" case.

In any case, the highest accuracy is for $X_0 = \bar{X}$, that is when the selected value of X is equal to the mean value of Xi on the sample.

– *"Mathematics/physics"*

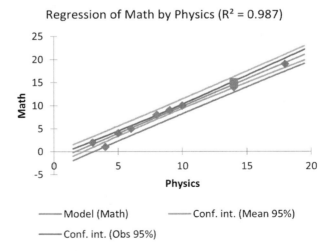

Regression of Math by Physics ($R^2 = 0.987$)

Figure 5.6. *Math/physics confidence interval and prediction interval. For a color version of this figure, see www.iste.co.uk/larini/education.zip*

– *"Mathematics/history–geography" case*

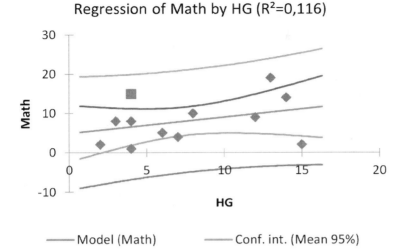

Regression of Math by HG (R²=0,116)

Figure 5.7. *Math/HG confidence interval and prediction interval. For a color version of this figure, see www.iste.co.uk/larini/education.zip*

The figures indicate that the two situations, at the level of the population, produce results that are very different. For the math/physics case, we have a very small margin of error on regression, so it is possible to make quality predictions. However, the math/HG case, for which it is recalled that the Fisher's test resulted in the conservation of the H_0 hypothesis (even though the representation exists), margins of error are wider. Moreover, there are doubts with regard to the relevance of regression; it is therefore advisable to use it with great caution or better to not use it.

5.1.4. *Explanatory power of the model*

We have just seen how to appreciate the accuracy of a linear relation that can exist between an explanatory variable X and an explained variable Y within a population. The question now arises as to what is the explanatory power d of the model found. Most often, a phenomenon depends on several variables and moreover the function that binds them is not necessarily linear. Thus, frequently, the relation found, even if it seems of good quality, only partly explains the variations of variable Y. The notions of accuracy and explicativity do not overlap completely, they complement each other; the fact that a representation is accurate does not guarantee the significance of the relation. In this section, we shall see how to express the explanatory power of a bivariate linear model. The method will be extended later to the case of several explanatory variables.

We start by defining the coefficient of determination R^2 whose value measures the explanatory power of a regression:

$$R^2 = 1 - \frac{\Sigma_i(Y_i - \widehat{Y_i})^2}{\Sigma_i(Y_i - \bar{Y})^2},$$

where Y_i are the values of the explained variable taken from the sample for the value X_i of the explanatory variable, $\widehat{Y_i}$ is the value of Y predicted by the model for the same value of X_i and $\bar{Y}$ is the mean value of Y_i. We find these variables in Figure 5.8.

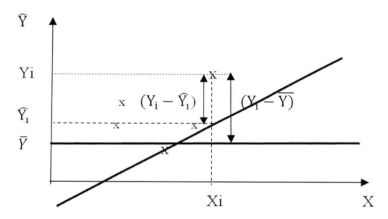

Figure 5.8. *Parameter involved in the explanatory power of the model*

The minimum value of $\Sigma_i(Y_i - \widehat{Y_i})^2$ is 0 and this corresponds to the perfect case where all the points of the cloud will be on the line. In this case, it can be said that the variable X fully explains the variable Y.

The maximum value of $\Sigma_i(Y_i - \widehat{Y_i})^2$ is $\Sigma_i(Y_i - \bar{Y})^2$, this corresponds to a case for which, whatever the value of X_i, Y will take the value $\bar{Y}$. In this case, there is no connection between the two variables: we say that X does not explain the variable Y.

So the value of R^2 varies between 0 and 1. At most, R^2 is close to 1 and at best X explains the variations of Y. Conversely, at most R^2 is close to 0 and at least X explains the variations of Y.

NOTE.– It is shown that the coefficient of determination, in the bivariate case, can be connected to already introduced basic variables. As a matter of fact:

$$Cor(X, Y) = \sqrt{R^2} \quad \text{and} \quad R^2 = a^2 \frac{Var(X)}{Var(Y)},$$

where a is the slope of the regression line.

EXAMPLE.– Here, we go back to our two examples. The coefficient of determination R^2 is returned directly by the XLSTAT software (Figures 5.6 and 5.7) and it is equally returned by the Excel spreadsheet when looking for the regression line of a point cloud.

For the mathematics/physics case, $R^2 = 0.987$. This means that the physics grade explains 98.7% of the mathematics grade, which is close to the ideal case. Thus, the representation is accurate and its explanatory power is big. This certainly means that the skills in the two subjects fall under the same logic.

For the mathematics/history–geography case, $R^2 = 0.116$. The history–geography grade only explains 11.6% of the mathematics grade and representation of the regression line is not accurate. This means that the skills in these two subjects do not pertain to the same logic. Thus, the HG grade is not enough to explain the mathematics mark. To improve on prediction, other explanatory variables need to be added and, using a generalized R^2, at more than two dimensions, the improvement that each of them contributes to the model needs to be tested.

5.2. Multiple linear regressions for quantitative explanatory variables

5.2.1. *Overview*

We shall now consider the case of multivariate linear regression for quantitative variables. The general theoretical principles were discussed in section 5.1, namely seeking for a representative function, accuracy of the representation and explicativity of the found law. These are the same principles for multivariate approaches; we shall not expatiate on these principles, as it will be enough to rely on a little more imagination in order to extend them to a number of explanatory variables greater than one.

At the end of this section, we shall briefly show, using an example, how it is possible to progressively build, by gradually adding variables, a more explanatory model.

The simplest case, which comes after the bivariate modeling, is the trivariate modeling for which we still have a graphic representation of the approach. This is why we start by mentioning this situation that, however, is representative of all multivariate cases.

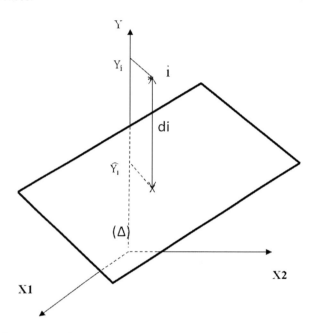

Figure 5.9. *Graphical representation for a trivariate problem*

Y is the variable to be explained and X1 and X2 are the two explanatory variables. Instead of looking for a straight line, we look for a plane (Δ) in a three-dimensional space. It is such that it minimizes the vertical distances "di" between point i of the cloud that represents the individuals in the sample. Its equation has the form: $Y = a_1X1 + a_2X2 + b$ and the coefficients a_1, a_2 and b are determined by the least squares method from data collected from the representative sample. The principle is the same as for the bivariate case but the calculations are more complex and we overlook them.

For each individual i, we have:

$$Yi = a_1 X1i + a_2 X2i + b + ei$$

with:

$$ei = \widehat{Yi} - Yi$$

Yi, X1i and X2i are the coordinates of the individual i in space, and $\widehat{Yi}$ is the value predicted by the regression equation for the values X1i and X2i of the two explanatory variables.

In this case, we shall limit our presentation to the analysis of the results returned by the software programs, and we used the SPHINX software to address an example concerning "graduation from school".

5.2.2. *Example: graduation from school*

We are resuming a study that we have already presented in chapter 4 on principal component analysis. It is a research work in sociology in which "the transition of young people from the education system to the professional world" for nine European countries was studied.

The nine countries studied were as follows: Austria, Belgium, Spain, Finland, France, Greece, Hungary, Italy and Sweden. They are considered as the nine individuals from whom five variables were taken.

The five variables selected were:

– V11: average age of young people graduating from school;

– V12: average age for obtaining a primary or secondary certificate;

– V13: average age for obtaining a degree at the undergraduate or graduate level;

– V31: % of parents with a primary or secondary level of education;

– V33: % of parents with an undergraduate or postgraduate level of education.

The variables result from surveys of a large number of individuals in each country.

The data table collected is presented in Table 5.6.

Var Country	V11	V12	V13	V31	V33
Austria	19.9	18	24.7	27	19
Belgium	20.6	18.3	22.8	45	26
Spain	19.1	15.2	22.5	80	10
Finland	21.6	16.9	25.3	21	36
France	20.8	17.9	23.2	51	15
Greece	19.4	14.5	23.3	66	9
Hungary	18.3	14.9	23.1	26	13
Italy	18.4	14.6	25	68	6
Sweden	23.9	22.6	26.4	26	36

Table 5.6. *Data table [I/V]: graduation from school in nine European countries*

Although this study was not organized for this, we propose to examine the extent to which it is possible to check, for all nine European countries (individuals), whether there is a law that explains the average age of young people (V11) graduating from school based on the four explanatory variables V12, V13, V31 and V33. The nine countries are considered as individuals.

In order to answer this question, we directly incorporated the above data table into the SPHINX software.

This is part of the results returned by the SPHINX software with some comments:

– *Multiple linear regression*

Linear regression consists of calculating the equation that enables a more accurate calculation of the value of the variable to be explained.

Thus, the following can be determined:

1) variables that have no influence. They are not represented in the equation;

2) the contribution of other variables. It measures their influence on the explanatory variable.

Survey: Number of complete observations: nine of a total of nine observations. Estimation of the value of the variable: V11 from the variables: V12, V13, V31, V33.

– *Non-influential variables*: Two variables do not contribute to explanation (at 5% threshold): V13, V31.

NOTE.– Software indicates that variables V13 and V31 have no statistically significant actions on variable V11.

– *Influential variables*: Two variables contribute to explanation (at 5% threshold): V12, V33.

Equation of the model:

$$V11 = 12.22 + 0.40 \times V12 + 0.06 \times V33$$

	Coefficient	P-value	Standardized coefficient	Contribution
Const.	12.22	<0.01	–	–
V12	0.40	0.03	0.59	58.73
V33	0.06	0.09	0.41	41.27

Table 5.7. *Coefficient of explanatory variables of the regression model: actual weight of explanatory variables*

NOTE.– The coefficients of the regression model (0.40 and 0.06) do not tell us about the actual weight of variables V12 and V33 on the variation of V11. It is for this reason that the software calculates the standardized coefficients that provide the real contribution of explanatory variables on the variation of the variable V11. Thus, V12 contributes 59% to the variation of V11 and V33 contributes up to 41%.

The P-values relative to the coefficients of the regression equation indicate a 5% probability risk of being misled by accepting the values calculated for each coefficient. This is a calculation comparable to the one presented in the previous section.

– *Quality indicator of the model*

The model accounts for 89.94% of the variance of the variable to be explained.

– Multiple correlation coefficient: R = 0.95.

– P-value of R: p (R) = <0.01.

– Fisher coefficient: F = 26.81.

– P-value of F: p (F) = <0.01.

NOTE.– The software indicated that the two variables V12 and V33 explain 89.94% of the variations of V11. Thus, only 10.06% of its variations can be explained otherwise.

The *P*-values returned by the software provide information on the confidence that can be given to the value of R obtained and to the regression equation taken as a whole using a Fisher test.

Representation of estimated Y

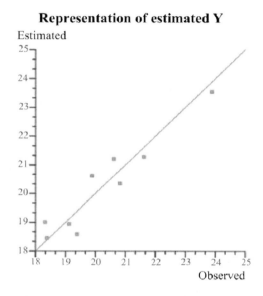

Figure 5.10. *Predicted Y (estimated) based on observed Y; ideally all points are strung together on the line (100% of the variable is explained)*

NOTE.– For multidimensional regression, representations equivalent to confidence intervals are not available. However, if predicted Y is drawn, by multiple correlation based on observed Y ($\hat{Y} = F(Y_{obs})$), this facilitates the visualization of the quality of the representation. No matter the regression function for a perfect representation, we must obtain a straight line and the more the points are scattered the lesser the quality of the representation. It is understood that the calculation of the linear correlation coefficient Cor ($\hat{Y}, Y_{obs}$) provides a good indication of the quality of the representation.

Such an approach is also possible for simple bivariate regression. It has the advantage of being easier to understand and implement, but it is less explicit than the representation by confidence intervals, and moreover, the interval depends on the explanatory variable X.

CONCLUSION OF THE CALCULATION.– It can be formally concluded that the data suggest that the age of graduating from school depends positively on the average age of primary or secondary school graduation and the percentage of parents who have an undergraduate or graduate level of education. However, no conclusions were drawn from it because it was not the purpose of the study.

5.2.3. Progressive development of a multivariate model

Let us go back to the previous study. It would have been logical to start by looking for the simplest relation(s) between variable V11 and other variables taken one by one. The following are the results obtained.

$$V11 = F(V12): \quad V11 = 9.74 + 0.62 \times V12 \quad\quad R^2 = 0.831$$

$$V11 = F(V33): \quad V11 = 17.66 + 0.14 \times V33 \quad\quad R^2 = 0.761$$

$$V11 = F(V13): \quad V11 = 1.00 + 0.80 \times V13 \quad\quad R^2 = 0.373$$

$$V11 = F(V31): \quad V11 = 22.06 - 4.0 \times 10^{-02} \times V31 \quad R^2 = 0.252$$

The first observation was that the last two relations clearly confirmed that the variations of V11 could not be well explained by the variations of V13 and V31, which is very much in line with the previous study.

It was noted that the first two relations correctly explained the variations of V11. However, one can question the fact that V11 strongly depends on both V12 and V33. This is certainly due to the fact that V12 and V33 are not independent of each other and that any variation of one must be accompanied by a variation of the other variable.

Now it makes sense to continue with the analysis and see if the multivariate model V11 = F (V12, V33) does not explain its variations even better. This is the result of the study of the previous section:

$$V11 = 12.22 + 0.40 \times V12 + 0.06 \times V33 \quad\quad R^2 = 0.90$$

This approach illustrates what the search for the best multivariate model could be in a more complex study context.

5.3. Modeling with qualitative explanatory variables

Taking into account a qualitative explanatory variable significantly expands the field of application of statistical modeling. For example, gender effects (M, F), group effects (control group, experimental group) and effects due to socioprofessional categories (managers, workers, secretaries, farmers, etc.) can be included.

This problem will be addressed by starting with the simplest case, quantitative explanatory variable and a dichotomous qualitative explanatory variable, that is two modalities. Subsequently, more complex situations will be discussed.

5.3.1. *Quantitative explanatory variable and dichotomous qualitative variable*

5.3.1.1. *Introduction*

To illustrate this situation, we consider a case encountered by many researchers when comparing the behavior of a control group and an experimental group.

The case presented is an adaptation of a work in progress at Université Aix-Marseille. We wanted to compare the effectiveness of a university education in mechanical engineering through "problem-based learning (PBL)" with a conventional education through classes, tutorials and practicum. In PBL, it is the students who must gather and/or acquire, on their own, the knowledge they need to solve a complete, more or less complex problem that is proposed to them. In addition, they organized themselves in small groups to develop a method in order to provide answers to the problem. This type of education is meant to promote self-employment and the ability to solve unguided complex problems.

On the basis of the same content to be acquired, we have two groups of students: the experimental group (EG) that follows PBL and the control group (CG) that follows conventional education. A quantitative indicator (X), between 0 and 1, obtained during a pretest, carried out before the training, made it possible to characterize the "level" of each student. After training, a complex unguided problem relating to the knowledge studied is proposed to each student in both groups. A quantitative indicator (Y), between 0 and 1, measured the mark scored by each student in this test.

Students who underwent a PBL program were expected to perform better in this type of test because they have been prepared compared to the control group. But is this the case for all students, regardless of their initial level? This is the research question that was asked.

The first approach to the problem is to compare separately the two regressions YEG = f(X) and YCG = g(X) obtained separately for each of the two groups. The second is to directly look for the relation of two explanatory variables Y = h (X, Gpe), where Gpe is a two-modality qualitative variable, EG and CG.

5.3.1.2. *Separate search for YEG and YCG*

The first idea that comes to mind is to separately carry out a simple regression of individuals from the experimental and control groups. This approach has not been criticized and the result below will serve as a reference.

Calculations using the XLSTAT software were as follows:

YEG = 0.95X – 0.08

YCG = 0.70X + 0.03

Figure 5.11 shows that for the students who did not obtain good marks on the level assessment test (X < 0.4), the results obtained for the control group are better than those of the experimental group. However, the trend is reversed for X > 0.4. The gap might go right up to 0.2 for the best. So we have a first answer to the question we asked: PBL is more effective for good students, but it seems to be disadvantageous to students with an inadequate initial level.

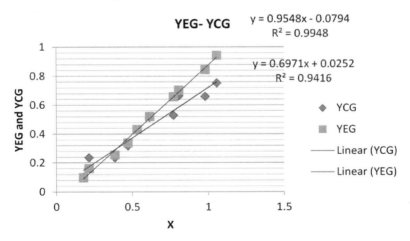

Figure 5.11. *YEG and YCG determined separately. For a color version of this figure, see www.iste.co.uk/larini/education.zip*

5.3.1.3. *Looking directly for the relation Y = h(X, Gpe)*

Now we were looking directly for the regression that linked the grade Y to both the initial level, X, of the students and group to which they belonged. For this reason, we introduced a new qualitative variable D (Dummy) that characterized the group to which the students belonged. Then, we looked for a function of type:

$$Y = a_1 X + a_2 D + b$$

Y is the quantitative variable to be explained, X is the explanatory quantitative variable and D is a qualitative variable. At this level, we had no other choice but to define D as a dummy variable such as D = 1 if the student belonged to the experimental group and D = 0 if the student belonged to the control group.

Calculation of the regression led to:

$$Y = 0.83X + 0.05D - 0.05$$

For each of the two groups:

$$YEG = 0.83X + 0 \text{ and } YCG = 0.83X - 0.05$$

For both groups, the lines had the same slope, they were parallel and they were distinguished only by their y-intercepts. Regardless of the initial level of students, the marks obtained by the experimental group were better by 0.05 points compared to those obtained by the control group. For our case, this result was not satisfactory. It did not show the crossing of the two lines highlighting that students in the experimental group, who obtained an initial grade X <0.4, were less successful than those in the control group.

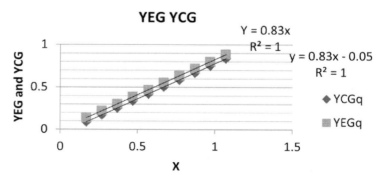

Figure 5.12. *YEG and YCG determined simultaneously*

To solve this problem, a model was needed in order to change the slope a_1. We have shown in section 5.4 that this is possible by introducing the notion of model with "interacting variables".

5.3.2. *Quantitative explanatory variable and polytomous qualitative variable*

We will discuss the case where the qualitative variable can have more than two modalities, it is said that it is polytomic. The method is an adaptation of the previous case where variable D had two modalities.

That is a group of n individuals, divided into J subgroups determined by a qualitative variable with j modalities. In this case, the variable Y to be explained depends on the quantitative explanatory variable X and a qualitative variable with J modalities (D1, D2,..., Dj). Thus, we are looking for a regression of the form:

$$Y = a\,X + a^1 D1 + a^2 D2 + \cdots + a^J Dj + b$$

The data table for n individuals is presented in Table 5.8.

Individuals	Y	X	D1	D2	...	Dj − 1	Dj
1	Y1	X1	0	1	...	0	0
2	Y2	X2	0	0	...	1	0
...	...	...	...	...	...	...	0
I	Yi	Xi	0	...	...	0	0
...	...	...	...	...	...	...	0
n − 1	Yn − 1	Xn − 1	0	0	...	0	0
N	Yn	Xn	0	0	...	1	0

Table 5.8. *Generic table [I/V]: quantitative explanatory variable polytomic explanatory variable*

Modalities D1, D2, ..., DJ take the value 1 if the individual belongs to the group and 0 in the opposite case. For example, individual 1 belongs to group 1 and individual n belongs to group $j − 1$.

NOTE.– For individuals belonging to group j, all values are equal to 0. This is what characterizes this group; it is said that it constitutes the "reference" because in this case, regression for group j takes the form: $Yj = a\,X + b$.

5.4. Considering interactions between variables

5.4.1. *Overview*

We talk of interaction between two variables when the effect of one variable on another varies according to the values or modalities of a third variable. The term value corresponds to quantitative variables and modalities correspond to qualitative variables. To illustrate, let us take a particular example where Y, the quantitative variable to be explained, varies under the direct influence of two explanatory variables X1 and X2, but variable X1 is also influenced by variable X2. It is said that variable X2 acts as a moderator variable. The situation is demonstrated in Figure 5.13.

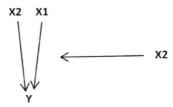

Figure 5.13. *Interaction of explanatory variable X2 on explanatory variable X1*

In order to consider this interaction, we introduced a new variable called interaction $I = X1 \times X2$. Thus, we are looking for a regression of the form:

$$Y = a_1 X1 + a_2 X2 + a_3 I + b$$

Various situations can arise; they correspond to the nature of variables involved.

5.4.2. *Quantitative variable and dichotomous qualitative variable*

For example, we come back to the problem in the previous section where we are looking for a model to describe the behavior of the control group CG and the experimental group EG. In this case, the variable X2 is the dichotomous dummy variable D that takes the value 1 if the student belongs to the experimental group and 0 if he/she belongs to the control group, X is the pretest grade and Y is the test grade, after training, relating to the unguided complex problem. The sought regression has the form:

$$Y = a_1 X + a_2 D + a_3 I + b$$

with: $I = X \times D$.

Thus:

$$YEG = a_1 X + b \quad \text{and} \quad YCG = (a_1 + a_3) X + (a_2 + b).$$

Consideration of the interaction of D on X led to a model that differentiated the two regression lines; they do not have the same slopes and do not have the same y-intercepts. This solved the above-mentioned problem.

Calculation resulted in complete regression:

$$Y = 0.025 - 0.105 \times D + 0.697 \times X + 0.258 \times I$$

that is:

$$YCG = 0.697X + 0.025 \text{ and } YEG = 0.955X - 0.08$$

This result is remarkable; the same results were obtained when calculating the two simple regressions taken separately (see section 3.3.1) for each group. This result is not by chance; it can be mathematically proven that the two approaches are equivalent. This raises the following question: is it more interesting to perform the two simple regressions separately for each of the groups or work with the interacting model? The tendency is that simple regressions are more natural, but some authors argue that the interacting model is preferable because it allows a more "attractive", statistical inference approach than separate regressions by performing tests of equality for constants or slopes. This is difficult to justify, because at this level we did not address the inference problems for such a modeling approach, which should be recalled; we measure the risk that one takes by agreeing to adopt the results obtained.

5.4.3. *Other types of interactions*

We have just presented interactions between a quantitative variable and a dichotomous qualitative variable. But other situations may arise. We simply mentioned them in order to show that they exist and we call on readers, if necessary, to refer to the book by Pascal Bressoux that has already been mentioned, where all these situations are widely addressed and illustrated.

5.4.3.1. *Interaction between two dichotomous qualitative variables*

It is possible to model an interaction between two dichotomous qualitative variables D1 and D2. For example, in the context of the previous example, if we wanted to consider the effect of gender in interaction with the group effect, both dummy variables would have been introduced. D1 (0 or 1) based on the individual's belonging or non-belonging to the control or experimental group and D2 (0 or 1) depending on whether it is a girl or a boy. In this case, the regression would take the following form (interaction between X and the group effect is not mentioned):

$$Y = a\,X + a_1 D1 + a_2 D2 + a_3 D1 D2 + b$$

X is always the initial level of the students and Y is the mark obtained, after training and solving the unguided problem.

NOTE.– It is possible to consider interactions between qualitative variables with more than two modalities. In principle, the problem is no longer complicated but the introduction of a large number of dummy variables makes writing and analysis more cumbersome.

5.4.3.2. *Interaction between two dichotomous qualitative variables*

The case where the moderator variable is a quantitative variable has not yet been addressed. The first way to do this is to "categorize" one of the two variables, that is, make it qualitative by defining categories. For example, if the height of individuals is a quantitative variable, we can define height categories: [less than 1.50]; [1.50–1.60]; [1.60–1.70]; [1.70–1.80]; [greater than 1.80]. The quantitative variable has been transformed into a qualitative variable with five modalities.

It takes us back to a case already presented, namely interaction between a quantitative variable and a qualitative variable (polytomic in this case). If only two categories had been defined, the qualitative variable would have been dichotomous. This approach has a simplicity advantage at the theoretical level, but it brings about loss of information, because a quantitative variable bears more information than the same variable that has been rendered categorical qualitative.

For this reason, a quantitative variable cannot be categorized and maintained in its original quantitative form and thus keep all the information it contains. In this case, it can directly be written as:

$$Y = a_1 X1 + a_2 X2 + a_3 X1 X2 + b$$

Unlike all the cases already presented, the relation is no longer linear, it is bilinear and it requires a different process from a mathematical point of view. An overview is provided in section 5.5, which deals with the modeling of nonlinearities.

NOTE.– It is possible to imagine several (3, 4, 5, etc.) quantitative explanatory variables in interaction, that is, acting on a major explanatory variable. But interpretation of the results quickly becomes complex, and moreover, as recommended by Pascal Bressoux, be careful not to fall into an overspecification that, given the accuracy of data, quickly becomes an illusion.

5.5. Complex modeling

So far, consideration has been given to situations with linear relations between the variable to be explained and the explanatory variable. More complex situations will be presented here. First of all, it is common that the link between two variables is not linear and in which case, the representative function is no longer a straight line but a curve. To address these nonlinearities, a number of possible situations, some of which are simple and others more complex, shall be discussed. Then, focus shall be on the multilevel approach that makes it possible to introduce into the modeling process, the influence of "context" from which data are taken. Finally, there is the logistic regression that deals with cases where the variable to be explained Y is a qualitative variable with p modalities.

5.5.1. *Nonlinear modeling*

5.5.1.1. *Interval-based nonlinear approach*

Figure 5.14 shows a variable to be explained Y depending on the explanatory variable X. It can be seen that in the full interval, the relation between these two variables is clearly not linear. Modeling, in this case, of the point clouds with a straight line would lead to an approximate representation that would betray the nature of the link. However, if we define two intervals, in each of them it is possible to correctly approximate the curve by a line as long as the variable X belongs to this interval. Each of the two straight lines has a validity domain, X belongs to the interval 1 and 2.

This procedure, which consists of splitting the curve into pieces, for each of which it can be approximated to a straight line, can be generalized to more complex cases where we can introduce a larger number of intervals, and thus several line segments to represent the curve. To complete the model, it would be necessary to give meaning to the slope discontinuity.

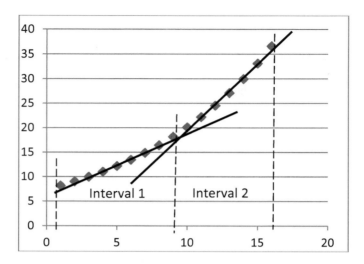

Figure 5.14. *Interval-based nonlinear approach*

5.5.1.2. *Quadratic regression*

Another way to approach the nonlinearities between the variable to be explained and the explanatory variable is to model the point clouds using a polynomial form of degree *n*. The simplest and most often encountered case in the human and social sciences is a second-order polynomial, also called a quadratic form. It is presented in the following form:

$$Y = aX^2 + bX + c$$

This is the equation of a parable. To determine coefficients a, b, c, the ordinary least squares (OLS) method is used in the same way as for the determination of the coefficients of a line, that is, by minimizing the sum of squares of the vertical distances of the points of the cloud to the parabola. Thus, if Q is the sum of the squares of these distances, then a, b and c must satisfy the three equations:

$$\frac{\partial Q}{\partial a} = 0 \qquad \frac{\partial Q}{\partial b} = 0 \qquad \frac{\partial Q}{\partial c} = 0$$

They form a system of three equations with three unknowns from which the values of a, b and c are deduced.

5.5.1.3. *Polynomial regression*

There may be situations where the connection between variables Y and X cannot be represented by a straight line or part of parabola. We can look for a polynomial representation of degree greater than 2, it takes the general form:

$$Y = a_n X^n + a_{n-1} X^{n-1} + \cdots + a_1 X + b$$

Figure 5.15 shows an example or a polynomial of degree 4; it accurately represents the experimental points (Internet source: http://webapps.fundp.ac.be/umdb/biostats/?q=book/export/html/263).

Many software programs perform these quadratic regressions and more generally polynomial regressions (XLSTAT, SPHINX, Moda Lisa, SPSS, R, etc.).

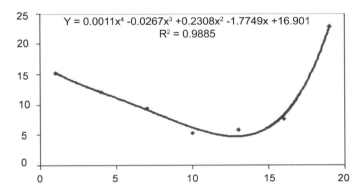

$$Y = 0.0011x^4 - 0.0267x^3 + 0.2308x^2 - 1.7749x + 16.901$$
$$R^2 = 0.9885$$

Figure 5.15. *Modeling from a four-degree polynomial*

5.5.1.4. *Regression from complex functions*

Although most of the time, in human and social sciences, the linear, quadratic or polynomial regressions are sufficient to provide a representative model of the points of a representative cloud of an experiment, one can in certain cases look for regression directly in the form of a complex function. For example, in an exponential and logarithmic form as well as in the form of a trigonometric function. Software programs, after having selected the desired function type, calculate adjustment coefficients. Figure 5.15 illustrates such a calculation when looking for an exponential regression, which represents the evolution of the Montréal population between 1801 and 1931[1].

---

1 Internet source: ville de Montréal : http://www.jybaudot.fr/httpdocs/index.html.

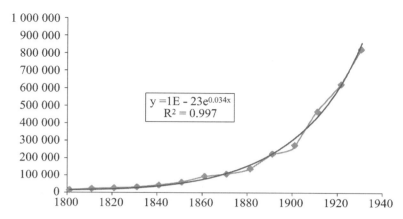

Figure 5.16. *Modeling from an exponential function. For a color version of this figure, see www.iste.co.uk/larini/education.zip*

5.5.2. *Multilevel approach*

This chapter cannot be concluded without mentioning the multilevel approach that makes it possible to introduce the effects of "context" during a modeling process. We just mentioned it without expatiating because a complete and effective presentation would be too long to develop. However, it is possible that within the context of a research project, the reader will come across studies that will be enriched by a multilevel analysis.

The multilevel approach integrates the notion of "context" where experimental data are collected. It came to light in the mid-1980s as part of research in education. Many publications have been written on this subject and we recommend reading the book already quoted several times by Pascal Bressoux.

In order to understand the advantage of this approach, we presented a sample problem that it can solve. We want to develop a model that can mold a satisfaction index, Y, expressed by students in a large city in terms of their education, for example on a scale of 1–10. To address this situation, the first level is that of the students themselves to whom we associate one or more variables that can explain their answer, for example the marks they obtain. If, in a conventional manner, we limit the analysis to the cohort of N students, we do not take into account the "context" in which each student finds himself/herself and which may have an influence on his/her choice. For example, influence of the class (and/or the teacher) in which he or she is found, or influence of his/her school, which can often be associated with the neighborhood in its appreciation. We have just presented three overlapping levels. The first consists of all students, the second level is the class to which the student belongs and finally the third level is the school to which the class belongs.

At each level, we must associate one or more explanatory variables characterizing it: for the "student level", we can choose the mean grade of each student; for the "class level", it can be a mean grade indicating the level of each class; and for the "school level", a qualitative variable indicating the neighborhood to which they belong.

We then search, in a conventional manner, for a linear regression that connects the variable to be explained Y to a linear combination of variables characterizing the different levels.

5.5.3. *Logistic regression*

Logistic regression is concerned with the case where the explained variable Y is a qualitative variable with two or more modalities. We are looking for a linear relation that enables us to predict the modality of the variable to be explained based on one or more explanatory variables.

As for the previous section and for the same reasons, the purpose of the presentation is limited to an understanding of the potential of logistic regression within the context of a research work and the basis of this approach. We limit our presentation in the case where the variable Y to be predicted is a dichotomous variable, that is to say, with two modalities. However, the case of a polytomous variable can also be considered.

We start by applying the linear probability model, which is why we shall try to determine a linear relation that expresses the probability of belonging to a modality based on explanatory variables.

This is the example presented by Pascal Bressoux: we want to express a dichotomous qualitative variable Y, for example "pass to third year", it takes the value 1 if the student passes and 0 if he/she fails. We want to express this variable according to the quantitative variable AVG (continuous assessment average) and qualitative variable PRIVATE (type of school) with two modalities PRIVATE $= 1$ if the student is in a private school and PRIVATE $= 0$ if he/she is in a public school. Thus, we are looking, in the sample, for a relation as follows:

$$P = a_1 AVG + a_2 PRIVATE + b,$$

where P is the probability that the student will be admitted into the third year.

Using the least squares method, we look for the line closest to the point cloud. The following result is obtained:

$$P = 0.198 \text{xAVG} - 0.161 \text{xPRIVATE} - 0.364$$

The variable to be explained Y has only two values (0 or 1), whereas prediction P is continuous, with the possibility of obtaining values lower than 0 or greater than 1 within the interval of defining explanatory variables. However, this information may be useful, but it cannot always be considered satisfactory, and particularly when the slope of the regression is too low.

To improve the model, one can work directly with the "occurrence probability" $O = P/(1 - P)$ or use its logarithmic natural log $(P/(1 - P))$ called logit (P). We can then look for a linear regression that connects logit (P) to the explanatory variables. The results must then be interpreted to go back to the initial dichotomous variable Y.

6

Toward the Robustness in Studies in Education by the Quantitative Approach

Education sciences have their own methods and knowledge, resulting from quantitative and qualitative studies. Among the qualitative approaches, many can benefit from a quantitative complement that can improve their robustness, and thus their reproducibility for evolutionary or contextual studies – in comparative education, for example. Without discussing in detail the many possibilities that quantitative approaches can bring in complement to or for exploring an educational problem, we provide some examples in the following.

6.1. Quantitative approach to social representations in education

Social representations, considered as powerful knowledge analysis tools, can be used in different ways in the issues related to education and its societal challenges. A few are mentioned here for information purposes:

– knowing the information that is acquired, the fields of representation, attitudes, specificities of human groups studied, forms of knowledge mobilized, societal challenges they convey and their contradictions;

– comparing the social representations of specific groups to better understand the similarities and differences. For example, comparing the social representations of sustainable development of students in several countries requires cultural specificities to be taken into account. But these comparisons can be diachronic; for example, it is possible to compare a social representation of a concept in fifth grade 5 years apart to know its evolution. The comparison can also apply to different grades or social groups;

– this use allows by extension to study the conflicts of representations between different groups of actors, for example, between students and teachers, between different social classes, different users of a resource, etc. or even forms of power implemented in a specific situation. This use mobilizes socially dynamic issues (SDIs):

- comparing knowledge acquisitions before and after a course to analyze students' outcomes, or between two courses using different pedagogies to understand how they affect outcomes;

- comparing prescribed/actual curriculum with students' knowledge;

- assisting in the implementation of didactic recommendations;

- understanding the hidden *curriculum* of concepts taught and value systems as well as educational purposes.

Studies that involve social representations in education are currently very empirical in general and could become more robust if given a little more quantitative characteristic.

6.1.1. *Methodological milestones of a quantitative approach to social representations*

The methodologies presented here are based on the structural approach to social representations as currently addressed in the field of social psychology, which have been adapted to prioritize quantitative and graphical methods, both for reproducible and communication purposes, to education issues [BAR 16].

Studying a social representation and understanding how it functions require studying its content and structure. To this end, Jean-Claude Abric explains that a "representation is a set of elements that are organized and hierarchically arranged around a central nucleus that gives the representation its meaning and coherence [...]". Peripheral elements are organized around this structuring nucleus, a true "keystone" of the representation.

The central nucleus is structuring, it provides an evidence status for the group or individual and constitutes a stable element. It therefore has a major role insofar as it provides the framework for categorizing new information proposed to the subject on the represented object. The nucleus contains a set of hierarchical elements, which are particularly significant in the representation since they give it meaning. The nucleus concept also refers to the identification of individuals to a social group, considering that it helps to ensure its homogeneity. The nucleus is thus determined not only by the nature of the represented object, but also by the relation that the subject or group has with it, and finally by the value system and standards defining the ideological context [ABR 94]. The nucleus provides two essential functions: a generating function, with the nucleus constituting "the element through which the meaning of the other constitutive elements of the representation is created or transformed" [ABR 94] and an organizing function where the latter, considered as the unifying and stabilizing element, "determines the nature of the links which unite the elements of the representation". The central nucleus is characterized by its stability since it ensures the sustainability of representations in rapidly changing worlds. It is therefore the identification of the central nucleus that makes the comparative study of representations possible. For two representations to be different, they have to be organized around two different nuclei.

Peripheral elements are organized around the central nucleus. When they are close to the central nucleus, they play an essential role in the realization of the meaning of the representation. More distanced, they illustrate or justify this meaning. Peripheral elements are the most accessible set of social representations because they are less stable and more dynamic. Concretely, new information is first elaborated by peripheral elements. They constitute a "set of judgments formulated about the represented object and its environment, stereotypes, beliefs" [ABR 94]. They have an essential role, and this role will be largely highlighted in the link between social representations and education for sustainable development, because the role they play is that of "interface between the central nucleus and the concrete situation in which the representation is developed or functions" [ABR 94]. The peripheral elements are directly dependent on the context and result from the anchoring of the representation into reality. They make it possible to render concrete, understandable and transmissible new information emanating from a specific and contextualized situation. In view of the stability of the central nucleus, they constitute the changing and evolutionary dimension of the representation, but they also provide a defense function to the central nucleus, which Flament [FLA 87] calls the "bumper" because the transformation of a social representation will possibly be made subsequently by the modification of its periphery. Claude Flament [FLA 94] considers that peripheral elements are "schemes" organized by the central nucleus, "instantly ensuring the functioning of the representation as decoding grid of a situation" [FLA 89]. They are behavior prescribers and instant reaction guides to a specific situation by designating what is normal to do or say in a particular situation. They also help, in this way, to instantly guide the reactions or action of subjects, without having to resort to central meanings. They thus constitute a customized modulation of central nuclei, more broadly socially developed and shared.

Social representations are therefore a double system consisting of the central nucleus and peripheral elements: the central nucleus is related to the historical, sociological and ideological context. It is strongly marked by the collective memory of the group. It defines the normative framework of the group. Associated with values and norms, it defines the fundamental elements around which consensual representations are developed that are relatively independent of immediate contexts. As Jean-Claude Abric points out, "the central system is thus stable, coherent, consensual and historically marked" [ABR 94]. The peripheral system is more individualized and contextualized, that is more related to individual characteristics and the immediate environment. Unlike the central system which is essentially normative, the peripheral system is, for its part, mainly functional. It is flexible and can integrate into the representation of individual variations that are related to the subjects' stories and personal experiences. This function therefore actually ensures the possibility of developing individualized social representations organized around a common central nucleus. "The peripheral system is indeed the essential complement to the central system on which it depends. The functioning of the nucleus can only be understood in continuous dialectic with the periphery" [FLA 94].

6.1.2. *Choice of study corpora, questionnaires and interviews*

In social representations analysis, there are two major categories of corpora: simple and complex corpora.

In simple corpora, the most common, the choice of the study individuals is made according to the types of knowledge that would be analyzed. A social representation always refers to a specific group, thus the individuals concerned all belong to this group, which is clearly defined in its characteristics. The group is investigated with a clarified objective. To have meaning, the social representation should have at least about 30 individuals per defined group. In this sense, adopting the usual classical approach of characterization questionnaires is a one-off support to interpretative analysis or to specify a corpus of social representations (examples: age, gender, social category, etc.).

In complex corpora, we find a prior undefined population that includes a large number of individuals, and the components of which will be sought through representational characteristics. There are many investigation methods on an *a priori* complex corpus that can be defined through crossed sorting, for example, or factorial correspondence analysis.

We do not intend to discuss all social representations study methods here, but to rather explain methods for examining quantitative methods related to the structural theory of social representations useful for knowledge analysis. In questionnaires or interviews not only the content of a representation or opinion of individuals, approached by questionnaires or conventional interviews are sought. An understanding of the organization of elements is also solicited, the objective being to highlight meanings and their ranking. In a first approach, we favor the quantitative perspective put in place by Pierre Vergès [VER 95, VER 01], for its reproducible nature that makes the comparison (temporal, intergroup, intercultural) and contrasting of reference systems possible. It is then possible to use questions having spontaneous responses such as: "What words or phrases come to mind when you hear about...". The respondent answers on the principle of anonymity in about a dozen words. Their non-binding nature allows us to decipher meanings, in such a way that the biases are minimized. Furthermore, this type of question allows "access to the figurative nuclei of the representation" [ABR 94, ABR 97].

If it is an interview, it should be borne in mind that interlocutor-related biases are more significant and they have to be considered in the analysis that will follow. The analysis must be weighted taking this factor into consideration. It is also possible to note the main words of a series of open-ended interviews. These questionnaires were reintroduced by Claude Flament [FLA 95] to verify the hypothesis of a collective raking of elements. They do not enable the construction of a notional network at the individual scale, but nevertheless offer a first approach to the definition of a social representation with reference to a specific corpus. In accordance with the Ecole of Aix, for the representation sample to be valid it must consist of about 30 individuals. Below this, the sample is considered to be non-representative. Beyond this, the representation is formed and cannot be modified. However, there is a debate regarding the ranking of terms, which should ultimately voluntarily be reorganized or not by the individual questioned.

6.1.3. *Graphical representation methods*

The presentation of social representations can take two distinct forms: simple and organizational graphs.

6.1.3.1. *Simple graph*

The first is a classical presentation in graphical form including the frequencies of the items evoked by all respondents on the y-axis and their citation rank (first, second, etc.) on the x-axis; it takes the following form: Item 1 (frequency, rank) or X (x, y) with x = frequency and y = rank. X_1 to X_n are then positioned on the graph.

This graph gives a directly readable approach to the information in four categories: a central nucleus and three peripheries: close, secondary, tertiary, discretized according to quartile methods. Only the items cited by at least 30% of individuals are included in the representation. We provide for information purposes the approximate reading grid of such a graph in table form.

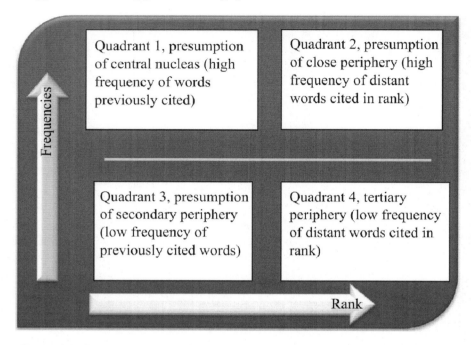

Figure 6.1. *Reading grid of a simple graph (frequency and rank of the items cited)*

The relationship between the items is not achieved, so the method does not enable access to the systemic nature of frames of thought of the social representation. On the contrary, we retained the graphical representation because of the ease of direct reading of a first indicative ranking. It also presents a more universal and open analytical approach to those who are unfamiliar with social representations. As this presentation is the most widespread, it equally allows comparative approaches with other similar studies, or with other lexical occurrence frequency studies carried out on analysis reference systems.

Though the manual method remains the same, several manual, semiautomatic or automatic techniques can be implemented to obtain results. It all depends on the number of responses that we have in order to carry out the processing.

Manual methods consist of placing all the words in columns on an Excel table. For each word, its frequency must be calculated (for example: the word is cited by 30% of respondents), and again, for each word, the rank average must be calculated (example, it is located on average in rank 3.4). For the calculation of rank, there is some debate among researchers on the validity of two methods: personally calculating the rank on a spontaneous ranking, or asking the respondents to make a classification of the importance of terms and to calculate the rank on this basis. Once the frequency and rank are calculated, a graph can be developed. There are software that can automatically do all calculations and figures, for example Modalisa (Kynos).

To comment on a social representations graph, the central nucleus and different peripheries should first be clearly defined, before explaining the meanings.

6.1.3.2. *Organizational graph*

The second presentation of social representations helps to more accurately approach the concept of organization of knowledge, allowing to act more easily on it, if we want a modification of the said social representations. It consists of the construction of a notional network in a graphical form. This approach presupposes establishing relationships between the different items through an analysis of similarities [DEG 73, VER 97]. The commonly proposed approach is that of the spontaneous classification of items by the respondents.

Here, the problem of recoding of terms equally arises, that is, grouping terms together. Recoding is often necessary, even just initially to group spellings that are close to responses. Direct analysis, which consists of developing co-occurrences tables from spontaneous responses without recoding, is the most reliable, but is often impossible, as the responses given can be close. The method here is still under debate in the spheres of research and is not always agreed upon. In this respect, we must keep a critical eye on what we do, keep in mind the various recoding made, be able to create several different recoding according to the study objectives and bear in mind the limits that they generate.

This graphical approach posits the hypothesis that the sum of co-occurrences over a sufficient number of individuals indicates the continuity of significant links in the representation object.

Just as with the first method, it is possible to use manual, automatic or semiautomatic methods. Manual methods consist of placing on an Excel table, all words on the x-axis and y-axis and placing the number of co-occurrences at the intersection of words... For example, if individual A has cited the term X , Y and Z in a question with spontaneous responses, individual B the term X, Y and W, and individual C, X, Y, Z and U, the table of responses is thus as follows (Table 6.1).

	X	Y	Z	W	U
X	0	3	2	1	1
Y	3	0	2	1	1
Z	2	2	0	0	1
W	1	1	0	0	0
U	1	1	1	0	0

Table 6.1. *Example of the construction of a co-occurrences table*

(Read: There are three co-occurrences between the term X and Y, that is three respondents who answered X also answered Y... or there are no co-occurrences between the term W and U, that is, none of the respondents who answered U answered W.)

The graph is then manually constructed on a conventional drawing software or on a specialized software "Free plane" type, knowing that a line thickness corresponds to a co-occurrence value. The lowest value corresponds to the minimum thickness, while the highest value corresponds to the maximum thickness. They can then be exported under Adobe Illustrator in order to be able to modify the visibility of the representation by modifying the discretization of links between items.

Semiautomatic methods involve using a classical statistical software that will automatically calculate the co-occurrences table, then the graphic representations are constructed as previously.

There are also software dedicated to this method such as "SIMILI 2003" and "EVOC 3000" developed within LAMES, MMSH, Aix-en-Provence [VER 01], which are equally free but not user-friendly. Most of the classical software on the market allow automatic data processing, like the "trees and networks" column of Modalisa software (Kynos). Manipulation is easy and simply requires the entry of a question and individuals.

Graphical results are presented in the form of interconnected word networks. They represent an image of the notional network. Words that are strongly interconnected and frequently cited are assumed to be part of the central nucleus; the more the connection of items are closer to it and strongly weighted, the more the periphery is closer and significant in the interpretation of social representations. Just as with the simple graph, to comment on a social representations graph, the central nucleus and different peripheries should first be clearly defined, before explaining the meanings, but the organizational graph provides additional information concerning the closeness of links between items and between the central nucleus and its peripheries.

It is possible to choose to represent cliques, rather than complete graphs. This means that the threshold for visualizing links is high. They represent the top two quartiles of co-occurrences in most cases, which gives the undeniable advantage of simplifying reading relative to graphs, though the complexity of the central nuclei is less obvious.

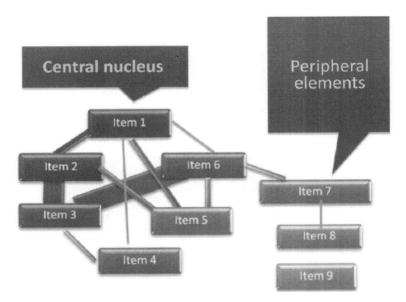

Figure 6.2. *Reading grid of a social representation in an organizational graph*

6.1.4. *Analytical model for explicitation of ideological loads*

6.1.4.1. *Overview*

In the genetic models of social representations, sorting of information according to social, cultural and normative determinants, their selection according to socially available norms [BON 99] amounts to saying that some information is prioritized to the detriment of others. The model retained the one that makes up the central nucleus of the social representation and system of thought, and comprises only a part of the complex set to which the representation object is related. Though this assertion may seem trivial, since any thought accesses the complex through simplification exercises, the modes of simplification used are however very significant.

Understanding the determinants that explain that a specific piece of information has been retained or not is a first step toward the analysis of the societal logics surrounding the representation object. Analyzing societal logics is tantamount to accepting to displace the perspective of analysis with regard to social representations studied and also to accept that they have an ideological load, which should be made explicit.

This approach assumes that the information collected as part of the formalization of a social representation must be analyzed. But if the representation is a reconstruction of the expressive object of a group or an individual, it amounts to saying that there is a discrepancy with the object. "This discrepancy may also be due to the specific intervention of collective values and codes, personal implications and the social commitments of individuals" [JOD 94].

6.1.4.2. Search for focal points, defalcations, supplementations and distortions

Analyzing this discrepancy requires the use of other social representations tools: focal points, defalcations, supplementations and distortions.

Focal points are found at the level of emergence of representations. Information focuses on certain aspects of the representation object "according to the interests and implication of subjects; inference pressure due to the need to act, taking a stand or achieving recognition and commitment of others" [JOD 89, JOD 94]. Moliner [MOL 96] holds that "it thus prevents individuals from having a global view of the object".

Defalcation corresponds to the suppression of information elements belonging to the representation object. "It results, in most cases, from the repressive effect of social norms" [JOD 94]. If this assertion is often understood from the social psychology perspective, the analogy can be quickly extended to normative social pressure, even when considered from its policy perspective. In the distortion process, all the attributes of the represented object are present but are accentuated or reduced in a specific way. The role of distortions is to reduce a cognitive dissonance in the evaluation of the qualities of an object. A set of distortion processes that strongly accentuate some elements over others may, to some extent, be more in line with the focal point process.

Supplementation consists of giving the representation object information that does not belong to it. It "proceeds from an addition of meanings due to the investment and imagination of the subject" [JOD 89, JOD 94]. The silent zone (hidden areas made up of available but non-verbalized elements of the representation because of their counter normative nature) or orthodoxy issues have not been discussed in this work, but research on them constitutes an interesting avenue for analysis.

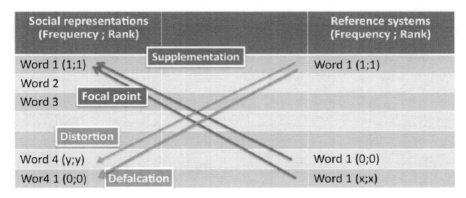

Figure 6.3. *Model of comparison of social representations with a reference system. For a color version of this figure, see www.iste.co.uk/larini/education.zip*

Focal points, distortions, supplementations and defalcations are technical tools that refer to the concept of a reference system of the representation object. The latter must be in line with the objectification of observations made and the theoretical interpretation of a reality. Objectification, as defined by Durkheim [DUR 94], then taken up in *Le Métier du sociologue* [BOU 68], characterizes the validity of knowledge or representation relating to an object. It depends, on the one hand, on what is meant by object and, on the other hand, on normative rules specific to the field concerned. This is basically a scientific approach. Objectification in the epistemological sense is not synonymous with truth, although usage tends to confuse them. It is more a "confidence index" or "quality" of knowledge and representations.

6.1.4.3. *Comparison approach to educational challenges: toward the analysis of conflicting elements and didactic recommendations*

The reference systems can then be subjected to a simple analysis of lexical occurrence frequencies. The advantage of this approach is that it does not just focus on a definition of a represented object that can be subject to debate, and this is the case for socially dynamic issues and sustainable development in particular. It avoids focal points, defalcations, supplementations and distortions, but above all it gives a quantitative formalization of results that are comparable with the analysis of social representations. Results are presented in the form of word lists with their lexical occurrence frequency. This approach enables an accumulation of reference systems.

Comparisons between reference systems and social representations are done by superimposing word lists (lexical occurrence frequencies) reported in terms of rank. The first step of the approach consists of identifying the words that are missing in one of the lists compared to the other, and then, second, the differential between the ranks is analyzed. This approach makes it possible to identify focal points, defalcations, supplementations and distortions.

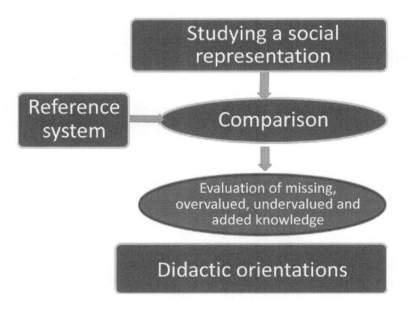

Figure 6.4. *Approach of comparison of knowledge with reference systems*

First, this involves analyzing the meaning of elements identified as missing, added, undervalued or overvalued. The questions are as follows: Why did they undergo changes with regard to reference systems? What societal, cultural or political determinants explain them? Then the societal educational challenges underlying these meanings are brought out.

Second, it concerns the identification of the role of previous knowledge, thus studied on future teachings that refer here to "education for..." or "socially dynamic issues".

Third, this includes proposing, in view of the meaning and structuring of social representations, didactic recommendations or strategies that teachers can use to actually position themselves toward teaching.

6.1.5. *Comparative analytical model*

6.1.5.1. *Corpus similarities and differences*

In the analytical model of explicitation of ideological loads, the selection of information according to socially available norms [BON 99] is paramount. In the comparative model, the issue particularly involves making comparisons between several social representations by the corpus similarities and differences method. All the corpus similarities and differences can be analyzed, that is we will look for the central nuclei and peripheral hierarchies and the analysis will focus on the comparison of their similarities or differences. But this analysis can be conducted in detail: the differences can be ranked and the social representation compared with a reference system. Regarding relationship graphs, these differences can also concern the closeness of relations between the items cited, with strong consequences on how to consider, for example, a didactic recommendation.

6.1.5.2. *In which cases are comparative methods used?*

There are many cases where comparative methods may be useful, but they are grouped under three categories: diachronic, intergroup and comparison methods.

In diachronic analyses, we analyze a single corpus (or similar) at different periods and see the evolution of the social representation over time of this group. It can concern the analysis of a concept over several years and for a specific social group (in society, at school, etc.). This may also involve assessing the scope of an event (an educational action, a trip and confrontation with a particular situation) to evaluate the impact. Studying the social representations of a concept before and after a lesson, for example, facilitates a partial evaluation of the effects.

Intergroup methods consist of analyzing several corpora on the same study object in order to determine the similarities and differences between the different social, cultural and situational groups but which are not particularly required to be in contact. These methods can be the basis of intercultural comparisons, for example.

Conversely, comparison methods are based on the same principle, that is analyzing several corpora on the same study object, but the groups are required to be in contact within the framework of a specific situation, and their differences and similarities in social representations will then be used as a guide for analyzing actors' logics. These methods can be used to understand intercultural, intersocial and situational conflicts, or even to resolve them in some cases, if the underlying issues are secondary.

6.1.6. *Case study*

6.1.6.1. *First step: study of students' social representations*

The comprehensive study can be found in the book on the use of social representations in education [BAR 16]. We reproduce a simplified path here as an example. The social representations of the sustainable development of students in the urban planning vocational field ($n = 66$) are mainly analyzed on the basis of the open question: What words or phrases come to mind when you think about sustainable development? This question specifies the field of representation and provides a first approach to the information selected by students as well as their structuring. It makes it possible to approach the systemic coherence of students' frame of thought and the normative framework in which the anchoring process takes place. Analysis of the information level and attitude are then complemented by additional questions.

To the first open question, we obtained 308 responses, recoded into 74 modalities and then calculated the co-occurrences, which are 2,748 in number. From the recoded responses, we developed a classical frequencies and ranks graph of the responses that give a first approach to the importance of collected items. Though it may not be possible to use it as such for the analysis of social representations, we retained it because it is easier to read at first glance due to the reading grid of a simple graph (frequency and rank of the items cited). But it is especially useful in the analysis of focal points, because the items in frequencies and ranks are comparable to others.

Percentage of times cited

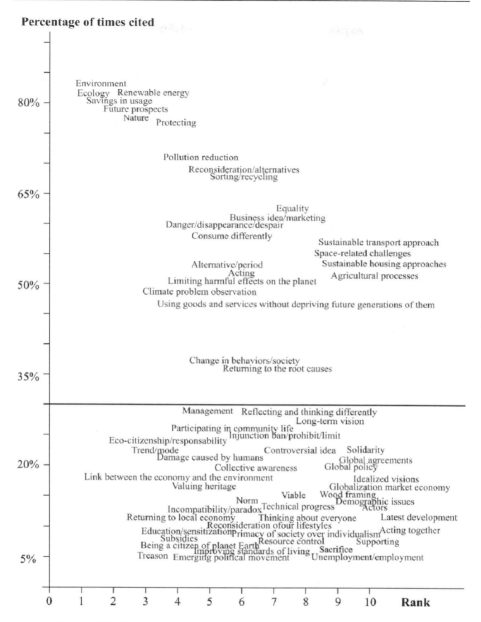

Figure 6.5. *Frequencies and ranks graph of spontaneous responses to the sustainable development of students in the urban planning vocational field (n = 66)*

We then developed, from co-occurrences, a graph of similarities allowing us to visualize the social representations of students in the urban planning vocational field. We reproduced and commented it here.

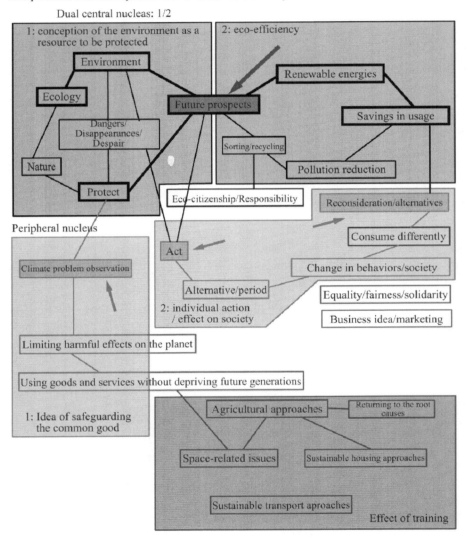

Interpretation of social representation of sustainable development

Figure 6.6. *Relationship graph of commented social representations of the sustainable development of students in the urban planning vocational field (n = 66). For a color version of this figure, see www.iste.co.uk/larini/education.zip*

The social representation of sustainable development shows a dual polarized structuring of the frame of thought: the central nucleus (represented by a double frame at the top) integrates two well-structured and differentiated fields.

The first field (1) structures the conception of the environment as a resource to be protected: this idea includes several terms such as "danger, disappearance, despair", which highlight its implicitly imperative nature, but also that of "nature" in its idealized version.

The second field (2) falls within the eco-efficiency area and technically means to be implemented "sorting/recycling, renewable energy, etc.". Eco-efficiency also involves a reduction in secondary production costs such as "pollution reduction".

This dual structuring is linked by the concept of "future prospects", which implies prospects as well as concern with regard to the future. It is directly related to the word "act", considered mainly in its imprecise collective form: "we must act", and with the imperative idea (duty).

For the students' group, the environment as a resource to be protected and the solution to this end, eco-efficiency, have evidence status. It does not however refer to the scientific field of knowledge. They offer to the social representation of sustainable development, the stable elements of its meaning, elements through which all new information may be organized. These two elements, related to the historical, sociological and ideological context of sustainable development, strongly mark collective memory. They define the normative framework of the group.

The peripheral nucleus (represented by middle frames) is also structured into two distinct parts. The first is based on the idea of safeguarding the common good, involving observations of the major problems of the planet as a whole and the need to counter them (limiting harmful effects on the planet and using property without depriving future generations of them). The second relates to the idea of individual and collective action necessarily involving a "change in behavior".

The concept of eco-citizenship, which is very often associated with responsibility or civic responsibility, is connected to the field of eco-efficiency through sorting and recycling, which constitutes the entry through which the concept of responsibility seems to be most accessible. The periphery of the representation around sustainable development is mainly functional and re-values the role of the individual within *a priori* inaccessible global issues. The representation of sustainable development therefore offers anchoring into reality that is particularly valuable for the individual. It solidifies new information and prescribes adapted behaviors.

Thus, the normative frame of thought of sustainable development is coupled with a functional periphery including acting in a particularly efficient and valuable way for the individual.

Two isolates are individualized in the peripheral system: one containing the concepts of equality/equity/solidarity and the other relating to the idea of trade and marketing around sustainable development. These two concepts are sometimes found in individuals and act as a justifying function of the central nucleus.

Finally, we note (represented in the lowest frame) an extension that forms part of the training effect.

6.1.6.2. *Second step: comparing social representations with a reference system to search for educational challenges*

Information such as is apprehended in the social representations of students has to be placed in the real context of the representation object for them to be compared. Comparison is done through the evaluation of focal point, defalcation and distortion processes whose social representations constituted the object when they were designed. Examining these processes involves an evaluation of the information retained and not retained, and this exercise takes a quantitative and reproducible methodological orientation, based on the frequencies of lexical occurrences and their ranking.

Second, it will be necessary to understand the determinants that explain why a specific information was or was not retained. This is a first step toward the analysis of societal logics within which the representation object falls. We will not discuss in detail the epistemological issue of the choice of reference systems because it is not the problem here, but these choices must be justified in any study carried out. We simply show quantitative results here as an example on a "case study"; it includes in this case an institutional reference system comprising one of the founding texts of sustainable development (the Brundtland report, 1987). Real studies generally require multiple reference systems.

The texts, taken as reference systems, are subjected to a simple analysis of lexical occurrence frequencies from the "Timmy miner" software (there are many other software that perform the same function, Tropes, Wordle, Pearl, etc.). This approach makes it possible to give a quantitative formalization of results comparable with the social representations analysis. The first results concerning reference systems are presented in the form of word lists with their lexical occurrence frequency. Processing however requires some adjustments, such as the elimination of words with less than three letters, places and dates, insignificant details (however, but, then, etc.). It is then appropriate to make an analysis of focal points, defalcations, supplementations and distortions according to the model presented above. Below is a graphical result for the focal point of students with regard to the selected reference system.

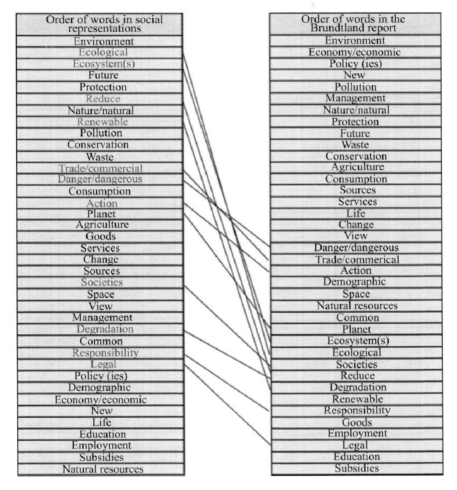

Figure 6.7. *Focal points of social representations of sustainable development with regard to Brundtland reference system. For a color version of this figure, see www.iste.co.uk/larini/education.zip*

Focal points are identified by words present both in the social representations of sustainable development and in the reference system, but which have wide rank differences. In theory, the words linked in larger characters in the first table are those that are overvalued by students. The concepts concerned are therefore the subject of focal points to the detriment of others and "prevent individuals from having a global vision of the object" [MOL 96]. In this sense, the analysis of focal points is of increasing importance. We will not provide details on the analyses that are made; for more details, the reader can refer to [BAR 16]. We simply illustrate using one of the curricular reorganization sheets for the proposed discussion, which resulted from the work concerning this education within the framework of the professional trainings analyzed.

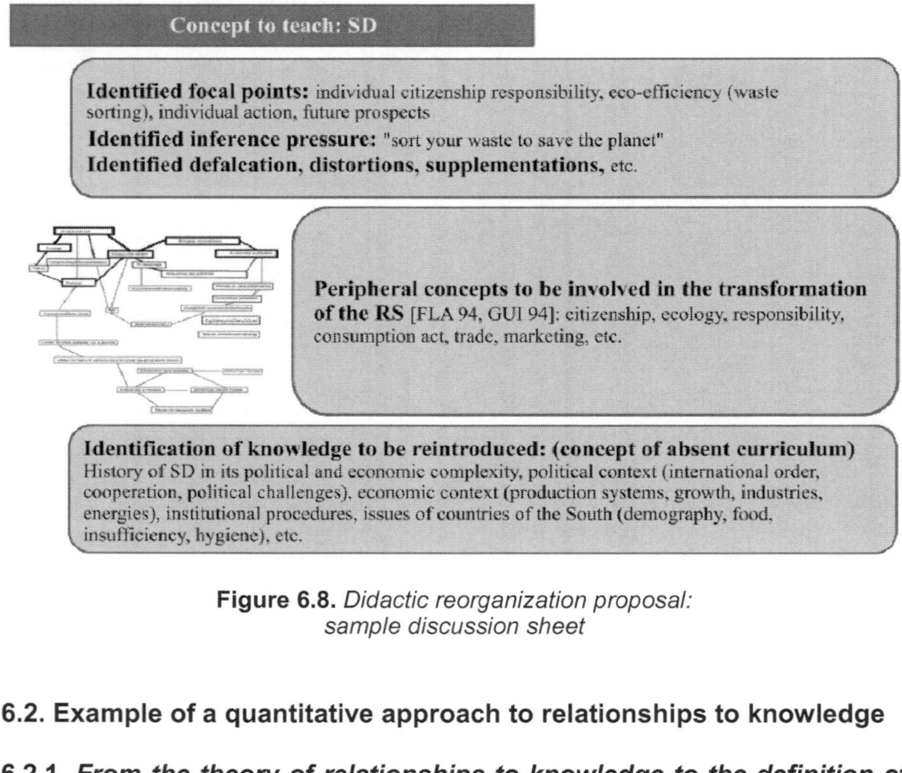

Concept to teach: SD

Identified focal points: individual citizenship responsibility, eco-efficiency (waste sorting), individual action, future prospects
Identified inference pressure: "sort your waste to save the planet"
Identified defalcation, distortions, supplementations, etc.

Peripheral concepts to be involved in the transformation of the RS [FLA 94, GUI 94]: citizenship, ecology, responsibility, consumption act, trade, marketing, etc.

Identification of knowledge to be reintroduced: (concept of absent curriculum)
History of SD in its political and economic complexity, political context (international order, cooperation, political challenges), economic context (production systems, growth, industries, energies), institutional procedures, issues of countries of the South (demography, food, insufficiency, hygiene), etc.

Figure 6.8. *Didactic reorganization proposal:*
sample discussion sheet

6.2. Example of a quantitative approach to relationships to knowledge

6.2.1. *From the theory of relationships to knowledge to the definition of variables*

The concept of "relationship to knowledge" has been the subject of numerous research and in different educational fields [BOU 00, BEI 89, CHA 97, CHA 99, CHE 92, CHA 03, CAI 01, VEN 17]. In order to bring assessment qualitative methods closer to relationships to knowledge, we rely on epistemological contributions to the socioanthropological aspect of relationships to knowledge [CHA 92, CHA 97, BAU 98, KAL 17].

The methodologies of the study on relationships to knowledge are usually focused on surveys (called knowledge assessments) that investigate individuals (sex, parents, ethnicity, prior history, social relations, self-image, personal and social identity skills, model of references, projection in the future, etc.) and their response to a given social situation – that makes sense or not – in a specific situation (very often, studies revolve around the relationship with the school, etc.). Note that knowledge assessments are not about evaluating what has been learned, but about what makes sense in what has been learned. Knowledge assessments are very complete, but on the one hand they are extremely time-consuming to manage and, on the other hand, they facilitate the analysis of situations, but are not very reproducible, for example, in comparative or evolutionary cases.

We therefore propose a method that can address and position the different dimensions of relationships to knowledge in a reproductive system. Each of its three dimensions defines analysis factors that can be quantified.

Thus, we shall proceed with a representation of relationships to knowledge, which will possibly be extended to several different knowledge objects and in different contexts, but on condition that they refer to very different situations that can be compared by the indicators created. These methods do not detract the importance of conventional knowledge assessments that provide accuracy in situations. This approach involves the devising of an operational analysis method – that is easy to implement as a first approach.

Based on Charlot's study [CHA 97, p. 122], "relationship to knowledge is a relationship of meaning, and therefore of value, between an individual (or a group) and the processes or products of knowledge [...]. Relationship to knowledge is rooted in the very identity of individuals: they bring into play their models, expectations of life".

Studying relationships with knowledge is about exploring the articulation of single stories and social relationships – this work is often carried out in order to understand school situations of success or failure (especially school dropouts). Thus, the study of relationships to knowledge is aimed at understanding the articulations of social meaning (usually in connection with a goal) with a personal meaning [VYG 77]. Social relationships are constructed within the context of a collective story, social models and relation with these social models.

On the other hand, considering relationships to knowledge implies understanding the knowledge appropriation activity known as reflexive mobilization. In education, it is a relationship to a learning process; more broadly, it is an issue of having control of a reflection activity in a situation. This is the definition that is used here because it also applies to the fields of non-formal and informal education that we are concerned with in this study.

Thus, according to the socioanthropological aspect of relationships to knowledge, there are three dimensions to consider: the relation of subject meaning vis-à-vis its knowledge object; relationship with social models and relationship with the process appropriation. In terms of relationships to knowledge, it is dimensions called identity, social and epistemic. We will be contented with the terms "individual relationships" (the individual is considered here in the statistical sense of the term) or relationships of meaning, relationship or relation with the models of society, relationship or relation to knowledge appropriation in situation or more simply mobilization of reflexive activity.

Thus, we started from these three dimensions that define relationships to knowledge: single stories and relationships of meaning, relationships with the social spheres that surround the subject, collective stories and their norms, reflexive mobilizations or relationships to knowledge appropriation in situation.

This enables us to represent the relationships to knowledge along three axes, that of the individual sense (we start from the assumption that the more a situation is intelligible, the more it can be meaningful and make sense to an individual), that of social positioning in relation to a social system on knowledge objects (we start from the hypothesis that the more the models of the individual are in line with the reference(s) – (for example those of the school) – the easier his/her relationship with the society. We will call this second axis social positioning (it must refer to a context or a well-defined situation). The third axis corresponds to reflexive mobilization. If we want to maintain the usual vocabulary of relationships to knowledge, then it is the identity, social and epistemic axis.

Thus, the formulation of a quantitative method of relationships to knowledge consists of finding indicators that give a relative weight to each of the factorial axes. We come back to the conventional situation of principal component analysis (PCA) or factorial multiple correspondence analysis (FMCA) (depending on the nature of the variables), where the different variables (quantitative or qualitative) are related in order to understand a little better the components of relationships to knowledge.

Therefore, it is a question of characterizing the intensity of the various relationships of the individual with three variables by identifying all possible categories independently of each other for a given problem. For each of the studies, the categories may be adapted to the situation identified, or may be derived from previous research on the issue.

Schematically, for the first variable, the first category hypothetically corresponds to: no relationship of meaning or disinterestedness, little interest, average interest, strong interest, strong interest and identity mobilization.

Schematically, for the second variable: no social positioning, limited positioning, distanced or mitigated positioning, strong positioning with adherence to the social system, strong positioning with rejection of the social system, strong positioning but non-stabilized reference system.

Categories of variable 1: individual meaning axis (or identity axis)					
No meaning (total disintegration)	Little meaning	Average interest	Proven meaning for the individual without visible identity interference	Strong interest and proven sense of identity	
Categories of variable 2: social positioning axis (or social axis)					
No social positioning	Limited positioning	Distanced or mitigated positioning	Strong positioning in line with the social system	Strong positioning with rejection of the social system	Strong positioning but non-stabilized reference system
Categories of variable 3: reflexive mobilization axis (or epistemic axis)					
No reflexive mobilization, no sensitive mobilization	Sensitive mobilization without reflexive mobilization	Preponderance of sensitive dimension and low reflective mobilization	Preponderance of reflexive mobilization	Utility reflexive mobilization	Strong reflexive mobilization

Table 6.2. *Variables and modality of relationships to knowledge*

Schematically, for the third variable: no reflexive mobilization, preponderance of sensitive dimension and low reflexive mobilization, sensitive and reflexive mobilization, strong reflexive mobilization.

Here is the table showing the different general categorizations of each axis. For each general categorization, it is, of course, necessary to add specifications according to each knowledge object in question, and then specify the possible categories based on the context.

6.2.2. *From the definition of variables to quantitative tools*

If it is possible to carry out a first PCA or factorial component analysis (FCA) taking into account these three variables, we have taken the analysis further by dividing the variables into several subvariables in order to apply the Likert scale, and therefore, in this case, lead to a PCA. On the one hand, this potentially provides more information and, on the other hand, it facilitates a more precise variation of the variables. In addition to the issue of relationships to knowledge substantiated by Charlot, we felt the need to add a variable, which is a knowledge level because it makes it possible to specify educational goals as well.

The divided variables are presented in Table 6.3.

Identity variables
Variable 1: measures the meaning that an individual attributes to knowledge Variable 2: measures the relationship with one's identity
Social variables
Variable 3: measures one's social positioning Variable 4: measures the rejection of social project Variable 5: measures the adherence to social project
Epistemic variables
Variable 6: measures sensitivity Variable 7: measures cognitive learning Variable 8: measure utility learning Variable 9: measures knowledge level

Table 6.3. *Variables of relationships to knowledge*

We transcribe using the Likert scale from 1 to 4 so that we can later on process the variables with a PCA.

Level		1	2	3	4
Identity variables	Variable 1	No meaning	Little meaning	Average proven meaning	Strong proven meaning
	Variable 2	No identity interference	Low identity interferences	Average identity interferences	Strong identity interferences
Social variables	Variable 3	No social positioning	Limited positioning	Average positioning	Strong social positioning
	Variable 4	No social project rejection	Low rejection	Average rejection	Strong rejection of social project
	Variable 5	No adherence	Low adherence	Average adherence	Strong adherence to social project
Epistemic variables	Variable 6	No sensitive mobilization	Low sensitive mobilization	Average sensitive mobilization	Strong sensitive mobilization
	Variable 7	No cognitive reflexive mobilization	Low cognitive reflexive mobilization	Average cognitive reflexive mobilization	Strong cognitive reflexive mobilization
	Variable 8	No utility reflexive mobilization	Low utility reflexive mobilization	Average utility reflexive mobilization	Strong utility reflexive mobilization
Knowledge level variable	Variable 9	No expressed knowledge	Low mobilization of knowledge	Average mobilization of knowledge	Many expressed knowledge

Table 6.4. *Likert's scale of relationship to knowledge*

The instrument thus designed makes it possible to measure what happens as a result of an educational mechanism for a series of individuals. Within this context, the question would be: did the educational mechanism make it possible to mobilize students' reflection, give meaning and social positioning to the student and increase his/her knowledge? The quantitative dimension allows a more robust comparison between students' relationship to knowledge before and after the mechanism. Analyzing evolutions becomes, on the one hand, more robust and, on the other hand, more visible from visually interpretable graphs.

6.2.3. *Case study of heritage education*

Here, a simple case study is presented to show a quantitative analysis of relationships to knowledge intended for a comparison of different sociocultural groups.

The case study concerns heritage education in the Moroccan Atlas as part of the establishment of a UNESCO-Geopark mechanism and teaching needs on the fossilized footprints of dinosaurs in Demnate[1].

The goal was to question the relationship to heritage knowledge of different population groups in order to possibly identify educational problems that may arise as a result of the implementation of mechanisms related to the Geopark.

Four groups of different individuals were interviewed: villagers who live in the immediate vicinity of dinosaur tracks in the Demnate municipality; life and earth sciences teachers to teach geoheritage in Demnate and Marrakech; rural students around Demnate; urban students from Marrakech.

The dataset used here involves 100 individuals belonging to four groups (4 × 25) described above. This includes transposing a study of social representations carried out on these individuals to analyze their relationships to knowledge. Spontaneous evocation questionnaires (see social representations) were used with the various groups concerned relating to the local project on the promotion of dinosaur footprints. This is not an assertion that only spontaneous evocations can answer precisely to the question on relationships to knowledge, but a consideration to the fact that they are an approach that makes it possible above all to see what dominates *a priori* in the individuals concerned, putting aside any specific call for reflexive exercise. It is used here as an illustration of a statistical method, and it is appropriate within a research framework to supplement the information obtained by other crossed approaches: explicit interviews or analysis of students' outputs, for example.

Here, individuals answered using about 10 words each to the question: what do you think about the dinosaur footprints of the Demnate site (give 10 words). Then we attributed "points" to each of nine variables involved based on the answers

---

1 Available at: http://www.unesco.org/new/en/natural-sciences/environment/earth-sciences/unesco-global-geoparks/list-of-unesco-global-geoparks/morocco/mgoun/.

obtained. This means, in statistical terms, that we have attributed scores to each individual and each variable. For example, the answer "beautiful" refers to sensitivity and we attributed a point on Likert's scale on variable 6 (sensitive mobilization). The answer "tourism" refers to a perceived utility function, and we attributed a point to variable 8 (utility mobilization). The answer "prevent grazing" refers to the social project rejection variable and we attributed a point to variable 4, etc., and so on for all the words associated with the different variables.

The data set is oriented; it aims at highlighting, on the one hand, the cultural difference between the groups concerned by the project and thus the heterogeneity to be taken into account in promoting the resource, but especially in the modalities that should be developed for the acceptability of the project conducted according to UNESCO's international standards. Moreover, the goal is to position the group of life and earth sciences teachers with regard to the other three groups, which are considered as learners in the mechanism put in place. The final idea is to build a training curriculum tailored to the prerequisites of the groups

Our goal is to show how a PCA can highlight the differences between groups and characteristics for each of them by using the approach already presented in section 4.1 of Chapter 4 of this book. Through this example, we also want to show how the PCA can be used to describe different relationships to knowledge and how this can be done prior to curriculum studies.

We first made an individual-variable table by attributing a score to each variable as shown in Table 6.5 for the first 10 individuals.

Then we moved to data processing in sequential phases.

	Var1	Var2	Var3	Var4	Var5	Var6	Var7	Var8	Var9
1	1	1	3	2	1	2	2	4	4
2	1	1	3	1	1	1	1	4	4
3	1	1	3	1	1	1	2	4	4
4	1	1	3	1	1	1	1	4	3
5	1	1	3	2	1	1	1	4	3
6	1	1	2	1	1	1	1	4	3
7	1	1	2	1	1	1	1	4	3
8	1	1	2	2	1	2	2	4	4
9	2	1	2	1	2	1	2	3	2
10	2	1	2	1	2	1	3	4	2
11	2	1	2	1	2	2	2	3	2

Table 6.5. *Example of table of [I/V] for relationships to knowledge for 10 individuals*

6.2.4. *Conduct a quantitative study of relationships to knowledge*

We first proceeded with a simple conventional tabulation. As a matter of fact, it is recommended to proceed gradually, starting with a monovariate (tabulation) and then bivariate (cross-tabulation) analysis and whenever necessary, a multivariate analysis (FCA–PCA) can be conducted. Each step provides its own teaching that makes it easy to better format the next phase. The goal is to make data meaningful at each phase.

6.2.4.1. *Monovariate analysis of relationships to knowledge*

We first define the mean value of the variables for each group:

	Var1	Var2	Var3	Var4	Var5	Var6	Var7	Var8	Var9
Villagers	1.36	1.00	2.6	1.52	1.28	1.2	1.32	3.56	2.8
Life and earth sciences teachers	2.68	2.36	2.68	1	2.88	2.32	3.56	1.96	3.68
Rural Students	1.32	1.08	2.12	1.08	2.48	1.16	1.16	2.16	1.32
Urban students	3	3	2.36	1	3.2	3.36	1.16	2.16	1.32
Total	2.09	1.86	2.44	1.15	2.46	2.01	1.80	2.46	2.28

Table 6.6. *Mean value of variables per group of individuals*

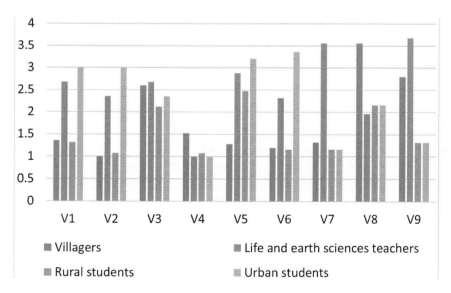

Figure 6.9. *Mean value of variables per group of individuals. For a color version of this figure, see www.iste.co.uk/larini/education.zip*

Thus, interpretation lessons can be drawn as an example:

– V1: The meaning given to local heritages is average with a strong disparity amongst the groups. It makes sense for people with an urban culture (teachers and students), who are geographically distant from the said heritages, but adhere more to values that I describe as western, while rural people living nearby do not really find it meaningful.

– V2: Ditto for the question of identity. This heritage is an identity only for those who are physically distant, in relation to their values rather than their local involvement, while it involves very little identity from the rural population (villagers and students).

– V3: An average social positioning with a more frequent rejection at the level of villagers (V4) for which this causes conflicts over the use of spaces and greater acceptability (V5) at the level of urban dwellers.

It is especially at the level of epistemic variables that we find the greatest differences. As a matter of fact, sensitive dimensions are present among urban dwellers, which is likely to be related to the values they develop with repercussions on the meaning (V1) of the heritage concerned. Cognitive mobilization is much more present in adults than in children, but villagers adopt a dominant utility dimension (V7), even though heritage makes no sense to them, while teachers have a cognitive relationship to this knowledge. Knowledge vis-à-vis heritage is important to adults and much less important to children (V9), as if the transfer of heritage knowledge (inheritance) had not been done in informal education. This does not seem surprising considering the real meaning that the local population attributes to these heritages. Formal (school) and non-formal (geopark) education is thus mobilized at the service of a social project, in this case, from rural valorization to tourism purposes, etc.

6.2.4.2. *Bivariate analysis of relationships to knowledge*

This analysis makes it possible to understand the positive or negative correlation links that exist between two variables taken two by two. The closer the figures are to 1 (or –1), the greater the correlation; the closer the figures are to 0, the smaller the correlations between the variables.

We will comment on some prominent results, not in terms of statistics, but in terms of significance as an example, knowing that it is potentially possible to analyze all the results one by one, although it is not the object of this study.

	C1	C2	C3	C4	C5	C6	C7	C8	C9
C1: Axis 1	1								
C2: Axis 2	0.761	1							
C3: Axis 3	0.172	0.114	1						
C4: Axis 4	−0.346	−0.381	0.216	1					
C5: Axis 5	0.488	0.55	−0.124	−0.599	1				
C6: Axis 6	0.639	0.729	0.091	−0.343	0.542	1			
C7: Axis 7	0.299	0.199	0.09	−0.255	0.254	0.126	1		
C8: Axis 6	−0.317	−0.312	0.206	0.476	−0.496	−0.286	−0.277	1	
C9: Axis 9	0.08	0.036	0.358	0.164	−0.184	−0.099	0.674	0.293	1

Table 6.7. *Correlation matrix of relationships to knowledge*

(V1, V2, V6): We noticed for example, a quite strong correlation (V1 and V6) or (V2 and V6), which shows that the "sensitivity to local heritage" factor is probably related to values that give them meaning and identity vis-à-vis heritage.

(V9–V7): On the other hand, it is because the individuals mobilize knowledge from a cognitive point of view that one tends toward their know-how. In other words, it is the project of cognitive use of knowledge that is important to the utility usage project it bears that allows access to a learning process.

(V6-V9): There is very little correlation between sensitivity and quantity of knowledge, which seems to challenge experiential approaches (conventional in some environmental education programs) as a potentially interesting learning mode in this case.

(V4–V8): Rejection of the social project requires cognitive mobilization, etc.

6.2.4.3. *Multivariate analysis of relationships to knowledge*

6.2.4.3.1. Complete PCA (nine variables)

We first proceeded with a PCA on all defined variables. The crosses represent the centers of gravity of the four groups of individuals. Based on the same scheme, there are urban students from Marrakech; rural students around Demnate; villagers who live in the immediate vicinity of dinosaur tracks in the Demnate municipality and life and earth sciences teachers to teach geo-heritage in Demnate.

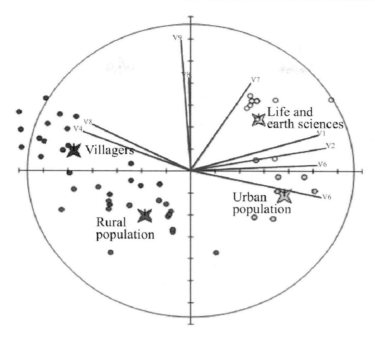

Figure 6.10. *Correlation circle of relationships*
to knowledge on all variables. For a color version
of this figure, see www.iste.co.uk/larini/education.zip

A first intuitive reading of the correlation circle indicates that the individuals of each of the four populations are grouped together and the four populations are concentrated in different quadrants; the position of the centers of gravity of each of the groups (stars) confirms this. This means that the groups have clearly distinct relationships to knowledge in terms of the heritage concerned, and the variables that contribute to it are also very different.

Variables 1 and 7 are "close" to life and earth sciences teachers, showing that geological heritage does not only make sense to them (V1), but they also mobilize their cognitive thinking on it (V7).

As for the villagers who live near dinosaur tracks in the Demnate municipality, reflexive utility mobilization (V8) is mostly identified (in the sense that it will attract tourists), but the heritage concerned has no meaning for them, and there is sometimes a rejection of the social project relative to the development of this heritage (V4), which concretely contradicts the usual agricultural activities.

As for students, what they have in common is little knowledge of heritage. They are the opposite of V9 which is the measurement of know-how on the knowledge, dinosaurs' footprints in this case. Their approach is sensitive for the urban people and that can make sense and identity for them (V1 and V2), whereas the rural people are not sensitive to it (the countryside and its heritage are synonymous with lack of modernity), but they may see it as useful in terms of economic opportunity (V8).

The interpretation of results on the simple intuitive reading of the correlation circle is based solely on the grouping of projected individuals and their visual proximity to the variables. But we must be careful, and we should make sure that the graphical representation of quality, that is, the first factorial plane observed, contains a sufficiently large % of the initial information in the table [I/V].

Analysis of the variance (see Table 6.8) informs us of the % of information that each factorial axis bears. The information contained in each of the nine factorial axes shows that the first two axes, which define the first factorial plane, to which we restrict the analysis, have a total of 61.2% of the information contained in the initial cloud. The value of 61.2% is not negligible, but we must not lose sight of the fact that 38.8% of the information was lost. Moreover, this results in moderately and even poorly represented variables.

	f1	f2	f3	f4	f5	f6	f7	f8	f9
Explained %	39.7	21.45	14.1	7.0	6.0	4.2	3.4	2.5	1.1
Cumulated %	39.7	61.2	75.3	82.4	88.5	92.5	96.3	98.84	100

Table 6.8. *Variance explained by components*

Under these conditions, it is difficult to go further with the analysis, because an increase in the number of variables (nine) does not give a clear meaning of the first two factorial axes f1 and f2.

6.2.4.3.2. Reduced PCA (V1, V3, V7, V9)

In this situation, it is possible to reduce the number of variables. For example, we decide to perform a partial PCA on only four variables and the choice of the variables is based first on the educational purpose, which is (at least in what is displayed) geared toward increased knowledge (V9), and cognitive mobilization relative to knowledge object (V7). The idea is to understand what could be the contributions and obstacles to the implementation of educational content in relation to these heritages. The other two variables selected are V1 and V3, which measure the individual's involvement in the knowledge at issue and the importance that he/she grants at the social level.

The group of teachers and more specifically variable 7, which normally corresponds to the major educational purpose – that is, obtain a cognitive reflexive mobilization around heritages – will serve as comparative benchmarks with the characteristics of the other populations.

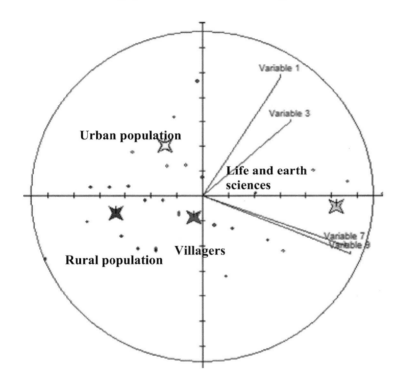

Figure 6.11. *Partial PCA V1, V3, V7, V9 relationships to knowledge. For a color version of this figure, see www.iste.co.uk/larini/education.zip*

From a simple reading of the correlation circle, one sees that V7 and V9 are well represented and strongly linked, indicating the link between the will to increase one's knowledge (V9) and the will to learn (V7). The group of teachers is indeed close, and the other three groups are distant but in a different way. The group of villagers (in red) is the one that appears the least distant from the group of life and earth sciences teachers. As for the students (yellow and purple), they are more clearly withdrawn from cognitive mobilization and know little.

As for variables V1 and V3, which relate to the meaning of knowledge for the individual (V1) and the meaning he/she gives to it at the social level (V3), they have a certain proximity and impact the first dial.

6.2.4.3.3. Interpretation of axes and meaning of dials

After this quick view, to say further and particularly to see what differentiates village, rural and urban populations, we must try to give meaning to each of the two factorial axes. But before that, it is necessary to be sure of the quality of the first factorial plane, that is, make sure that it contains enough information on nine dimensional initial point clouds.

	f1	f2	f3	f4
Eigenvalue	1.908	0.944	0.922	0.227
Explained %	47.694	23.595	23.045	5.665
Cumulated %	47.694	71.289	94.335	100

Table 6.9. *Duality of representation: variance explained by components*

The two factorial axes contain more than 71% of the initial information; it is better than the previous case with nine variables. This is not surprising, the more the variables, the least the information contained in the first factorial plane.

We are now looking for the contribution of variables to the meaning of the first two factorial axes. The software produces Table 6.10 on the contributions of variables to the first two factorial axes.

	Axis 1 +47.69%		Axis 2 +23.59%	
Positive contributions	Variable 9	+38.0%	Variable 1	+55.0%
	Variable 7	+36.0%	Variable 3	+21.0%
Negative contributions			Variable 9	−13.0%
			Variable 7	−9.0%

Table 6.10. *Contribution of factorial axes of partial PCA for relationships to knowledge*

The table expresses, in percentage, the contributions (positive at the top, negative at the bottom) of variables at the first and second factorial axes (f1 and f2).

If one relies on the contribution of the variables produced by the software considering that V7 and V9 contribute positively to the first factorial axis (Ax1), we move more toward positive f1, that is, to the right, and at most we find individuals who consider that we must study to better understand the knowledge in question (V7) and have good expertise relative to this knowledge (V9).

If we limit ourselves to the contribution of variables produced by the software, and if, to simplify, as a first approximation, we acknowledge that the negative contributions to the second factorial axis (V7 and V9) are negligible compared to the positive contributions of V1 and V2, then we move more toward positive f2, that is, upwards, and at the most we find individuals who consider that the knowledge at issue makes sense to them (V1) and who also consider that this knowledge is important at the social level (V3) .

CAUTION.– The graph represents standard scores, so the values close to 0 correspond to values of the initial variables close to the mean, the positive values correspond to values higher than the mean value and if they have a negative value they are below the mean.

Thus, we can attempt to provide a trend for each of the four dials. The first corresponds to individuals who have positive (above average) scores for variables (V7 and V9), but also for variables (V1 and V3). The second dial corresponds to individuals who have positive scores for variables (V1 and V3), but negative values for variables (V7 and V9). The third dial is characterized by negative values (V1 and V3) as well as negative for (V7 and V9) and finally in the fourth dial, we find individuals with positive values for (V7 and V9), but negative for (V1 and V3).

6.2.4.3.4. Group analysis

We will focus on the position of the centers of gravity of each group.

The group of life and earth sciences teachers falls under the fourth dial and therefore (V7 and V9) > 0 and (V1 and V3) < 0 but with absolute values important for (V7 and V9), but small for (V1 and V3). It can therefore be said that life and earth sciences teachers are mainly concerned with the cognitive approach of learning relative to heritage, and the issue of known knowledge is central. This corresponds to the idea that one could have of this group and the role it can play in the project.

The group of villagers falls under the third dial and therefore is characterized by negative values for (V1 and V3) as for (V7 and V9). But its position near the point of origin indicates that although negative, the values of the initial variables are close to the mean and so it is the closest to life and earth sciences for (V7 and V9). We notice that for (V1 and V3) life and earth sciences, the rural and urban populations are significantly at the same level. It can therefore be said that local heritage has little meaning for the villagers, and consequently, the heritage building that is proposed here is completely of exogenous origin to the village concerned (UNESCO-Geopark), or even, moderate forms of project acceptance (negative value of V3) are identified within this population. On the other hand, if it has no sense or identity link, it is nevertheless identified as being useful, and it is invested in this respect (V7). Knowledge, although not the same as that of the teachers, is however considerable (V9).

The group of urban students falls under the second dial and therefore is characterized by positive values for (V1 and V3) but negative for (V7 and V9). As for (V1 and V3), it is the only group that has positive values. For variables (V7 and V9), it is between the villagers and rural students. This shows, on the one hand, that the heritage project has meaning for them (positive value of V1) and that they accept it (positive value of V3). They are therefore culturally closer to the group of teachers, even though results show that the knowledge expressed is very low (V9).

Finally, the group of rural students also falls under the third dial. It is further away from life and earth sciences teachers than urban students. Since (V1 and V3) is negative, the project makes little sense to them. There is a chance that educating rural students on local heritage will be a more complex task than urban students who are more distant. Rural students have little knowledge, unlike their elders, the village adults.

To conclude, the analysis shows that relationships to knowledge are very different from one group to another and the consequences need to be considered in learning. Surprise is mainly due to the fact that for the local population who is more culturally distant from international heritage standards than the urban population, the heritage to be promoted makes no sense, and this is some kind of a challenge for teachers who are mainly concerned with learning and its cognitive dimension.

Beyond this case, the study thus conducted shows the complexity of the relationships between social groups with different relationships with knowledge. These differences constitute, as the case may be, a handicap in view of the dissemination of the international values promoted by the valorization project.

6.2.4.4. *Conclusion of case study*

The case study presented is not a complete study; however, it highlighted the differences between the four groups and gave them meaning based on the different variables. The nine-variable PCA has an interesting intuitive reading, but the high number of variables does not allow for further analysis because the factorial plane is of mean quality and the interpretation of axes is very difficult under these conditions. By reducing the number of variables to four, the quality of the factorial plane is better and the axes can be interpreted more easily, thus leading to a better analysis of the results.

The method can certainly be improved by defining steps in the analysis while reorganizing and prioritizing the variables based on the problems pertaining to the study. This would reduce, at each step, the number of variables, and thus, on the one hand, increase the significance of the first factorial plane and, on the other hand, enable a better interpretation of the factorial axes.

References

[ABD 87] ABDI H., *Introduction au traitement statistique des données expérimentales*, PUG, Grenoble, 1987.

[ABR 94] ABRIC J.C., *Pratiques sociales et représentations*, PUF, Paris, 1994.

[ABR 97] ABRIC J.C., "Méthodologie de recueil des représentations sociales", in ABRIC J.C. (ed.), *Pratiques sociales et représentations*, PUF, Paris, 1997.

[AIT 86] AITKIN M., LONGFORD N.T., "Statistical modeling in school effectiveness studies", *Journal of the Royal Statistical Society, Series A*, vol. 149, no. 1, pp. 1–43, 1986.

[ALB 07] ALBARELLO L., BOURGEOIS E., GUYOT J.L., *Statistique descriptive : un outil pour les praticiens et les chercheurs*, De Boeck, Brussels, 2007.

[ALI 14] ALINAT S., BARTHES A., "Apports de la cartographie aux recherches sur l'école rurale", in BARTHES A., CHAMPOLLION P. (eds), *L'École rurale et montagnarde en contexte méditerranéen: approches socio-spatiales*, PUFC, Besançon, 2014.

[BAC 10a] BACCINI A., *Statistique descriptive élémentaire*, Publications de l'Institut de mathématiques de Toulouse, Toulouse, 2010.

[BAC 10b] BACCINI A., *Statistique descriptive multidimensionnelle : Pour les nuls*, Publications de l'Institut de mathématiques de Toulouse, Toulouse, 2010.

[BAG 17] BAGGIO S., DELINE S., ROTHEN S., *Statistique descriptive-L1/L2 psycho*, De Boeck, Brussels, 2017.

[BAR 14] BARTHES A., "Comment réintroduire les savoirs face à l'éducation au développement durable? Exemple des filières professionnelles d'aménagement des territoires", *Éducation au développement durable et à la biodiversité : concepts, questions vives, outils et pratiques*, available at: https://hal.archives-ouvertes.fr/halshs-00957808/document, 2014.

[BAR 16] BARTHES A., ALPE Y., *Utiliser les représentations sociales en éducation*, L'Harmattan, Paris, 2016.

[BAU 98] BAUTIER E., ROCHEX J.-Y., *L'expérience scolaire des nouveaux lycéens, Démocratisation ou massification?*, Armand Colin, Paris, 1998.

[BEG 10] BEGUIN M., PUMAIN D., *La Représentation des données géographiques : statistique et cartographie*, Armand Colin, Paris, 2010.

[BEI 00] BEILLEROT J., "Le rapport au savoir", in MOSCONI N., BEILLEROT J., BLANCHARD-LAVILLE C. (eds), *Formes et formations du rapport au savoir*, L'Harmattan, Paris, 2000.

[BEN 73a] BENZECRI J.P., *L'analyse des données, tome 1 : La taxinomie*, Dunod, Paris, 1973.

[BEN 73b] BENZECRI J.P., *L'analyse des données, tome 2 : L'analyse des correspondances*, Dunod, Paris, 1973.

[BER 14] BERTRAND F., MAUMY-BERTRAND M., *Initiation à la statistique avec R : cours et exercices corrigés*, Dunod, Paris, 2014.

[BLA 84] BLALOCK H.M., "Contextual effect model: theoretical and methodological issues", *Annual Review of Sociology*, vol. 10, pp. 353–372, 1984.

[BON 99] BONARDI C., ROUSSIAU N., *Les Représentations sociales*, Dunod, Paris, 1999.

[BOU 68] BOURDIEU P., CHAMBOREDON J.-C., PASSERON J.-P., *Le Métier du sociologue*, Mouton de Gruyter/EHESS, Paris, 1968.

[BOU 00] BOURDIEU P., "L'inconscient d'école", *Actes de la recherche en sciences sociales*, vol. 135, no. 12, pp. 3–5, 2000.

[BOU 15] BOULAN H., *Le Questionnaire d'enquête : les clés d'une étude marketing ou d'opinion réussie*, Dunod, Paris, 2015.

[BRE 04] BRESSOUX P., BIANCO M., "Long term effect on pupils learning gains", *Oxford Review of Education*, vol. 30, no. 3, pp. 27–34, 2004.

[BRE 10] BRESSOUX P., *Modélisation statistique appliquée aux sciences sociales*, De Boeck, Brussels, 2010.

[BUS 09] BUSCA D., TOUTAIN S., *Analyse factorielle simple en sociologie : méthodes d'interprétation et études de cas*, De Boeck, Brussels, 2009.

[CAI 01] CAILLOT M., "Y a-t-il des élèves en didactique des sciences ? Ou quelles références pour l'élève ?", in TERRISSE A. (ed.), *Didactique des disciplines, Les références au savoir*, De Boeck Université, Brussels, 2001.

[CHA 92] CHARLOT B., BAUTIER E., ROCHEX J.-Y., *École et savoir dans les banlieues et ailleurs*, Armand Colin, Paris, 1992.

[CHA 97] CHARLOT B., *Du rapport au savoir, Éléments pour une théorie*, Anthropos, Paris, 1997.

[CHA 99] CHARLOT B., *Le rapport au savoir en milieu populaire, Une recherche dans les lycées professionnels de banlieue*, Anthropos, Paris, 1999.

[CHA 03] CHARTRAIN J.-L., Rôle du rapport au savoir dans l'évolution différenciée des conceptions scientifiques des élèves, Un exemple du volcanisme au cours moyen 2, unpublished PhD Thesis, Université Paris-V, 2003.

[CHE 92] CHEVALLARD Y., "Concepts fondamentaux de la didactique : perspectives apportées par une approche anthropologique", *Recherches en didactique des mathématiques*, vol. 12, no. 1, pp. 73–112, 1992.

[CIB 94] CIBOIS P., *Analyse en composante principale et analyse des correspondances*, PUF, Paris, 1994.

[COR 12] CORNILLON P.A., GUYADER A., HUSSON F. *et al.*, *Statistiques avec R : 3e édition revue et augmentée*, PUR, Rennes, 2012.

[COS 13] COSTA R., *Analyser les données en sciences sociales : de la préparation des données à l'analyse multivariée*, Peter Lang, Bern, 2013.

[COU 15] COUPAUD M., LARINI M., CASTERA J. *et al.*, "Méthode d'analyse exploratoire pour une étude comparative sur les représentations de la démarche d'investigation d'enseignants de collèges", *Review of Science Mathematics and ICT Education*, vol. 9, no. 2, pp. 99–114, 2015.

[DAG 07] DAGNELIE P., *Statistique théorique et appliquée : 1. Statistique descriptive et bases de l'inférence statistique*, De Boeck, Brussels, 2007.

[DAG 11] DAGNELIE P., *Statistique théorique et appliquée : 2. Inférence statistique à une et à deux dimensions*, De Boeck, Brussels, 2011.

[DEG 73] DEGENNE A., VERGES P., "Introduction à l'analyse de similitude", *Revue française de sociologie*, vol. XIV, pp. 471–512, 1973.

[DUM 11] DUMOLARD P., *Données géographiques : Analyse statistique multivariée*, Hermes-Lavoisier, Paris, 2011.

[DUR 94] DURKHEIM E., *Les Règles de la méthode sociologique*, PUF, Paris, 1894.

[ESC 16] ESCOFIER B., PAGES J., *Analyse factorielle simple et multiple : cours et étude de cas*, Dunod, Paris, 2016.

[FLA 87] FLAMENT C., "Pratiques et représentations sociales", in BEAUVOIS J.L., JOULE R.V., MONTEIL J.M. (eds), *Perspectives cognitives et conduites sociales, I. Théories implicites et conflits cognitifs*, PUF, Paris, 1987.

[FLA 94] FLAMENT C., "Structure, dynamique et transformation des représentations sociales", in ABRIC J.C. (ed.), *Pratiques sociales et représentations*, PUF, Paris, 1994.

[FLA 95] FLAMENT C., "Approche expérimentale de type psychologique dans l'étude d'une représentation sociale", *Les Cahiers internationaux de psychologie sociale*, vol. 4, no. 28, pp. 67–76, 1995.

[GER 15] GERARD F., *Conduite d'enquête par questionnaire*, Éditions du robot furieux, 2015.

[GUE 97] GUEGUEN N., *Manuel de statistique pour psychologues*, Dunod, Paris, 1997.

[HOF 03] HOFFMANN J.P., *Generalised Linear Model: An Applied Approach*, Pearson, London, 2003.

[HOW 10] HOWELL D.C., *Fundamental Statistics for the Behavioral Sciences*, Wadsworth Publishing, Boston, 2010.

[JOD 89] JODELET D., "Représentations sociales : un domaine en expansion", in JODELET D. (ed.), *Les représentations sociales*, PUF, Paris, 1989.

[JOD 94] JODELET D., *Les représentations sociales*, PUF, Paris, 1994.

[KAL 17] KALALI F., "Rapports aux savoirs", in BARTHES A., LANGE J.M., TUTIAUX-GUILLON N. (eds), *Dictionnaire critique des enjeux et concepts des éducations*, L'Harmattan, Paris, 2017.

[MAA 16] MAALOUF J.P., "Introduction aux statistiques descriptive", *XLSTAT*, available at: www.xlstat.com, 2016.

[MAR 12] MARTIN O., *L'Analyse quantitative des données : l'enquête et ses méthodes*, Armand Colin, Paris, 2012.

[MIL 09] MILOT G., *Comprendre et réaliser les tests statistiques avec R.*, De Boeck, Brussels, 2009.

[MOL 96] MOLINER P., *Images et représentations sociales, De la théorie des représentations à l'étude des images sociales*, PUG, Grenoble, 1996.

[MUN 09] MUNOZ F., BORGNER F., CLEMENT PP. *et al.*, "Teachers' conceptions of nature and environment in 16 countries", *Journal of Environmental Psychology*, vol. 29, pp. 407–413, 2009.

[PRU 10] PRUM B., *La démarche statistique*, Cépaduès, Toulouse, 2010.

[PUM 01] PUMAIN D., SAINT-JULIEN T., *Les Interactions spatiales*, Armand Colin, Paris, 2001.

[PY 07a] PY P., *Exercices corrigés de statistique descriptive*, Economica, Paris, 2007.

[PY 07b] PY P., *Statistique descriptive*, Economica, Paris, 2007.

[RAM 96] RAMOUSSE R., LE BERRE M., LE GUELTE L., Introduction aux statistiques, 3. Choisir le test statistique approprié, available at: www.cons-ev.org/elearning/stat/St2b.htlm, 1996.

[RAU 89] RAUDENBUSH S.W., "The analysis of longitudinal multilevel data", *International Journal of Educational research*, vol. 13, no. 17, pp. 721–740, 1989.

[STA 05] STAFFORD J., BODSON P., *Analyse multivariée avec SPSS*, PUQ, Quebec, 2005.

[VAN 14] VAN DER MAREN J.M., *La Recherche appliquée pour les professionnels : Éducation, (para)médical, travail social*, De Boeck, Brussels, 2014.

[VEN 07] VENTURINI P., *L'envie d'apprendre les sciences, Motivation, attitudes, rapport aux savoirs scientifiques*, Édition Fabert, Paris, 2007.

[VER 94] VERGES P., "Approche du noyau central : propriétés quantitatives et structurales", in GUIMELLI C. (ed), *Structures et transformations des représentations sociales*, Delachaux et Niestlé, Lausanne, 1994.

[VER 97] VERGES P., FLAMENT C., "Comparaisons de méthode : à propos de l'article 'Apport des modèles graphiques gaussiens en analyse de similitude'", *Papers on Social Representations*, vol. 6, no. 1, pp. 73–87, 1997.

[VER 01] VERGES P., "L'analyse des représentations sociales par questionnaires", *Revue française de sociologie*, vol. 42, no. 3, pp. 537–561, 2001.

[VYG 78] VYGOTSKY L., *Mind in Society: The Development of Higher Psychological Processes*, Harvard University Press, Cambridge, 1978.

[WEI 97] WEIL-BARAIS A., *Les Méthodes en psychologie : observation, expérimentation, enquête, travaux d'étude et de recherche*, Éditions Bréal, Paris, 1997.

Index

A

anchoring, 242, 245
ANOVA, 81, 99–103, 105, 106, 108, 110, 111, 118
approach
  multilevel, 194, 223, 226
  quantitative, 229, 230, 233, 248
average, 18, 29, 32–34, 36

C, D

cartography, 41–43
central nucleus, 245, 246
chance, 50–52, 55, 61, 64, 76–78, 112, 113
circle of correlations, 151, 153, 159, 166
comparative analytical model, 241
corpus, 242
correlation coefficient, 29, 38, 39, 40, 41
curriculum, 230
didactic recommendations, 230

E

eco-citizenship, 245
eco-efficiency, 245
education databases, 2, 3
experimental approach, 10, 11
explanatory power, 207–209

F, G

FCA, 141, 173, 175–177, 180, 181, 183, 186–188
FMCA, 141, 173, 186–188, 190, 191
focal points, 242, 247
geographic information systems, 46
graph, 237, 242, 244

I, K

idealogical loads, 237, 241
individuals, 15–21, 27, 29–33, 37
interval
  confidence, 193, 204–206
  prediction, 204–207
khi^2, 50, 52, 69, 118–126, 128, 129–136, 138–140
knowledge, 229, 230
  relationships, 249

L

large numbers, 50, 52, 54, 58, 60
law
  normal, 52, 64–69, 75, 79, 81, 83, 84, 87, 94, 97, 100, 106, 121, 124, 126
  probability, 51, 52, 58, 61, 71, 77, 79

Other titles from

in

Science, Society and New Technologies

2018

BARTHES Angela, CHAMPOLLION Pierre, ALPE Yves
Evolutions of the Complex Relationship Between Education and Territories
(Education Set - Volume 1)

BÉRANGER Jérôme
The Algorithmic Code of Ethics: Ethics at the Bedside of the Digital Revolution
(Technological Prospects and Social Applications Set – Volume 2)

DUGUÉ Bernard
Time, Emergences and Communications
(Engineering, Energy and Architecture Set – Volume 4)

GEORGANTOPOULOU Christina G., GEORGANTOPOULOS George A.
Fluid Mechanics in Channel, Pipe and Aerodynamic Design Geometries 1
(Engineering, Energy and Architecture Set – Volume 2)

GEORGANTOPOULOU Christina G., GEORGANTOPOULOS George A.
Fluid Mechanics in Channel, Pipe and Aerodynamic Design Geometries 2
(Engineering, Energy and Architecture Set – Volume 3)

LELEU-MERVIEL Sylvie
Informational Tracking
(Traces Set – Volume 1)

SALGUES Bruno
Society 5.0: Industry of the Future, Technologies, Methods and Tools
(Technological Prospects and Social Applications Set – Volume 1)

2017

ANICHINI Giulia, CARRARO Flavia, GESLIN Philippe,
GUILLE-ESCURET Georges
Technicity vs Scientificity – Complementarities and Rivalries
(Social Interdisciplinarity Set – Volume 2)

DUGUÉ Bernard
Information and the World Stage – From Philosophy to Science,
the World of Forms and Communications
(Engineering, Energy and Architecture Set – Volume 1)

GESLIN Philippe
Inside Anthropotechnology – User and Culture Centered Experience
(Social Interdisciplinarity Set – Volume 1)

GORIA Stéphane
Methods and Tools for Creative Competitive Intelligence

KEMBELLEC Gérald, BROUDOUS EVELYNE
Reading and Writing Knowledge in Scientific Communities– Digital
Humanities and Knowledge Construction

MAESSCHALCK Marc
Reflexive Governance for Research and Innovative Knowledge
(Responsible Research and Innovation Set - Volume 6)

PARK Sejin, GUILLE-ESCURET Georges
Sociobiology vs Socioecology – Consequences of an Unraveling Debate
(Interdisciplinarity between Biological Sciences and Social Sciences Set -
Volume 1)

PELLÉ Sophie
Business, Innovation and Responsibility
(Responsible Research and Innovation Set - Volume 7)

2016

BRONNER Gérald
Belief and Misbelief Asymmetry on the Internet

EL FALLAH SEGHROUCHNI Amal, ISHIKAWA Fuyuki, HÉRAULT Laurent,
TOKUDA Hideyuki
Enablers for Smart Cities

GIANNI Robert
Responsibility and Freedom
(Responsible Research and Innovation Set - Volume 2)

GRUNWALD Armin
The Hermeneutic Side of Responsible Research and Innovation
(Responsible Research and Innovation Set - Volume 5)

LAGRANA Fernando
*E-mail and Behavioral Changes – Uses and Misuses of Electronic
Communications*

LENOIR Virgil Cristian
Ethical Efficiency – Responsibility and Contingency
(Responsible Research and Innovation Set - Volume 1)

MAESSCHALCK Marc
Reflexive Governance for Research and Innovative Knowledge
(Responsible Research and Innovation Set - Volume 6)

PELLÉ Sophie, REBER Bernard
From Ethical Review to Responsible Research and Innovation
(Responsible Research and Innovation Set - Volume 3)

Printed and bound by CPI Group (UK) Ltd, Croydon, CR0 4YY